Miriam Corke

# THE AMERICANS

# ALISTAIR COOKE

## The Americans

*Fifty Letters from America
on Our Life and Times*

**THE BODLEY HEAD**
LONDON SYDNEY
TORONTO

British Library Cataloguing
in Publication Data
Cooke, Alistair
The Americans
1. United States – Social life and customs – 1971
2. United States – Social life and customs – 1945–1970
I. Title
973.92'092'4        E169.02

ISBN 0–370–30163–3

Printed in Great Britain for
The Bodley Head Ltd
9 Bow Street, London WC2E 7AL
by William Clowes & Sons Ltd, Beccles
set in Clowes Ehrhardt
*First Published 1979*

# CONTENTS

# A Note to the Reader

The word 'reader' ought to be in strong italics. For these are talks meant to be listened to. And the job of writing—and then performing—a radio talk has been for me, down forty-odd years, by far the most challenging and satisfying craft of any I have attempted in a lifetime of journalism.

The challenge is not to write for your friends, or the intelligentsia, or your newspaper editor, but for an audience that spans the human gamut in very many countries. For these weekly thirteen-and-a-half-minute talks were broadcast first in the Home Service of the British Broadcasting Corporation and then aired, through the overseas services of the BBC, on every continent (they can be heard in the United States only on the short-wave). It is a great privilege to have the ear, at least the opportunity to entice the ear, of ordinary people and extraordinary people in countries as far apart as Scotland and Malaysia. I stress the unique satisfactions of the medium because nothing could be more rewarding than the sort of letter which acknowledges that a German grocer has been touched by an obituary piece on Dean Acheson or a Lord Chief Justice moved by the story of an illiterate black girl who swiped a baby from the incubator of a New York hospital.

Radio is literature for, so to speak, the blind. For one friend sitting in a room, not for any large collective audience that might be assembled in Madison Square Garden. And because the 'one friend in a room' may be of any colour, any station in life, any sort of education, the radio talker must try to write in an idiom acceptable to almost everybody who normally speaks the language. There are vocabularies, such as you would write for your newspaper or for a serious periodical, which are taboo as talk. Ideally, one ought to be Daniel Defoe, or John Bunyan, or Pepys, or Mark Twain, or the Jacobean translators of the

*Book of Genesis.* This is, of course, an almost impossible challenge, and it is rarely met and conquered. Consequently, in going over these talks for publication I have made the most of the privilege of print to straighten out the syntax (which one doesn't do in conversation) and to introduce occasionally literary words that are more exact and that will not throw the much smaller race of book-readers.

During the Second World War, I did a weekly broadcast from America that concentrated, understandably, on the progress of the war effort and on its human exasperations. Once the war was over, I was invited by the BBC to forget our preoccupation with Armageddon and talk about anything and everything that occurred to me about life in America. The series, called *Letter From America*, started in March, 1946, for a preliminary try-out of thirteen weeks. I hope it will not sound vain if I say that nothing I have done in journalism, or in the past few years in television, has given me more pride than the fact that the series still goes on and is now in its thirty-fourth year.

The talks were done once a week when I was busy with other things. For twenty-five years I was writing a daily report for the (*Manchester*) *Guardian* as its chief correspondent in the United States. For more than two years, between 1969 and 1972, I was trekking across and around the United States writing and filming the television series, *America.* The talks were, and are, never prepared. They offer the relief and the exhilaration of sitting down once a week and writing what comes to mind about the American scene, usually no more than a couple of hours before they are taped and flown to London to be broadcast. More often than not, I have little idea, as I sit down to the typewriter, what I am going to talk about. This, I believe, is the proper psychological condition for composing a talk: we do not go out to dinner with a little agenda in our pockets of what the evening's conversation is to be about.

Like the talks in two previous collections (*Letters from*

*America* and *Talk About America*) these appear in chronological order, with three exceptions. The first talk (which combines two talks) seemed to be a proper introduction to the whole book. The second 'Letter From Long Island' assumed you knew things elaborated on in the first. And it seemed sensible to put the so-called 'Epilogue' to Watergate immediately after the last talk on the whole episode rather than in its historical place, three years later.

Otherwise, there is only one other thing to say, which I can't say better than I did in the preface to a previous collection: 'Most Americans, in spite of the evangelism of bloodshot politicians, live their lives without any feeling of "national destiny" and without seeing their country as the big brutal world power of the nasty cartoons. My aim is still what it was when these talks began: to run up and down the human scale that unites a Lancashireman to a Texan and a German to a Siamese.'

A.C.

Nassau Point, Long Island.
Summer, 1979.

# Telling One
# Country About Another

## 2 March 1969

A year or two ago, I had an invitation to go and talk to the
cadets at West Point, which is the Sandhurst or St Cyr of the
United States. The letter was signed by a general. It was the
first time a general had invited me to anything, though more
years ago than I care to say I did get a letter from the President
of the United States which began: 'Greetings!'—with a cordial
exclamation mark, too.

The general even sent a car to drive me up the Hudson. If
I'd been going to talk to the Arts Club, or whatever, of Long
Beach, California, I'd have put on a pair of golfing slacks and
a blazer. But I was not going to be found guilty, at West Point,
of what my headmaster called 'the supreme act of rudeness:
casualness' and I decked myself out in a suit and a tie bearing
the three cocks (the cock crowed three times) and weeping
crowns of Jesus College, Cambridge. This badge offered the
only possibility open to me of pulling rank. I also practised
saying 'Yes, sir', 'No, sir' and 'Not at all, sir'.

When I got up there, I was the one who was called sir. The
commanding general, it happened, was about five years
younger than I and on the verge of retirement. He wondered
if there was anything he might do to make me comfortable.
This alarming deference made me think back to an afternoon,
in 1962, aboard the USS *Kitty Hawk*, a super aircraft carrier.
I was along with the White House press corps at a
demonstration of missile firing being put on for President
Kennedy. When it was all over, and the twilight was dropping
over the Pacific, I was nearly knocked down by a hefty slap on

the back. It came from the Admiral of the Pacific Fleet. 'Hi, there!' he said, 'You old bastard.' I had known him twenty years before as a humble lieutenant, and we had had one or two memorable raucous evenings together.

There seem, indeed, to be fewer men around than there used to be to whom I feel I ought to defer. By the same token, there are more and more men, going from grey to white at that, who come to me and seek advice. It is a mixed compliment. I now get calls from incoming foreign correspondents who wonder how to go about acquainting themselves with the Presidency, the Congress, investigating committees and the rest of it. The other day, one of them asked me to tell him the main differences between reporting the America of today and the America of thirty years ago. It is worth a passing thought or two.

To begin with, I could say, and truly, that the job is always the same: to say, or write, what you see and hear and relate it to what you know of the country's traditional behaviour. 'Traditional behaviour' may sound a little clumsy. But I'm trying to avoid the trap of what is called 'national character'. Whenever you are really baffled, it is always safe to put it all down to national character. I have come to think that a strong belief in national character is the first refuge of the anxious. For the moment, we'll let that pass.

A foreign correspondent, then, is both an interpreter and a victim of his subject matter. He must be aware of his own changing view of the country he's assigned to. And the danger here is that of assuming that the longer you stay in a country, the truer will be your perspective. As the Pope said to the earnest visitor who wondered how long he ought to stay in Rome to know it well: 'Two days, very good. Two weeks, better. Two years, not long enough.'

More important still, the reporter must always have in mind the settled view that his readers or listeners hold of the country he's writing about. The home reader, whether a simpleton or an intellectual, a Socialist or a Tory, wants—like a tourist—to find what he's looking for. He doesn't want to be startled out of his preconceptions. It is the correspondent's job to startle preconceptions. And, I must admit, sometimes to say that they're right.

There was, twenty odd years ago, the instructive case of a Hungarian refugee from his Communist country. He had been a Communist himself, till he saw Communism in action. Then he escaped to Britain. He was a journalist, a brilliant intellectual, and a Jew. When, after the Second World War, the British Labour government had to try and establish a policy for Palestine, a British editor decided that this man was the ideal outsider to report on the anarchy and ill-will that had set in between the British and the Jews. The editor gently suggested that it would be a fine thing if he could incidentally expose the 'lies' that the Palestinian Jews were spreading abroad. The 'lies' included the notion that Mr Ernest Bevin, the Foreign Secretary, in trying to hold on to Palestine, and the support of the Arabs, and the goodwill of the Jews, was attempting an impossibility that was involving him in ruthless treatment of the Jews. The Hungarian was told to spend a few weeks feeling his way into the situation and then to begin filing his series of articles. He stayed a month, five weeks, six weeks, and nothing was heard from him. When the editor cabled, 'What happened? Where is the series?' he cabled back, 'Sorry, no series, all the lies are true.'

Luckily no such bad blood has soured the relations between Britain and the United States in the past thirty years, except during the first three or four years of the 1950s, when the British view of the late Senator Joseph McCarthy blew up the only blizzard of disgusted mail I have ever received. But, more recently, there have been delicate problems involved in reporting a first-rate power that was once a second-rate power to a second-rate power that was once first-rate. For many years after the Second World War, Britons refused to acknowledge their fading influence. And for a blazing month or two the most unpopular American in Britain was Dean

13

Acheson, simply for having expressed his glimpse of the obvious: 'Britain has lost an empire and not yet found a role.'

When I arrived in Washington in the late Thirties, I was one of only four British correspondents. Today, there must be forty or fifty, if you count reporters on particular assignment, and the enlarged radio and television staffs of the BBC and the British commercial television companies. This trek followed a simple law of politics: the best reporters, like the best chefs, gravitate toward the centres of power. (The Australians today complain, as Americans did fifty years ago, that the foreign press corps in their country is unreasonably small.) When Britain really ruled the waves, in good King George V's glorious reign, London was the capital of foreign correspondence. The Foreign Office briefings were attended by a pack of correspondents from nations big and small. And the Foreign Office, being the repository of all wise and relevant information, felt no call to bandy debating points with the press. The Foreign Office distributed handouts, no questions asked. It did not justify its policies. It announced them. And I remember how American correspondents, newly arrived in London, used to fume in their impotence when they found it was not possible to have a private word with a Cabinet minister. To have invited him to lunch would have thrown him into a coronary.

A young Texan, a journalist, who is now a distinguished American magazine editor, stayed with me in London when I was back there in the early, dark spring of 1938. He was an inquisitive and typically courteous Texan, and one night he had a message from his New York office asking him to look into a rumour, a correct rumour as it turned out, that the Nazis were about to invade Austria. It sounded pretty melodramatic to me, but in those days we were not yet accustomed to the idea that gangsterism was a working technique of international politics. My friend mulled over the cable from New York and his instincts as an Associated Press stringer got the better of him. He asked to use my telephone and he rang up the Foreign Office, an impulse which to me was as bizarre as phoning Buckingham Palace. When the FO answered he asked to talk to Lord Halifax, who had just then become the Foreign Secretary. I was agog with admiration. I was at the time a political innocent, a film critic, but I knew my Hitchcock movies well enough to know that that was exactly how Joel McCrea in a raincoat went about his business.

It was soon obvious that my friend was having a rough time with the other end of the wire. 'Yes, sir,' he kept saying in courteous variations, 'I know it's very late in the evening, but this is not the sort of rumour the Associated Press can just forget.' Somehow, he managed to get Lord Halifax's home number, a remarkable feat in itself. He re-dialled and there was a crackle and a pause and a respectful fluting sound from the other end. It was the butler, who had a strangulated moment or two while, I imagine, he was being revived by the rest of the household staff. At last, he pronounced the definitive sentence: 'I'm sorry, sir, his Lordship is in his bath.'

This is still not an approach I'd be inclined to take, though in failing to be so brash I no longer feel merely courteous: I feel I'm neglecting my duty. Because I now take for granted the ease of access to people in government in America. Americans had, and have, a quite different feeling about the press. In many countries, and Britain used to be one of them, a reporter is a potential enemy. The Americans, however, feel it is better to have a friend in print than an enemy. And this, too, is a great danger, for nothing castrates a reporter so easily as flattery. But the main thing is, the politicians tend to look on you as a camp follower through the maze of politics, and if they can help you find your way out, without trading the Pentagon secret file, they will do it. Nowadays, of course, even dictators have to pretend to welcome cosy conversations with television interviewers.

America, from the beginning of my time, was an open book to a reporter. The people were there to mix with, and the landscape and its troubles and pleasures, and a reporter with

15

the most modest credentials could get to talk to everybody from the Governor, the local Congressman, the Chamber of Commerce, the saloon keepers, the local madams. Huey Long stretched out on a bed barefoot in the Roosevelt Hotel in New Orleans and picked his toes while he enlarged on the glorious future he had in mind for Everyman and Everywoman in Louisiana. I once asked the late Governor Talmadge of Georgia how the (since abolished) 'county unit' system worked in his state. He sucked his teeth and ordered up a car, oddly—it seemed to me then—a humble jalopy. We jumped in and he drove me into the corners of three counties that fringed Atlanta. In each of them he dropped in on a couple of farmers on the pretence of needing to relieve himself. When we were back in the city, he said, 'I got myself six unit votes right there, and them students and doctors and Commies in Atlanta can shout themselves hoarse—it's more votes than they have.' Once, I was driving across Nevada and noticed from the map that I was close by Hawthorne, and that it was the site of the US Naval Ammunition Depot. I asked to look in on it, and I did. I am a little awestruck now to reflect that a Japanese reporter could probably have done the same right up to the eve of Pearl Harbor.

In the Thirties you required no confidential sources to straighten you out on the condition of the country. The country was racked by depression. On several trips around the United States, in the South more than anywhere, I was physically nauseated by the people I saw in the country towns and in the workless cities: the absolutely drained look of mothers nourishing babies at shrunken breasts, the general coma of the rural poor, with the tell-tale rash of scurvy or pellagra on the back of their necks. Today there is very little, if any, scurvy or pellagra in the South, because they varied the crops and learned about green vegetables, and the cities turned to textiles. They were no longer doomed to plates of rice and corn and potatoes and hominy grits—a feast, whenever it was a feast, of nothing but starch.

The first year I drove around the whole country, about one family in four was on the breadline or just above it. Yet, while we totted up the grim statistics, we wrote little about these things for foreign consumption. The foreign consumers too had their silent factories and marching miners, and they had bemused and stumbling leaders. The great news from America was that the country was galvanised by the new President into a prospect of greener pastures. The story was the exhilaration of the Roosevelt era: the public works, the dams and new housing, the first national network of concrete highways, the poor boys planting millions of trees. These things excited us more than the conditions they were meant to cure depressed us. If thirty or forty per cent of the population was then at some stage of need, today only eleven per cent falls below the government's rather generous definition of a subsistence income of $2,200 a year. And though that may sound like small pickings, there has never been a time in this country's history, or perhaps in human history, when more people in one nation were better off, never a smaller percentage of two hundred millions who could be called poor. Yet there is less complacency, I believe, than there ever was. As I talk, the cities tremble and the countryside groans over the shame of it.

In case my drift is being misunderstood, let me say that this trembling and groaning is a good thing too. If God observes the fall of one sparrow, it is right in a prosperous time that we should feel not only that we are our brother's keeper but that our brother is the whole of society. I think it must be the first time in history that the so-called civilised nations have felt this way. Why? Are we more humane, more sensitive than we used to be? I think not. The world's population of the starving and near-starving at the height of the Victorian age must have been beyond our imagining. But the point is, the Victorians had to imagine it, or read the fine print, or take the progressive magazines or dig out—from some encyclopedia—the infant mortality rates. Statistics make few people bleed or weep. Today all of us, in a castle or a cottage, can see every night the

17

warped skeletons of the children of Biafra. Thirty students up at Columbia University paralysed for a time the education of several thousand, and it looked and sounded, on the evening news, like the siege of Mafeking. A hundred cops go berserk on an August night in Chicago, and next day it's the scandal of the world. Television, whatever its faults and banalities, is the new conscience—or nagger—of mankind. I am frankly relieved to reflect that in the early Hitler days we had no television. The news dispatches of brave men had to be read by choice. The television scene of Nazism, as filmed by the devilishly skilled Leni Riefenstahl, could have recruited millions of disciples. It might, of course, have made people stop and listen to Winston Churchill, who went on and on, a croaking old orator, about the threat of a frightful regime he had evidently pictured in his mind.

This, I am sure, is the single greatest change that has come over our society's awareness of what is going on everywhere. The sight of violence has quite likely upset our sense of proportion just as badly as the assumption of general calm upset it by default. If so, we are upset in the right way.

The effect on the foreign correspondent has been revolutionary. All newspaper reporters, whether they know it or not, are competing with the television news, which has a daily audience bigger than the most famous newspaper correspondent ever dreamed of. The sheer pungency of television, of the thing seen, invokes not meditation but partisanship: that is to say, instant ideology. The newspapers, to stay solvent, try to match this emotional appeal. The result is that—in Britain, for example—the best papers are more and more turning into daily magazines of opinion, and the worst make the crudest, the most blatant, appeal to the seven deadly sins.

Consequently, while the scope of a foreign correspondent has not been narrowed (he's still expected to take all knowledge for his province) the reader's expectations of him are narrower, more ideological. When I began, it was possible to present the awkward complexity of a political story without any side being taken. And then to move on to any number of what were called 'colour' pieces: on the landscape, the livelihood of a region, sport, odd characters, the history of this custom and that place. Today, you write about these things and the partisan oldsters say you are fiddling while Washington or Chicago burns. The young say you've got a hang-up on whimsy.

A year ago, I was talking to a forum of Californians about the rape of their beautiful landscape by the developers. The tidal wave of new arrivals. The mania for city ways. The universal obsession with industry as the only true form of progress. When it was over, a handsome nineteen-, twenty-, year-old girl came up to me and said, 'I understood most of it except for one thing.' What's that, I said. She said, 'You have a thing about trees, don't you?' That's right, I said.

In these talks, and at the risk of seeming callous or whimsical, I propose to go on having a thing about many other matters than Soviet expansionism, and the plight of the cities, and the nuclear arms race, and who—after the next Presidential election—is going to be the lord and master of us all.

# Making a
# Home of a House

It obviously takes a little time to be able to judge the political style of any new President, because he suddenly has more power inside the White House than he'd ever guessed. But less power outside the White House than he'd hoped.

In the meantime, there are other changes, from one White Housekeeper to the next, that are more likely, I believe, to fascinate more people than those who are interested only in political programmes. I mean, quite simply, the way the man lives, or is made to live by what we call 'maintenance' and once called a wife. What he does with his day, the gadgets and objects he likes to have around him, the sort of midnight snack he chooses to steal from the icebox.

Five Presidents and thirty-five years ago, the chief White House usher brought forth a book of reminiscences covering nine Presidents and forty-two years in the White House. 'Ike' Hoover, as he was familiarly known, was a sharp-eyed man who had quiet but definite ideas on dignity, eccentricity, what was becoming in a President and what was not. His book is a mine of off-hand observation not unlike, I imagine, the notebooks that Dickens kept on names, characters, foibles, for novels he died too soon to write. Ike Hoover's is a proper book and anyone looking for keyhole confidences or coy sexual innuendo is going to be disappointed. Ike Hoover would have despised such stuff. Nevertheless, what stays in my memory more than all the Cabinet crises or the State dinners are his small observations about character and taste. He never hesitates to draw comparisons. Such as, that Wilson was the only President who cared for the theatre (though Harding 'liked vaudeville'), and that nearly all of them were voracious readers of detective stories. As for diversions, he records—without irony—that whereas for Wilson it was 'much motoring, golf, and solitaire', and for Harding 'golf, poker and lots of company', Coolidge indulged in 'some smoking, sleep and jigsaw puzzles'.

Ike Hoover puts down whatever comes to mind always with propriety but never with censorship. It will be hard to forget the off-hand note that Herbert Hoover seldom noticed the staff and never said 'Good morning', 'Good evening', 'Merry Christmas' or 'Happy New Year'. Ike Hoover also seemed to feel an historian's responsibility to deliver a final judgment on every man he served. He announced that 'The nine Presidents whom I have known seem to me just about average men.' But having obliterated them under a blanket of ordinariness, he then pulled them out again and assigned them marks for human qualities that meant much to him. Egotism? Coolidge had most, Hoover least. Self-control? 'Those who saw Coolidge in a rage were simply startled for life.' Laughter? Taft was a hearty laugher. Hoover, he says, never laughed at all. Fondness for the ladies? 'Theodore Roosevelt was a man's man, through and through. Taft was a ladies' man, pure and simple. Harding was a sporting ladies' man.' Food fads? 'Harding liked fancy food ... Roosevelt would make a whole meal on pork and beans ... Coolidge enjoyed cheese and would eat it by the slice like pie ... Hoover just ate.' Sleeping habits? Teddy Roosevelt never slept by day, Taft 'could sleep at any old time', Wilson could take a nap 'when he had large affairs to deal with ... (he could) go right to sleep as soon as he lay down on the couch. It was part of his plan of self-control.' The report on Calvin Coolidge amounts to a revelation. He went to bed at ten and got up between seven and nine. 'In the afternoon he would without fail take a nap lasting from two to four hours, going from one-thirty to ... sometimes five o'clock.' I have forgotten many things about Calvin Coolidge, but I shall not readily lose the picture of a President of the United States who on principle slept between eleven and fifteen hours a day.

Well, Ike Hoover is long gone, and we shall never have the pleasure of his clean but odious comparisons between, say, Truman and Eisenhower. Even though we've had a spate of memoirs and torrents of gossip, we still don't have as memorable a domestic picture of the newcomers.

A few of us were sitting around the other evening indulging a fantasy that millions of Americans must have been enjoying in secret this week: What would you do if the impossible office came your way? What's the first thing you'd do if you moved into the White House? A pretty brunette with a fine chin knew at once: 'I'd get rid of those damn Remingtons.'

Frederic Remington was an American painter and sculptor of the old West, born just at the right time, the year of the outbreak of the Civil War, to see the last upsurge of the old boisterous life on the plains. If he'd been born out West, he no doubt would have taken for granted the old corral, and the trail herd, and the branding, and the buffalo range, and the occasional Indian massacre. But he was born in New York State and, following the rule that no true believer is so bigoted as a convert, he did over two thousand, seven hundred paintings and drawings of horses, cattle, cowboys, Indians, soldiers, and horses, horses, horses. They were done with almost painful realism, every hoof and muscle and lariat and nostril painted as if by a photographer who was not satisfied with the print until he had pencilled in all the creases. Yet Remington prompted in strong, simple men the thrill of recognition that comes to yachtsmen when they see a painting, good or awful, which reflects the sunset light on ballooning sails.

Today, Remington's pictures bring incredible prices. Two of them were loaned to the White House at the insistence of President Johnson and hung in a room outside his big office. It was a compulsory routine, if you were a visitor to Johnson's White House, to be led at the end out of the office and planted in front of these broncos and urged to admire them. The President would look at them as other men look at a Rubens or a photograph of their grandmother, and a tear would form in the corner of one eye. He would sniff like a gusting wind and brush away the tear with the back of a hand the size of a cod.

Now, if one thing is more certain than another in the transfer of power from Johnson to Nixon, it is that the style and flavour of White House family life will change. It always does, of course, though there have been new occupants too timorous to change anything for a while. Mrs Truman was one. For six weeks, she nibbled away at cold, hard dinner rolls of a kind surely very familiar to English-speaking and French-speaking people. But she'd been brought up in Missouri and inherited the Southern taste for hot, crumbly rolls. It was only on the command of President Truman that her recipe was passed on to the chef, and the Trumans reverted to breaking the bread of their fathers.

I don't suppose any of us would dare to say yet what changes the Nixons are likely to make. In spite of the loving work done on the Nixon image by advertising men and similar plastic surgeons we really know very little about his tastes and private prejudices. He was so anxious for so long to be all things to all men that he seemed to have no preferences whatsoever. In, for instance, food. On his campaign trips his enthusiasm was carefully prepared for the regional foods that came his way. In Idaho, he simply craved a baked potato. In the state of Washington, he couldn't get enough apple and boysenberry pie. In Maryland, he drooled to get at the crabs (and in that, we must admit, he was at one with the best crab-fanciers on earth). In his native state of California—which grows an alarming variety of food—he knew enough to be pretty spry. Praise an orange in Merced County, for example, and you're likely to lose the votes of all the Armenians who pack apricots. When in doubt he settled for plastic hamburgers everywhere, and in Southern California, his home ground, he made a big thing of wolfing *chili con carne* in the Mexican districts, even though it is a Texas and not a Mexican dish. But now he's in his own large home, and he can do what comes naturally, and it must be an immense relief.

First thing he did was to throw out those Remingtons, or rather send them back politely to the museum. Within twenty-four hours, he struck some other blows for liberty that wiped out the more theatrical memories of the Johnson reign. First, he announced that he's not comfortable working in a large, pretentious office. The President's office is a sumptuous and beautiful white oval room. It has two or three superb portraits of earlier Presidents, some elegant eighteenth-century furniture, and a great sofa, in front of which Johnson planted a massive white console. It looked like the computerised dashboard of a nuclear submarine, with many winking lights signifying all the people at home and abroad who were dying to phone the President. He used to gaze at it fondly, as a Roman emperor might have gazed at the roaring Colosseum begging him to elevate his thumb or invert it. Away off, and facing the sofa, were three television sets, each tuned to a different station, for if ever there was a man yearning to know what the world was saying about Lyndon Johnson on three networks, not to mention Telstar, that man was Lyndon Johnson.

Well, the console has gone, and so have the television sets. Mr Nixon hastened to remark that he was not against television. He just wants to turn an IBM headquarters into a home. The Oval Office will be used for ceremonial occasions. Mr Nixon has taken over a small office, where he can put his feet up and—a moving touch—have a fire, with the air-conditioning turned way up, even on the blistering days of midsummer.

These changes will be applauded, I believe, by both the citizens who voted for him and by those who didn't. Nixon is a smalltown boy, and in spite of the trappings of power that have surrounded him since he came to the Vice Presidency sixteen long years ago (he has been at the top or close to it as long as any politician in American history) he likes small surroundings and homely things. There is an anxiety among some old courtiers from Camelot that the Nixons will tear down the French eighteenth-century wallpapers, and dispose of the fine paintings, and otherwise reduce to a suburban 'den' all the other elegant fixings with which Mrs Kennedy did over the White House in the splendid Federal style. There's no sign of this at the moment.

But a President has considerable say in how he wants to have the house look while he's in it. Theodore Roosevelt, another New York convert to the muscle-flexing life of the Far West (and the jungles of Brazil), did over several rooms into menageries of moose and bison heads. His successor couldn't wait to ship them away and be free to walk through the place standing up straight. Harry Truman loved to sit in an old rocker in the evenings and face the lawns behind the White House. What he missed was a porch to rock on, so after a squabble with Congress and the architects (who said the second floor would look like a big Missouri back porch), he had some construction done under the back portico. It looked like a big Missouri back porch.

And how about the Vice President? Agnew is his name. In spite of the usual promise that he will be given vast new sovereign powers, he is tucked away in a tiny office he has commandeered from a secretary. He thus gives substance to Mencken's definition of a Vice President: 'He is a man who sits in the outer office of the White House hoping—to hear the President sneeze.'

# Pegler

*29 June 1969*

I'd like to tell you about an outrageous man who was one of the best American humorists of any time and even at his worst handled the American language with a free-wheeling audacity that has rarely been matched since Mark Twain.

Westbrook Pegler died suddenly the other day and I was saddened. I am puzzled to say why this should be so. I was never close to him, he was seventy-four, he'd been sick in more than a physical way for years, and he had not been seen in print much in a decade or so. Scurrility was his trade, you might say, and in the 1930s and '40s, it was a breathtaking thing to see how close he could sail to the wind of the libel laws. Long before the end, he lost all skill in coming about when the wind was raging. He grossly libelled an old newspaper friend by describing him, among other repulsive things, as a coward, a war profiteer, a fugitive from the London blitz in the bowels of comfortable hotels, 'an absentee war correspondent', and he wrote also that the man had once gone 'nuding along the road with a wench in the raw'. This spasm of whimsy and malice cost Pegler's employers $175,000 in the biggest libel settlement awarded up to that time.

He was always a scornful man, but after that his scorn turned rancid and he babbled on and on about old enemies, about both President and Mrs Roosevelt long after they were dead. His last years seemed to have been spent in fuming total recall of all the Presidents he had watched, from the first Roosevelt to John F. Kennedy, whom he called 'a mean, ratty, dough-heavy Boston gang politician'. Towards the end, even the monthly magazine of the John Birch Society found his last piece, on Chief Justice Warren, too raw to print.

You would think that here was the case of a great talent gone to seed. And, as a man certainly, he was for years simply thrashing in deep water and making incoherent sounds before he went under. Why, then, should I have felt sad at his going? It is because, I think, of a fact of relativity not mentioned in Einstein's theory. Some people are so bristling with life that when they have been dead for years they still seem to be on call, whereas many sweet but pallid people who are up and about have nothing more to offer.

Pegler, newspaperman, is the man I am talking about, and he had a lion's share of the vitality that outlasts its time and place. Picture him first. A big hulking man but erect as a guardee, with glimmering blue eyes that flashed an ultimatum to all simple believers and all secret slobs. A grim, mischievous Irish mouth. Two shaggy, forked eyebrows, to stress that the message—via Western Union—came from nobody but Mephistopheles. Plainly not the kind of reporter to be brushed off by a handout, or a telephone call, or a Presidential 'no comment'.

He was what they used to call a muckraker, and in his middle years he was the best. Once, over a drink in Denver, when I asked him what he was doing so far from his den in Connecticut, he said he'd heard that a couple of insurance companies had suddenly shown alarming fat profits. 'The trail led out here,' he said, 'and I thought I might come and—sink a pick. Could be pay dirt.' I imagined every insurance man in the West out of bed and doctoring the books.

When, soon after, he appeared in Hollywood to look into the way the motion picture unions worked, his hosts should have been warned. At that time, a man named Willie Bioff was the labour boss of the movie unions and a man highly thought of by the bigwigs of the New Deal. Pegler threatened nothing and nobody. He mooched around the studios and the houses in Beverly Hills and dingy offices downtown, and picked up a private scent that led him to Chicago and on to other, obscurer, towns in the hinterland. He pored over police blotters and old newspapers and tramped off to interview this anonymous old man and that forgotten old madam. And after six months of pick-sinking, he wrote a series of searing columns. The first began with the firecracker of a sentence: 'Willie Bioff is a convicted pimp.' Period. By the time Pegler was through, so was Bioff, whose shady past Pegler had reconstructed with the tedious accuracy of one of those picture puzzles in a hundred bits and pieces that emerges at last as the Taj Mahal. Bioff went to jail. So did the national president of a building employees' union, and the prison gates closed behind him on the whining phrase: 'I've been Peglerized.'

Pegler was born in Minneapolis, a skinny little runt, irascible at his first gasp. He delivered newspapers as a boy in the paralysing northern winters, and one day he was shoving his little wagon along in Chicago when the Arctic wind whistling in across the lake blew his papers away, and while he was chasing them his route book too took off in another direction. He was disgusted. He tore off home and when the route boss called him up and said, 'You're fined three dollars,' he shouted back, 'Oh, shut your face!' And that was the end of his first job.

He was the son of a newspaperman and he never thought there was any other trade to follow. He started, at sixteen, as a ten-dollar-a-week cub reporter and described himself as 'a raw kid as freckled as a guinea egg'. He was transferred to St Louis and at twenty-two was in London as a fledgling foreign correspondent. Then he went into the Navy in the First World War and after that turned sports reporter and in no time showed that he had a rowdy, biting style that was to make him a star. He moved up to a sports column, and when nothing much was happening he wrote about this and that and found himself sounding off about the cost of living, the gangsters and the man in the White House. In 1933, he set up shop as a national columnist with no illusions about the pretensions of the breed. He called all columnists 'myriad-minded us ... experts on the budget who can't balance an expense account, pundits on the technological age who can't put a fresh ribbon in their own typewriters, and resounding authorities on the problems of the farmer who never grew a geranium in a pot.'

The first fifteen years of his column were the great years. He wrote about everything with the unsleeping scepticism of a man in the bleachers who had watched many a dumbbell turn into a national hero on the baseball mound, who had seen many a horse race fixed and who was therefore quite ready to believe that a labour leader, a Governor, a Secretary of the Treasury or even a President might be no better than he should be.

He refused to be dazzled by the vocabulary of the sociologists or distracted from his own horse-sense by the hushed pronouncements of the Walter Lippmanns and the Arthur Krocks—what he used to call 'double-dome' commentators. Mussolini, for instance, at one time had very vocal admirers and detesters in the United States, but the role of his Black Shirts in the Spanish Civil War was thought to be a topic for exclusively military experts. To Pegler it was all very simple: 'In most invincible legions, the front rank is regarded as the post of maximum peril and honour. But at Guadalajara, when Mussolini's brave Black Shirts encountered the enemy, the men in the rear rank found themselves overwhelmed by the impetuous dash of their comrades in the forward positions ... it is reliably reported that most of the Black Shirts casualties were caused by hobnails.'

Off in Florida covering some labour conference, he took a day to explore the expensive magic of deep-sea fishing. He was not impressed. Listen to this: it might be out of *Life on the Mississippi*. 'We were going after tarpon and they kept telling me the water was absolutely reeking with all kinds of fish with queer names like dace, mace, plaice, reach, peach, gudgeon, mullet, grommet and shovel-nosed duebills ... we anchored in the barley water beside a channel and rigged up a lot of tackle with hooks the size of those on which they hang half-cows in butcher shops ... we didn't catch any fish on the first day or the second ... the third day we were burned as red as fire engines and the mosquitoes were coming up in clouds ... I can't play golf either ... when I was a kid, I was a punk ball player. Poker—the same story. I try to live right and follow the instructions, but it never makes any difference. Maybe this is what makes me so mean.'

Well, in time Pegler's meanness got to be a national scandal, and the obituary writers made much—too much I think—of his almost psychotic hatred of the Roosevelt family, and his ornery conviction that practically all Americans of Slavic origin were probably Communists. In life, in fact, he was most of the time, and in a private room, an amiable and surprisingly soft-spoken companion. But the path to his prose led through the bile duct. He had a perverse love of demoting all current heroes in a single phrase. Vice President Henry Wallace was 'old bubble-head'. J. Edgar Hoover, when everybody thought of him as the national scourge of all evil men, was put down as 'a nightclub fly-cop'. Mayor Fiorello LaGuardia, the plucky Little Flower to the citizens of New York, was to Pegler 'the little *padrone* of the Bolsheviki'. And though it may seem odd, his devotion to Franklin Roosevelt till America got into the war was an expression of this same contempt for people in power, for he saw Roosevelt as the champion of 'the hired help' against 'the meanness of a complacent upper class'.

He was brought up in the tough and talented school of Chicago reporters when Chicago was the best newspaper town in the country. And when he came East, he carried with him this air of being a prairie lad permanently unfooled by the rich, the genteel, the powerful and all foreigners. He must have adopted the manner early on, possibly as a small fry's defence against the jeering reminders of his gang that his father (a diligent and respectable Cockney immigrant) was English, and his mother was Canadian: Irish–Canadian but still Canadian. Like many other Midwesterners, Pegler was specially on his guard against any beguilements that came from England and the English. But unlike some Midwesterners, he was not exasperated by an English story that defeated the usual American preconceptions.

There was an unforgettable evening just after the Second World War when I was dining with a Midwesterner who had made a fortune in New York as an advertising tycoon. He was the son of a poor parson and he remained a lifelong rural Republican, and a fervent anti-Royalist with a very pat view of Europeans as the lackeys of kings and courts. The only other guest was Pegler. I had just returned from London and the bleakness of England in the winter after Harry Truman had abruptly cancelled the blessings of Lend–Lease. In material comforts the British were, if anything, worse off than they'd been during the war. But I had been struck, as all visitors were in those days, by a new and rousing social equality that the war had—you could almost say—enforced on the country: an equality of want. Pegler and the tycoon politely doubted it. I told them how I'd been invited by the Lord Privy Seal, no less (fifth in line of precedence after the King) to look over the bomb damage to the House of Commons and other ancient memorials. They visibly sniffed at my dragging in such a title. I couldn't think why I'd been chosen for this flattering grand tour until the Lord Privy Seal began to speculate aloud about the type of Englishman who might be best qualified to be the next ambassador to the United States. I said only that I wished for once he could be plain Mr Somebody, and not knighted beforehand, since Americans were fuzzy about titles and tended to think that even a knight was an eighth earl accustomed to whipping the peasants. Pegler and the host glared at their plates as if to challenge me to produce one common man in a society so notoriously class-ridden. Well, so what did Lord What's His Name say to that? He replied, I said, 'Ah dawn't want to goa to't friggin' Stairs, we've got a bloody sawcial revolution goin' on 'ere.' (The Lord Privy Seal was a poor boy from the woollen mills of Yorkshire.)

There was a long bristling silence. Then the tycoon said grimly, '*The Prisoner of Zenda* was the last good book to come out of Europe.' The tycoon glowered while Pegler bellowed. He told me much later he'd never forgotten it.

It's true that Pegler often got angry about many foolish things and never forgot a grudge. But just as often his indignation was nobly directed against unfashionable targets and sometimes his scorn made Dean Swift read like Lewis Carroll. He bucked the Ku Klux Klan when it was dangerously powerful, and he belaboured the ruthlessness of union leaders when their power was sacrosanct. He wrote withering pieces out of Nazi Germany, which was more than many resident correspondents did, but when Hitler was everybody's Evil Eye and Stalin was his benign counterpart, Pegler saw Stalin as at least an equal monster. Defending the American police in the gangster days against invidious comparisons with Scotland Yard, he pointed out the comparative amateurishness of English criminals and the probity of English courts, and ended with this blazing sentence: 'So the British hang their simpletons and Scotland Yard takes credit for another triumph, all to the great inferential disgrace of the American cops, who have to fight it out with Dillingers and Harvey Baileys and Vincent Colls and crooked lawyers, low-grade governors, sentimental juries and courts beneath contempt.'

If the spiritualists are right, and Pegler is somewhere within the sound of these words, he is certainly tearing at his robes and bashing in his harp. But those are the kinds of opinions for which he is to be honoured. All you can do with the talent is envy it.

# Liable to
# Get Your Head Broke

*7 September 1969*

I have just come across a little notebook that I bought soon
after I arrived in America, in 1932. It went with me
everywhere, like those phrase books through which foreigners
new to France, say, riffle in desperation in order to make
elementary contact with the natives. Into this notebook I put
down the prevailing American slang, and it is a deadening
thought that I find it is now quite useless. It was authentic
enough at the time, a time when a phoney was 'a four-flusher',
when people had 'the grippe' or felt 'logey', and when all good
things were either 'keen' or 'swell'. These words are now
hilariously old-fashioned to the young or quite simply baffling.

But I notice that one habit of popular speech—of popular
thinking—is as tenacious as ever, even though the words that
express it have changed. It is the habit of dividing the world,
its people, its books, music, clothes, slang itself, into two
opposing factions, signifying the good and the bad, or rather
the fashionable and the naive. Way back there, nearly forty
years ago, Robert Benchley said that nothing was easier in
America than the practice of dramatic criticism, 'since all
plays are either swell or lousy'. At Yale, we distinguished
between 'regular guys' and 'queers', and the latter term was
not restricted to homosexuals: it took in what would later be
called 'oddballs' or 'weirdos'.

The current prejudice is to divide human beings into the
hip and the square. 'Hip' started out as 'hep' and has gone
through several variations, but everybody will know what I
mean if I say that the American young in the main distinguish

33

between the swingers and the squares. Of course, in America as everywhere else, most of human life lies between these two extremes, or any extremes at all. But slang is not interested in defining the subtleties of the good life or the bad. Slang exists to boost the self-esteem of its users with the least possible effort. It is the handgun of the man who wants to put down his enemy in no time flat.

Now, you'd think you'd be safe in assuming that the squarest of all American institutions is that of the United States Marine Corps. The world's picture of these tough servants of the Republic was fixed in the 1930s and a little beyond by a dozen or more movies in which these most regular of regular guys put to flight the whole historical pack of their enemies: the Barbary pirates of Jefferson's time, the Mexicans of the 1840s, later the Cubans, in this century the bandits of Nicaragua and the Dominican Republic, and then the Japanese who had the gall to stay on their Pacific islands when the Marines were in the offing. Say 'an American Marine' to any regular moviegoer of the last three decades and he knows in a flash the types you have in mind. Victor McLaglen with fists like sledge-hammers, Pat O'Brien barking at his men in the last ditch and bowing his head only when the flag goes up, the undefeatable and forever cocky James Cagney, trading insults with the relish of a schoolboy swapping cigarette cards.

Think of the Marine in his off-hours, and all the technical resources of Warner Brothers and Twentieth Century Fox were available to show you how two honest men could demolish the furniture and fixings of a waterfront saloon whenever some wise guy cast the slightest slur on the Corps. Think of a Marine in the abstract, if that is possible, and you conjure up a man all muscle and nerve, pesky, fractious, quick-tempered and brave, but running reservoirs of simple goodness: a two hundred per cent male pitifully susceptible to every passing skirt.

You would have to be a foreigner, and a newcomer at that, not to know this hero when you saw one. I remember when the

New York headquarters of the United Nations was very new and security, though polite, was for a while rather jumpy. I went along to do a radio report on the first session of the General Assembly, and I had with me a recording engineer, a recent immigrant from Vienna. We were stopped at the outer gate—on the New York City edge of what was now an international zone—by a policeman. He looked at the engineer's impressive gear and said, 'I'm sorry, you can't take that stuff in there.' The Viennese showed his BBC credentials and suggested that 'Perhaps ze other policeman would give oss ze proper permission.' The cop fixed him with a solemn stare and said, 'Listen, sonny, that's not a policeman. That's a United States Marine. Liable to get your head broke.'

I should guess that few Americans ever get to see an actual Marine, so the popular preconception remains intact. Or did until last week, when General Leonard Chapman, the Commanding Officer of the Marine Corps, laid down this remarkable new regulation: 'Commanders will permit the Afro natural haircut providing it conforms with current Marine regulations. That is, if it is neatly trimmed on the sides and in the back and stands no more than three inches high on top.'

An Afro haircut, need I say, is that high foam of black hair, as fine as spun sugar, which was first sported a few years ago by American Negroes who—before they preferred to be called blacks—looked back with pride to their African origin and wanted to be known as Afro-Americans, as, indeed, many still do.

Well, though the Afro haircut was once a novelty, it is now a fashion with all sorts of blacks, most noticeably with the young, and most becomingly with young women. But hardly the most clairvoyant reader of racial relations could have guessed that it would become an issue in the United States Marine Corps. The Commandant's order, however, brought us up against one of the great and troublesome issues of our time, namely the daily relations between whites and blacks.

35

Lately, at Marine camps in several states, there have been sudden and violent brawls between them. There was recently a formal inquiry. The Commandant put out a message to all Marine commands in which he granted that there has been racial discrimination and violence 'unheard of among Marines in combat. Literally thousands of young Marines have quietly made the adjustment from combat and capably served stern and demanding tours of duty in a national atmosphere where expressions of appreciation for their services are hard to find.' As I learned to say forty years ago, Commandant, you said a mouthful.

This very restrained remark of the Commandant puts a brave face on what must be the present chronic indignity of the Marine Corps. If the Corps ever comes up as a topic among the rebellious young, I am sure it is thought of as the military equivalent of the policeman 'pig'. Inasmuch as the Marine Corps is the oldest military service in the country, it has become a symbol of what is most inflexible about the military establishment. Today, when an actual majority of college students have, to put it mildly, misgivings about military service, and the White House itself is pondering the virtues of a volunteer army, the Marines are seen as the most rigid, the most Prussian, unit in the services. I think that to appreciate the brave faint sigh that one can hear between the lines of the Commandant's message, we ought to consider briefly the history and traditions of the Corps, which, as I say, occupies pride of place in the military history of the United States.

They first appeared in the American War of Independence by a special act of the Continental, or provisional, Congress. As early as November 1775 they were, as they were with the British, auxiliary units of the Navy, and they had to be ready for the worst fighting on land or sea. When the war was over, the Americans did what Americans have done at the end of every war, including the Second World War. They never thought of themselves as a military nation. Soldiers were for emergencies, and when the emergency was over you disbanded and, in the early days of the Republic, actually abolished the service.

Once the United States was created, the Marines went out of existence. But the next emergency came very soon, within fifteen years, in a naval war with France. And since the only possibility of invasion came from overseas, the Marine Corps was set up once and for all as a permanent watchdog service. The Marines inscribed daredevil records in the war of 1812 and in the defence of Washington against the British two years later. They were rushed down to New Orleans to help Andrew Jackson, and for the next thirty years they helped the Army, alongside the frontiersmen, clear the frontier of the Indians. That's a rather complacent way of putting it. They did what the first generation pushing West did without scruple: they slaughtered and, over a vast region, banished or extinguished the American Indian.

The fine hours of the Marines were in the war with Mexico and then in the conquest of California. But the picture of the tough and valiant Marine that we started with was impressed on the folklore of America by three well-advertised episodes at the turn of the nineteenth century: they were the heroes of the Spanish-American war, of an insurrection in the Philippines, and of the besieged victims of the Boxer Rebellion. When the United States was for the first—and let us hope for the last—time thinking about having an empire, the Marines became the sentimental favourites of a nation that knew it had an army and a navy but couldn't quite recall many of their exploits. From about 1900 on, and into the 1930s, the United States assumed it was its duty to put down any internal trouble in the Caribbean. So whenever a bandit leader was on the loose in Haiti, or somebody seemed to be threatening the Panama Canal, or a dictator twirled his moustaches in Dominica, the word went out from the White House as thousands cheered— 'Send in the Marines!'

This status, which I suppose is unique among the armed

forces of the world, is what sets the US Marine Corps apart from all the American soldiers, sailors and airmen. They are unique also in the physical severity of their training, and not least in their pride. Commandant Chapman recalled the other day: 'The Corps has always demanded the highest standards in military appearance, military courtesy, and proficiency... standards that breed pride, and pride in turn builds the kind of discipline that is essential to battlefield success with minimum casualties. These qualities have always been the hallmarks of Marines, and no relaxation in our proven high standards will be condoned.' Afro hairdos or no Afro hairdos. Brave words, but the Commandant must know as well as the rest of us that after eight years of Vietnam, 'battlefield success' carries a whiff of sour grapes. The military is everywhere on the defensive.

But then the Commandant took the bit between his teeth and applied the iron discipline of the Marines to the new issue of race: 'Positive and overt efforts to eradicate every trace of discrimination, whether intentional or not, must be continued ... we are a band of comrades in arms. Every Marine must understand that the Corps does guarantee equal rights, equal opportunity, and equal protection without regard to race, and will continue to do so. We take care of our own.' In this day and age, it seems to me to be a remarkable pronouncement, not least for a literacy very rare nowadays in any officer of the government or member of the Congress.

You all no doubt remember the little boy, dragged bawling to the circus, who was told by a furious parent that 'You were brought here to enjoy yourself, and enjoy yourself you shall.' In the day of racial upheaval, there seems to me to be a sad and gallant irony in the warning of the Commandant that the Marine Corps is one place in America where, black or white, you are recruited to become an equal. And if you are not, by God, we'll break you.

# 'Eternal Vigilance'—By Whom?

*19 October 1969*

The other day I had a long talk with an attractive young American. The conversation divided between long sarcastic monologues on his part, and grunts of approval—more often of doubt—on mine. He was bemoaning, as we all should, the noisy and smelly flood of scandal and corruption that fills the papers these days, defaces the brightness of the television screen, and makes television commercials seem more smug and fatuous than ever. We touched on street crime, on the army sergeants swiping huge profits from overseas service clubs, the continuing proof about risky short-cuts in the manufacture of automobiles, the deep inroads the Mafia is making into big and respectable business. And so on and so on.

What bothered me was that he put all these things down, not to the corruption of any class but to 'middle-class values' in themselves. Before we come to that, I'd like to say that it was not only the substance of his jeremiad that upset me, the blanket indictment of a whole country. It was the muddy language that drooled from his lips. Nobody burgles a house any more: 'A kid I know was burglarised.' None of the statesmen we brought up ever met or tangled: they were involved in 'a confrontation'. He talked of 'interface' and 'feedback'. People were either 'committed' or 'alienated'. I said goodbye and went off. I believe he thought I was shaken and impressed. I was glad I'd not said what I was tempted to: that the whole burden of his song had been sung long ago—'It's the rich what gets the pleasure, it's the poor what gets the blame.'

I suppose that one way of explaining this unpleasant get-

39

together (confrontation?) was the so-called 'generation gap'. Well, in some things it is a fact, and always will be. In many more disputes, and strained relations, the generation gap is a lazy excuse for the age-old suspicion between parents and children. And today, certainly, there is a widening gap between the language the generations use. I throw it out as a suggestion merely that this may be due to the sudden eruption, in the past twenty years or so, of technology—the passing over, into ordinary speech, of the special vocabularies of advanced mathematics and computers, and the new and respectable status now given to the ghastly language of sociology and psychology. Most of the horrors that now befog the speech of students and politicians, not to mention advertising men, are a special lingo that the layman doesn't understand: like 'input', 'orientation', 'parameter'. 'Parameter' is a good example. In mathematics, it means a quantity constant in a given case, but one that varies in different cases. It is used by politicians and pundits to mean no more than limit, or boundary.

No wonder they talk about a failure of 'communication' (another stop-gap word between two thoughts) when they spend so long using words like communicate and verbalise. Only a year ago, I heard a qualified psychiatrist declare that his two-year-old was already talking. But he didn't say it that way. He said, 'Children of his age group don't usually verbalise at this stage.' Especially if there's a verbalising sibling in the familial situation. A gabby brother, that is.

Well, by way of thoughtful reacting, I can only say that things are bad and they'll probably get worse. There's just one point I'd like to make to people who despair of American society—and I have to confess it's a point I often forget myself. In a self-governing republic—good government in some places, dubious in others—three thousand miles wide, eighteen hundred miles long, with fifty separate states which in many important matters have almost absolute powers—with two hundred million people drawn from scores of nations, what is remarkable is not the conflict between them but the truce.

Enough is happening in America at any one time—enough that is exciting, frightening, funny, brutal, brave, intolerable, bizarre, dull, slavish, eccentric, inspiring and disastrous—that almost anything you care to say about the United States is true. You can make a case for thinking this the best, the worst, the most abject, the most alert democracy ever invented. Of course, this reflection doesn't help people bleeding in a riot or languishing in a sloppily run hospital at an outrageous daily rate. The great need for anyone in authority is courage. And the requirement for a reporter, an onlooker, is horse-sense and the ability to strike a true balance. I don't know any good reporter who would confidently claim these qualities.

Yet there is one whole class in America, and that the largest, which claims them and thinks of itself as the balance wheel of the American system. It is nothing more or less pretentious than the middle class. In America, it is not only huger—proportionately and absolutely—than anywhere else. It is not simply a large group of people who qualify by reason of income and social habits. It includes all the people who aspire to be in it, or think they are already there. In nearly forty years, I have never heard an American say, 'I am a working-class man.' I have often heard people say, 'So-and-So is looking out for the ordinary guy like me,' but that's not quite the same thing.

In all the great conflicts of the past ten years—of race, student rebellion, street crime, pornography—the middle class has not been much heard from. It has been, in fact, the besieged, the ridiculed victim—of the black leaders, the student leaders, the film makers, the intellectuals, all leftists and many liberals. Yet middle-class standards, as they were planted and have grown everywhere in this country, are the ones that have kept America a going concern. It is time to grit the teeth slightly, prepare for a shower of eggs, and say what those standards are. Fair wages for good work. Concern for the family and its good name. A distrust of extremes and often, perhaps, a lazy willingness to compromise. The hope of

41

owning your own house and improving it. The belief that the mother and father are the bosses, however easy-going, of the household and not simply pals. A pride in the whole country, often as canting and unreasonable as such patriotism can be. Vague but stubborn ideas about decency. An equally vague but untroubled belief in God. A natural sense of neighbourliness, fed by the assumption that your neighbour is much like you and is willing to share the same lawn (hedges are rare in American towns) or lend you a mower, a hammer or a bottle of milk.

Did you ever hear of qualities less heroic? Helpless laughter must be bellying up from almost any group of young people who happen to be hearing this recital. But there are signs, tentative and fumbled signs, that these people—who for too long have been called 'the silent majority'—are tired of being laughed at and frustrated. In desperate times, the meekest people show alarming symptoms of defiance. And, in the early races for the autumn elections, I notice that policemen are being elected as the mayors of cities. It should not yet give us cause to splutter. It is possible, I dare to say it is common, to find policemen who are fair, brave and level-headed.

However, it doesn't seem to me a good thing that the middle class, weary of violence and mockery as it may be, should turn to policemen as rulers, any more than that we should turn the government of the military over to the military. If war is too important to be left to the generals, the government of the people is too serious to be turned over to the police.

There is a more disturbing sign of the turning of the worm. Some cities are beginning to form vigilante committees. The most famous instance of this drastic remedy for lawlessness and disorder happened in San Francisco in the first furious years of its life as an El Dorado, after gold had been discovered nearby. San Francisco had been a shanty town on whistling sandhills. Then suddenly hundreds, and shortly thousands, of people from many states and several lands, came hurtling in to pan the rivers and get rich quick. The vast majority never made it but stayed. The garrison down the Peninsula deserted. The farmers quit. The shopkeepers closed down, and the laundries. The lucky new-rich sent their shirts to Hawaii—or even to China—to be washed.

When the ordinary, and pretty rude, services opened up again, the town was a combination of a doss house, a street bazaar, a mushrooming suburb and a brothel. At nightfall gangs roamed the streets, invaded stores, taverns and houses and beat up the inmates, especially if they were foreigners, and robbed them and quite often shot them. In two months, among a population of only 25,000, there were over a hundred murders, and no one had been executed. In the end, the silent majority rose up, held mass meetings, elected officials and formed what was known as the Vigilance Committee of San Francisco. In short order they tried, condemned and hanged all the notorious criminals they could catch.

Inevitably, the lust for justice, and quick justice, can be as insatiable as any other lust. When California came into the Union, it became possible within a year or two to suspend the committee and hand the law over to the State government. Not all San Franciscans thought this was a sensible, or even a decent, thing to do. In a report I have in front of me, written in 1856, the author has this to say about the Vigilance Committee of that year. It is quite an end-of-term report: 'Scorn and applause, exoneration and abuse, indignation and sympathy, have been the expressions of the civilised world in speaking of the Vigilance Committee of San Francisco. To law-loving and worthy people, it did seem strange that such an organisation which usurped, as it were, the laws of the land and inflicted the severest penalties, should exist without molestation at this time ... yet from this power California recognised her only protector of life and property, her only security for peace and virtue. Such was the object of the Society of Vigilantes. The remedy was violent but the result was good.'

The other day, the *Wall Street Journal* carried a long report on the growth of vigilante societies around the country. At present they take the form of night patrols. They mean to make the streets safe. Mostly, they go unarmed. But in some small towns they tote guns, and in others they are sufficiently in league with the police to ride around in police cars. In one place their targets are robbers or muggers, in another Negroes or radicals or homosexuals. Most of them protest that their aims are innocent. Conceivably, there are simple and just men who, like the sheriff's deputies in the old Western towns, feel they must fill in for the failure of law and order. Needless to say, the courts and the police and the Governors in most states are dead against them. Vigilantism is at best a mischievous pretension, at worst a seedbed for civil chaos.

It is a small, and understandable, but ugly symptom. It would be a tragic thing for America if the middle class, the silent majority, provoked by some appalling wave of rioting and violence, found its voice and used it not to preach but to improvise law and order. Those last three words have become a catch-phrase, used by the Right to argue for arbitrary restraints on the freedom of people you don't like. But the phrase has been taken up too by the Left, as a sneering put-down of ordinary people who question violence and the abuse of 'peaceable assembly'. I say, a plague on both your houses. Any society that hopes to be stable must surely yield its most passionate prejudices in the cause of getting law and order by consent of the majority. The only alternative is to get a very tough form of law and order imposed by a powerful minority. Sometimes, a minority of one.

# Massacre:
# An Act of War

*30 November 1969*

This is the weekend when Americans of all ages stream over the highways and pack the airports and criss-cross the continent in order to sit down with Mom or old Uncle Fred, or the recently divorced wife and the children in common, and celebrate the meagre first Thanksgiving of the first Massachusetts colonists with a gluttony of turkey and cranberry sauce and pumpkin pies and other dishes, succulent or barbarous, peculiar to the part of the country you were born in.

It used to be the weekend when the President, Franklin Roosevelt with more zest than anybody, sat by his fireside and carolled, 'My Friends', and went on, with lilting persuasiveness, about the hardiness and the essential benevolence of the American character. It is a national ceremony with which foreigners are either enchanted or uncomfortable. I suppose there are hardy festivals in Spain, saluting the independence of the Spanish character, that were not suspended during the years that Generalissimo Franco had all independent men and women under his heel.

I appreciate that this is not a happy comparison. But it did, after all, come to mind. Because the United States is cowed today, not by the rule of any single man but by its conscience. There must be very many homes in which the rich food and its fixings lie heavy not only on the stomach.

It is usually claptrap to say that a whole nation is haunted at any time by a single preoccupation. But I'm afraid this is one of those times. There is no need to go into details of the ghastly massacre of a village and all its inhabitants in South

Vietnam, which has only now come to light. It is a numbing story. What haunts Americans just now is why they weren't numbed long ago. For though the story, like all war stories, is probably very complicated and will be straightened out in the coming courts martial, the moral issue is simple in its challenge if not in its solution. Yet only in the past few days has it been brought home to people that the massacre at Songmy is not an isolated incident but a brazen variation on a regular policy of modern war. In spite of President Nixon's regretful statement to the effect that the massacre violated the 'American rules of war', the truth had already anticipated him: that the men of Company C, First Battalion, Twentieth Infantry, did with rifles what the Air Force and the artillery had been doing for years as standard procedure. That is, wiping out the people of any village that was suspected of harbouring, or being under the control of, the Vietcong.

Let us remember that the killing of civilians harbouring nothing more than their own goods and fears has for ages been a regulation practice of all armies. There would not, otherwise, have been any bombing in the Second World War. (Come to think of it, there would have been no city sieges in the Middle Ages.) But aerial bombing was defended, if not humanised, by a doctrine. In the Second World War, we called it 'strategic bombing'. Many good men and true laboured night and day over maps of Germany to pick out those industrial cities, shipyards, ammunition depots and the like whose destruction would most damage the enemy's war effort. Unfortunately, factories and shipyards are not always built in separate locations suitable for hygienic bombing. And the ghosts of the dead mothers and children of Southampton and Coventry and London could testify that in time the bombing of the people who do nothing but keep a home together becomes indistinguishable from the killing of the war workers and the young men who might turn into soldiers. Nobody who has seen the long, flat plain of Hiroshima rebuilt as a tacky neon city can doubt that strategic bombing can go beyond itself and ultimately, if the choice is between defeat or survival, be forgotten.

I have gone into this not at all to provide a plausible excuse for the fearful scenes that followed on the easing of, shall we say, the rules of strategic bombing. They are examples of how the self-propelling pace of total war can carry you beyond its declared aim. The so-called strategical bombing of Dresden is perhaps the most flagrant violation we know about. For it, too, was a military base. It was also the unique northern capital of baroque architecture. And while Hiroshima had its hundred and twenty thousand casualties, Dresden had its hundred and thirty thousand, a great many of them ordinary people so desperately scorched by the fires that they jumped in the river and were drowned. It may be cold-blooded to recall these famous devastations but I think they are relevant to the massacre at Songmy.

Now, in the Vietnam war, we have two related doctrines that sanction the killing of women and children and other non-combatants. There is the doctrine of 'search and destroy', and we think of it as a legitimate pretext for searching out the Vietcong in the rice paddies and the jungles and the bush and destroying him and his hideouts. But, fairly early on, 'search and destroy' was stretched to take in what is called 'a free-fire zone'. That is to say, a village presumed to be under Vietcong control. Consequently, to be a legitimate target for B-52s or artillery.

There is a knotty problem here for any company commander or roving squadron leader. How can you decide when a village is under enemy control, in a war whose villages are so often inhabited by young men who go about their work by day as peaceable South Vietnamese civilians and who by night turn into Vietcong, tossing hand grenades into the bunks of the resident US Marines? President Johnson heard of so many examples of this sort of thing that he used to put in regular sympathy calls to the relatives of the murdered men and suppress the word of the manner of their death. In

Songmy, the tactical decision must have been more heartrending still: the women and children left behind by day belonged to men who were off fighting *either* with the South Vietnamese or with the Vietcong. It is as if half the inhabitants of a village in the Cotswolds had been in the British Army and half in the German. (This split of allegiance was a regular thing in many towns of Tennessee in the American Civil War.)

Well, there is ample evidence to show that neither the American Air Force nor the South Vietnamese themselves agonised for too long about deciding whether or not a village was 'a free-fire zone'. A young sergeant, now back home, who was interviewed the other night on television, was asked if the villagers shot at Songmy were Vietcong. He replied with dry disgust, 'Most of them were too young to walk.'

Jonathan Schell, a gifted American in his middle twenties, has written two books that are full of bombing missions which unload their bombs, on the home run, on the people of villages that might or might not have housed the enemy. Mr Schell wrote a letter the other day to the *New York Times* 'in the hope,' he said, 'of dispelling two possible misapprehensions: that such executions are the fault of men like Calley and Mitchell alone' (the two men already accused of murder); 'and that the tragedy of Songmy is an isolated atrocity.' He tells of flying daily missions with Forward Air Control that utterly destroyed a whole province and its people. In the midsummer of 1967, Schell recalls, the so-called 'pacification camps' became 'so full that Army units in the field were ordered not to "generate"'—a delicate word—'any more refugees.' The Army complied. 'But search-and-destroy operations continued, only now the peasants were not warned before an airstrike was called on their villages. They were killed [there] because there was no room for them in the swamped "refugee camps". The usual warnings by helicopter loudspeaker or air-dropped leaflets were stopped. The civilians on the ground were assumed to be the enemy by the [fact] of their living in Quangngai, which was largely a free-fire zone.

Pilots—servicemen not unlike Calley and Mitchell—continued to carry out their orders. Village after village was destroyed from the air as a matter of *de facto* policy. Airstrikes on civilians became a matter of routine . . . Such atrocities were and are the logical consequences of a war directed against an enemy indistinguishable from the people.'

I am sure there must be hundreds of thousands of old people in Germany, and very old people in France, survivors of the Second World War and the First, who could say Amen. But the British people on the home front in the First World War, and the American people in the Second, never knew the confusion of military problems and moral problems that sets in when your home town comes under fire. Certainly, though Americans are dividing too simply into two indignant camps over Songmy, we are an age away from that ludicrous day in the First World War when the Germans dropped a bomb on the grounds of a hotel in a Yorkshire seaside resort, and shattered the eggcup of a resident old gentleman, causing him to rise in a purple rage and cry that the Huns had gone too far. But I honestly don't know if we are very much further away, in planned brutality, from the destruction on the ground of French and German villages in the First World War, or from the strategic bombing of the Second. Once the 'art' of war renounces the formal ultimatum, the attack at dawn, the digging of opposing trenches, the infantry lines drawn up to proceed in 'contact', the squadrons of airmen searching out a promising target below, and all the other arranged manoeuvres of soldier against soldier moving towards a piece of ground, or a town, which is presumed to be occupied by the enemy— once the battleground is any city and any village, and all its intermingled populations: the man who aligns the bombsight is saved only by the charity of distance from the charged crimes of Lieutenant Calley and Sergeant Mitchell.

I don't suppose it's a popular time to be asking mercy for these two men. But the moral riddle will not go away: is it valiant to bomb a hundred women and children from the air,

and despicable to shoot them on the ground? I leave it to you.
Like Pontius Pilate, I don't care to stay for an answer.

# La Fayette Si,
# Pompidou No!

*1 March 1970*

When I first arrived in the United States, one of the novelties that fascinated me was something called a 'greeter'. New York City had an appointed, indeed a salaried, official known as the town's greeter. His office has by now gone pretty much the way of the town crier, because—whereas they used to take five days to come from Europe, and several hours to sail up the bay—celebrities now whisk in and out of the city as nonchalantly as housewives bustle in and out of a supermarket.

But in those days, New York had a splendid greeter, a man named Grover Whalen, and his job was roughly, or smoothly, equivalent to that of the State Department's chief of protocol. His office was not, I believe, sanctioned by law or even by custom. It was the inspiration of one Mayor Hyland, a man who before he became Mayor had been a tram driver—or, as I was learning to say, a streetcar motorman. Mayor Hyland was what they used to call a rough diamond and at some point he yearned for a smooth diamond who might, on official occasions, put up a front worthy of the grandeur of New York City. Mr Whalen did not let him down. When some person of blinding glamour was sailing into the city—at various times, I remember, it was Queen Marie of Rumania, Lindbergh, Michael Arlen (and, some of you may tenderly recall, Chico Marx masquerading as an Italian aviator)—the great ship came sliding in when the tide was right, and tug boats hooted at it, and fireboats jetted fountains of water by way of salute, and the liner responded with a blast of the last trump. Either on the pier, or down at City Hall, there would be a welcoming committee headed by the wonderful Grover Whalen, a rare bloom amid the surrounding business suits—with his top hat, cutaway, striped trousers, toothbrush moustache, wing collar, grey stock, pearl stickpin and a white carnation in his buttonhole. He would make a mellifluous speech, and the ex-tram driver, or the ex-band leader, or the ex-con man, or whoever was Mayor, would nod and marvel that he had on hand a greeter worthy of the Earl Marshal at the coronation of an English king.

In those days the United States, for all its accession of financial and naval power, was not so obviously the world power it is today. And the city didn't think twice about the political implications of welcoming a distinguished German or a sheikh or a Frenchman or an Italian. There was always a special fuss reserved for the arrival of a Prime Minister of Ireland, a Cardinal from the Vatican or a Mayor of Jerusalem. For, considering the ethnic composition of the voters of New York, a Mayor of New York going to Europe for nothing but a holiday would—as one told me later on—'naturally make compulsory stops in Dublin, Rome and Tel Aviv'.

Today, it is all changed. New York has grown up in many ways. Mayor John Lindsay needs no social stand-in, being himself at once as gorgeous as Apollo and the very epitome of Eastern Establishment grace and confidence. But today, also, the Mayor and his staff must scrutinise very cagily the list of important people who are coming on state visits to the United States. For though they may fly in the first place to Washington, if they are political grandees they usually indicate that they would like to come to New York, and the city is required to arrange a banquet for them. In fact, the Mayor of New York sometimes finds himself on a more sensitive spot than the President of the United States. It is grudgingly admitted on all sides that President Nixon, by virtue of his office, cannot rudely ignore any head of state who chooses to come here, although there are times when a head of state, or a head of government, is quietly informed that the only welcome he is likely to get is a Bronx cheer. Plainly, the President cannot sacrifice common courtesy to some purely regional prejudice.

But the Mayor of New York is not, like the Lord Mayor of London, an anonymous figurehead. He is, after the President, the second most important executive in the country. He is the administrative head of the country's biggest city. He is also a practising politician and the chief citizen of a city that crackles at all times with political prejudice. There are in New York City resident colonies of almost any country and any religion that cares to send along a ruler or a delegate or a holy man. There are not too many Arabs in New York, but there are more Jews than there are in Tel Aviv. And on St Patrick's Day more Irish, it appears, than in the whole of Ireland. There was an awful to-do a few years ago about the state visit of an Arab king. When the Mayor let it be known that he would welcome the king in a cool correct way, there was such an uproar that the monarch confined himself to Washington.

Well, as everybody knows, M. Pompidou, the French President, arrived in the United States this week and presented a nasty problem to Mayor Lindsay, and a lesser problem to President Nixon and the Congress. President Pompidou's government had just sold some jet fighter planes to Libya. So? It is a deal that might have gone merely regretted, or barely mentioned, if the incoming President was anything but a Frenchman.

Because if there's one foreign dignitary more welcome in the United States than a Frenchman, it is hard to say who he might be. The French have always been envied, by Britons especially, because they have had an insurance policy in American goodwill which has not lapsed in two hundred years. The French had a shining hero who helped the colonies win their independence from Britain, and his fame and benevolence still brush off on the dullest French film director who condescends to visit us.

He was a stripling, a boy of nineteen who bore the

impressive name of Marie Joseph Paul Yves Roch Gilbert du Motier, Marquis de La Fayette. A captain of dragoons when he heard that the American colonies had proclaimed their independence of Great Britain. 'At the first news of this quarrel,' he wrote, 'my heart was enrolled in it.' He hastened off to an American agent in Paris and they made a deal whereby he would sail for America and be commissioned in the revolutionary army as a major-general. Flushed with as much rebel fervour as any hippie or Black Panther—though considerably more house-broken—La Fayette took leave of his friends, wrote a tender farewell to his seventeen-year-old wife, and was ready to sail when the word came in of very severe American defeats.

Benjamin Franklin, the American Minister in Paris, tried to dissuade his going, and the King himself forbade it. But La Fayette was young and bold and steaming with ideology, and so the opposition of the establishment fired him all the more. He started to fit out a ship in secret till the British Ambassador at Versailles got wind of it and La Fayette was arrested. The ship, however, slipped off to a Spanish port. And so, in a week or two, did La Fayette. He landed on the coast of South Carolina and journeyed for several weeks over rough roads with great good humour and with no more recognition than a tramp. He had the aristocratic habit of never needing to pull rank.

At last, he came to Philadelphia. He knew practically no English and the new Congress had more pressing things on its mind than the tattered letters of introduction he kept offering to show to bigwigs. So for several disheartening months he hung around, till the news began to spread that here in the capital city was a noble if slightly eccentric Frenchman, said to be an excellent soldier, a friend of Franklin and a very young man blazing with devotion to the American cause. In July, 1777, after much wangling and politicking, Congress passed a resolution accepting his services and giving him the rank of major-general. The next day he was taken to meet

George Washington, who gave him his first command. Within three months he'd been wounded but his enthusiasm overcame his convalescence, and Washington was so taken with his spirit that he gave him, what he'd prayed for, the command of a division. He was still only nineteen. And when you consider the huge stretch of territory over which the war was being fought, and the turtle's pace of communications in those days, it is an astonishing thing that his renown as a soldier spread throughout the colonies.

When at last the French declared war on England, La Fayette went home to report to the King and was received as a conquering hero. He was back, though, within six months and was now welcomed by the Congress as the incomparable foreign hero of the Revolution. It passed a resolution saying so. When the British surrendered he was twenty-four, and his military career was over. He visited the United States again, in 1784, as the twenty-six-year-old guest of the new nation.

Incidentally, he drafted the declaration of rights for the French Revolution and was the designer of the combination of royal white and red and blue that became the tricolour cockade of France. He is one of the best examples of an undying type: the highly idealistic young man who responds to a revolutionary cause and then recoils in horror from the savagery of his revolutionary heroes once they have carried their cause and taken over. I'm talking about the revolution in his own country. Three years after the fall of the Bastille, he was arrested and served five years in prison as a traitor to the Revolution, which to him had soured into a murderous betrayal of its promise. He was later set free and as an old man of sixty-seven he paid a last visit to America and was overwhelmed by a national reception which not all the American Presidents—with the aid of Grover Whalen—could have equalled.

The legend of La Fayette has never dwindled. When the first American troops arrived in France in the First World War, an aide to General Pershing had the happy thought of greeting the welcoming French general with the line: 'La Fayette, we are here!'

So the lingering memory of this impulsive nineteen-year-old has given France a prejudice in her favour till this day. Or perhaps we should say till last Wednesday, when President Pompidou got up before a wary and partly hostile Congress. It is true that General de Gaulle at the end was no idol either, and his quitting of the North Atlantic Treaty Alliance offended the government and the people. But M. Pompidou—simply by representing France—offended the nation and enraged New York. The glory of the Marquis de La Fayette, his two-hundred-year investment in Franco-American goodwill, appeared for the moment to have been liquidated in a day: the day the French sold those jets to Libya.

# Now Here is
# the Nightly News

*7 June 1970*

Every night the comfortable people who have no personal link
with Vietnam, and surely the anxious who do, settle down to
one of the three television networks that put on, at seven
o'clock, a half hour of world and domestic news. The other
night one of their Vietnam correspondents poked his camera
into a small jungle clearing in an unnamed and probably
unpronounceable corner of Cambodia, and asked four or five
American soldiers who were squatting there how they felt
about crossing yet another Asian border, or should we say
entering a new country? One of them smiled wanly and said,
'We ought to get back home where we belong, in Vietnam.' It
was the only faint attempt at a joke. All the others were sad
and sore. To put it mildly, they violently disagreed with their
Commander-in-Chief who, as you may recall, is the President
of the United States. They not only had no taste for war in
general, they thought the Cambodian adventure was a mess
and a mistake.

This fragment of face-to-face reporting was seen, I suppose,
by about twenty-five or thirty million Americans, and it sent
me by morbid association to my bookshelves and one particular
book, a slim, crisp and marvellously cool account of one stage
of the Flanders campaign in the First World War. At the end
of it, its author sums it all up: 'It is possible to arrive at some
conclusions as to whether the [1917] Flanders Operations did
contribute to the victory achieved the following year. It is true
that the British casualties during this period, 31st of July to
10th November, were actually 238,000. But in spite of the

57

heavy casualties and hardships experienced during 1917, the morale of the British and Commonwealth troops remained remarkably high.' That, surely, is the last word, since it comes from the man who was the director of Military Operations at General Headquarters in France.

Well, not quite. I turned to the memoirs of David Lloyd George, the wartime Prime Minister: 'For the massacre of brave men, who won just four miles of indefensible mud, the Government were not prepared by any warning or prediction given us by the military leaders. The total British casualties on the whole British front during the progress of that battle amounted to the appalling figure of 399,000 men—three times the official military estimate. Divisions were sent in time after time to face the same slaughter in their ranks. And they always did their intrepid best to obey the fatuous orders.'

How come the morale of these foredoomed, mole-like men held? It didn't. GHQ simply said it did and GHQ was closer to the home front than to the front lines. There was no television to move into the trenches and have the men speak their mind. There were correspondents, and they either toed the drastic line of censorship or gave up. The stuff of the best of them—Philip Gibbs, for instance—is now shameful to read, full of chin-up officers and comical Cockneys ('We won't 'arf give it to the Kaiser when we get 'old of 'im'). But when the war was over, one or two of them wrote what they knew. Gibbs, in a book significantly called *Now It Can Be Told*, had his own sharp recollections of the troops' morale. He noted— and none of us on the home front could know it—the increasing number of arrests and executions for desertion. And he recalled, as it might have been a nightmare, 'the deadly depression in the ranks among men who could see no future but bloodshed. They shrank from what was to come, and above all they hated the salient with a despair reflected even in the place names—Suicide Corner, Idiot Crossroads, Hell Fire Crossroads, Stinking Farm.'

We return the books to the shelf and go back to our

television. Night after night it tolls the bell of the dead. Twenty-eight Americans killed yesterday, sixteen the day before, 110 the day before that. How would it be if the figure was 399,000 in eleven weeks—which is precisely three times the Confederate losses in the whole American Civil War? Or, let us stay with the official figure for the Flanders campaign, only 238,000, which is almost 100,000 more than *all* the American casualties in the Korean War. Yet the repetition of these comparatively minute numbers, and the nightly sight and sound of the men in motion, have succeeded better than any enemy propaganda in dividing the two hundred million Americans left at home, and noticeably enraging many of the young whose number is coming up, like no other war of our time.

I'd no sooner wondered about this, and wondered at the ease with which we have come to accept a living picture of a group of genuine malcontents as an implied cross-section of the troops in Cambodia, or for that matter in all of South Vietnam, when I picked up the *New York Times* and read a dispatch from a correspondent in Oakland, California. That is the location of Travis Air Force Base. And that is where twenty odd buses a day pick up troops from the airport coming in from all over the country and fit them out in combat uniforms and jungle boots before they are flown off to South Vietnam. 35,000 a month come in and are made ready to go. Now—you may ask: I thought the President was withdrawing a quarter of a million men from Vietnam? That's right. But these withdrawals simply reduce the total force. The rest have a limited period of service—one year, two years at most—an indulgence that the men in the trenches would never have believed possible. The men withdrawn have to be replaced, and the 35,000 coming in every month to Oakland are the fill-ins, the new boys. We're told that about five per cent of the replacements have tinkered with the idea of not showing up in Oakland. And as many as fifteen per cent have tried to wangle a deferment through their parents, doctors or

Congressmen on various grounds: conscience, illness, psychiatric troubles, the sudden urge to do university graduate work. This spring there were so many of them that the Army gave out a bit of advice: if a recruit was going to exhibit a conscience, he had better acquire it before he left home.

There are people who say that the television networks in general, and the *New York Times* in particular, are liberal in their bent. But there are other stations, other newspapers, which convey the clear impression that the war is an exercise in rescuing Asia for life, liberty and the pursuit of happiness. There would seem to be nowhere to go for the uncomfortable truth but the public opinion polls. While they can often adulterate their samples by asking leading questions, they are far more objective than your wishes or mine. It is strange but true that in spite of all you hear about 'the American people' being in a paroxysm of rage against the war, here in 1970 President Nixon has well over sixty per cent of the country believing he is doing a good job. This is as high a percentage of public backing as Eisenhower or Kennedy had—and in peacetime—in all but their early honeymoon days in the Presidency. So when President Nixon decided he had to go into Cambodia he knew what you would never gather from much of the press and television—that most Americans were prepared to trust him.

However, it was a bold risk, because he didn't ask the people to trust him in perpetuity. He announced a deadline, something no President and none of the generals has done in the whole history of the Vietnam war, or—not to be too parochial about it—in the history of war: all the men to be out of Cambodia by the 30th of June. As the date came near, Nixon said that the Cambodian adventure had been the most successful operation of the war, so much so that he would promise to have another 50,000 men out of Vietnam by October. He has maintained all along that what he was doing was destroying the enemy's occupation of his left flank and so protecting the lives of the remaining 400,000 Americans.

Even sympathetic wiseacres have said that what he's really doing is protecting a strategic withdrawal, and at some time in the next year or so the protesters will be embarrassed to discover that the United States has indeed brought all its men home. Of course, they won't be embarrassed, they'll say it's too late.

But what is unique about the public conflict over the war is its openness, which I think is a direct reflection of the openness of the reporting of the war. Nobody seems disturbed, or writes about, the sudden abandonment of what have always been thought to be disciplines, or if you like cover-ups, essential to the conduct of a war: official secrets acts, front-line censorship, aiding the enemy laws, indeed almost the whole code of treason. In no previous war could men at the front say aloud what was on their minds for immediate, or even delayed, transmission to the home front. And though in most wars there have been sporadic civilian riots, there never was a time when people at home could rip up the flag or burn down recruiting offices and generally raise hell with impunity.

Some people say that these protests on the home front are uniquely ferocious and widespread because we live in a uniquely violent age such as our grandfathers could never have guessed at. I wonder.

The Victorians had to read a serious newspaper to know that in one evening in the 1870s South Carolina had just barred whites from voting, that there had been a revolution in Bulgaria with many attendant atrocities, that 40,000 people had died in India from starvation, that in Wyoming a whole valley of homesteaders had been massacred by cattlemen.

Come closer to our own time and consider the contrast between the old and the new traditions of war reporting. It is 1916. John Chancellor and David Brinkley, today's nightly NBC news team, are reporting on the opening day of the Battle of the Somme: 'The British and French armies began today the long awaited Allied Big Push, with the French claiming an early breakthrough at Hardecourt and Curlu

61

north of the river. Further to the north, the British infantry advanced into the German lines. Garrick Utley, who is following the British advance, has that story.'

The camera dollies up a trench of packed corpses. Follows a long raking shot of thousands of dead men on open ground, and hundreds more skewered on the barbed wire defences. Utley appears: 'Beginning at 7.28 this morning, the first of July, the British infantry went over the top, wave on wave, into the German lines. They were, however, well fortified by double trenches, belts of barbed wire and machine-gun nests at high points. Our correspondent with the German army has no figures yet on the German losses, though they are known to be high. But I'm afraid this has been a bad day for the British. The command at GHQ would not offer an official estimate, but the British losses for the day are thought to be somewhere between 55,000 and 60,000 men. Garrick Utley, at British GHQ on the Somme.' (When that battle was over, the British would have taken just over eight miles of ground, which the Germans had abandoned, devastated and heavily mined. The total British losses were close to a quarter of a million.)

Is it conceivable that if there had been a population of British viewers to see and hear this sort of thing, they would have simply shaken their heads and gone off to the railway stations to wave their boys off on the troop trains? The Pope, who knew these things, begged the combatants in that year of 1916 simply to stop 'while there are still any young men left in Europe'.

Ninety-one years ago, a commencement speaker stood up before the graduating class of the Michigan Military Academy. This is what he told the newly-fledged soldiers, in the confident high noon of the Victorian age: 'War is at best barbarism. I am tired and sick of war. Its glory is all moonshine. It is only those who have neither fired a shot nor heard the shrieks and groans of the wounded who cry aloud for blood, more vengeance, more desolation. War is hell.'

The speaker was the man who fourteen years before had desolated the cities of the South, a man whose name cannot be lightly pronounced south of the Potomac even to this day. He was General William Tecumseh Sherman.

You'll notice that he waited fourteen years to speak these passionate lines. Philip Gibbs waited four years to report the despair and the deep depression of the men in Flanders. The young American correspondents in sweaty sports shirts in Vietnam see and hear it in the morning and tell us that night. There is no gap now between the battlefields and the memoirs. I don't think it possible to exaggerate the shattering capacity of television to tell it—now. And what is shattered, I suspect, is morale, both at the front and at home. It puts a crippling burden on the generals and the politicians who in a democracy are trying to conduct any war.

Field-Marshal Haig could assure all and sundry that the morale of his men was splendid, since we were not in touch (nor, by the way, was he) with the feelings of the 100,000 men moving up into the graves of 238,000. It raises the profound question of whether any nation not under a dictatorship can ever again fight a war with a steady spirit. And this, I believe, is something new under the sun.

# Final Health Warning

*9 January 1971*

Some studious type on the radio thought to greet the New Year by reciting Tennyson's *Ring Out Wild Bells*. But on television the New Year was rung in with the wildest, certainly the most expensive, burst of cigarette advertising since Sir Walter Raleigh returned from Virginia and started up the unending debate about tobacco: whether, as Raleigh thought, it was a delicious medicine with a most soothing effect on the nerves; or whether, as King James I insisted to the point of hysteria in his famous *Counterblaste to Tobacco*, it was a 'moste abominable and noxious weede'.

Anyway, as you may have heard, cigarette advertising on television and radio was banned by Act of Congress—beginning not on January the first but January the second. There is a very important difference here. In some countries, New Year's Day is given over to recovering from New Year's Eve, also to the making of resolutions, like giving up smoking. In the United States, New Year's Day is a national holiday given over entirely to the last orgy of football before we retire to our caves to sit out the winter snows and the zero temperatures. We still go by a calendar—or by a view of the calendar—invented in temperate countries. And nature sometimes doesn't oblige. Football games had to be postponed for a couple of days the other week when twenty inches of snow were dumped on the Eastern seaboard. Just before that the English papers reported that Southern England was 'paralysed'—was the word—by three inches of snow. I had a heartbreaking letter from an American now living in England.

He said, 'Two inches of snow fell on London a day or two ago. It must be one of the most pitiful catastrophes since the Black Death. Trains stopped. Highways closed. Little men scraping snow off railroad tracks with penknives, with shovels at least. Parliament at a standstill. You have no idea.' Anyway, the climatic theory is sound, most of the time. In most places where American football is played, the weather is comparatively mild through December. Then comes the Ice Age.

Forty years ago, big-time football was college football. All the movies and musical comedies about football were about a clean young stripling giving his all for old Winsockie and the clean young soprano in the stands. Today, college football excites the great public about as much as college baseball. The big time is professional football, and the stars are rangy young gorillas who will give their all for four or five years at most to achieve the ambition of any self-respecting sportsman today, which is to make a million dollars and, a little later on, to emulate the two most famous living golfers—Arnold Palmer and Jack Nicklaus—and buy their own private jet.

I'd better say, before a universal prejudice sets in, that no American institution is worse understood abroad than American football. British sportsmen who know their way around a rugby field, a billiard table and even a chess board succumb without a second thought to the facetious view of American football as a mindless bout of mayhem between brutes got up in spacemen outfits. But it would not take more than a couple of weeks of careful instruction from a coach or a fan to realise that American football is an open-air chess game disguised as warfare. It is without question the most scientific of all outdoor games. There is a lexicon of 'plays', known to any decent footballer, as premeditated as the Ruy Lopez opening, the Petroff Defence, the Sicilian Defence, the Muzio Gambit, the Queen's Gambit Declined. Most of them are not only learned for the purpose of using them but of declining them on the spur of the moment. Hence the extraordinary, and to the foreigner, bewildering sight of men

65

running off in circles and tangents with no apparent relation to the ball or the man who's holding it. For weeks before a big game, the players practise these plays and feints, and fake plays, and in the evenings they attend sessions of instruction, in strategy and tactics, following hieroglyphics on a blackboard with which Einstein would have been quite at home.

What makes footballers more than usually susceptible to physical injury is the fact that they never forget they are engaged in warfare and that the switch from planned to impromptu tactics requires them to break, twist, crash or swerve on a signal from a man thirty yards away or a map of the game inside their heads. And they do seem to suffer more than most athletes from characteristic and innumerable injuries. As much as baseball players, who also are required to practise hairsbreadth plunges and turns that, in cricket, for instance, would be mad and dangerous improvisations. The dazzling standard of fielding in baseball is not due to any native physical superiority of baseball players over cricketers. A fielder practises down in Florida for half the winter, timing his run to a ball to catch it on the bounce and return it with a single reflex. And when a runner literally dives full length into third base he is not being desperately brave, he is doing something he is expected to do after hundreds of rehearsals on dry ground.

Consequently, while football and baseball may be recommended by muscular parsons as splendid ways to build up health and strength of character, they also tend to produce dislocated elbows, chronic trouble with the knee-cap and damage to the spurs of the heel. Top golfers, of course, because they must regularly perform the damaging movement of pivoting around a braced spine, are frequently laid low with muscle spasms, disintegrated discs and bursitis. Somebody said Arnold Palmer would refuse to appear on the first tee without a bursa. And show me a top-notch footballer, and I'll show you a top-notch collection of torn cartilages, bruised tendons and wobbly knee-caps. Think of Joe Namath, the greatest living American footballer. To a stranger, he appears to be a lanky, loping, heavy-lidded, shaggy-haired young man who throws a long ball in any direction his fancy suggests. But I gather he is a tactician unrivalled since Napoleon or Alexander the Great. He is, however, not expected to be out on the field for more than two or three seasons. And why? His knees have been operated on three times. They are braced and bandaged before every game, and at the end he staggers off like an infantryman on the last lap of the retreat from Moscow. But he is a wise sportsman of the late twentieth-century variety: he has formed a syndicate. To make footballs? Endorse cigarettes? No. He does endorse—wait for it—panty hose. But he is going to start an employment agency. Or a nightclub. He may yet come to rival the chain of fish and chip joints started by Arthur Treacher, the old English movie butler. Or the tea shops of Japan: Arnold Palmer tea shops.

So no one is more aware of the tribute the nation owes to its footballers, its supreme gladiators, than the cigarette manufacturers. They knew that for about twelve hours on New Year's Day the living-rooms of America would resound with the cheers of the crowds, the blare of the bands, the gabble of commentators, the rise and fall of famous plays, and, occasionally, with the smart crack of a breaking heel or a slipping knee-cap. There was probably a larger audience watching television than for anything so comparatively placid as a landing on the moon. The cigarette manufacturers, consequently, had a day and a night to get across their last inspirational message. Once for all, let every nation know that this brand is sweeter, better, milder, tastier (than what they never tell us).

On the second of January, you wouldn't have known that smoking had ever been discovered. The silence fell like a great snow, but not before one tobacco firm had spent a million and a quarter dollars making one last heartrending pitch. Next day, they laid their plans to increase cigarette advertising on billboards, on buses, in papers, magazines, and—what do you know?—through the sponsoring of sports events.

During all this, I expect the class has been thinking of the recent report of the Royal College of Physicians, which reinforces practically everything that has been said since the American Cancer Society got out its first, and frightening, report in 1954. By now everybody except people whose livelihood depends on the tobacco industry agrees that the damaging evidence against cigarette smoking is overwhelming. Even in America, where trade lobbies are immensely powerful, the tobacco industry failed a year ago to stop Congress passing a law which requires the printing on every pack of cigarettes of a warning: 'The Surgeon General has determined that cigarette smoking is dangerous to your health.' What I don't think is likely to happen here, or even in England, where it's been proposed, is the banning not only of all cigarette advertising but the public prohibition of smoking. However noble the impulse may be to save people from themselves, the Americans remember only too well the disasters that followed on the noblest experiment of them all: the national prohibition of all alcoholic liquors. Which, within a year or two, had every other sixteen-year-old carrying a hip flask of bootleg liquor even if he or she was travelling only two blocks.

Once you start stamping health warnings on things that have harmed a lot of people, I frankly don't know where you'd stop. A helping of Christmas pudding could mean sudden death to a man with a high cholesterol count. Should we have to trace in creamy white sauce on every plum pudding the warning: 'This pudding may be hazardous to health'? I was brought up in a city where black smog, which reduced visibility to about fifty yards on the winter days, was known as 'fresh air'. ('Get out in the fresh air, now, don't sit here watching your father smoke.') I have lately thought of suing the town council—retrospectively, of course—for poisoning my youth and stunting my growth. If we start a campaign of wholesale, wholesome health warnings, I don't see why every

68

industrial town in the Western world shouldn't be compelled to erect public signs which say: 'Warning. Breathing our air may be hazardous to health.' Hazardous to health, indeed. As the man said, the mortality rate from breathing is one hundred per cent.

# Judgment Day's A-Comin'

*13 February 1971*

'Five o'clock in the morning, and all well. Families of artisans and mechanics living in homes and lodging houses south of Market Street were bestirring themselves. Oil stoves were lighted and smoke was curling out of kitchen chimneys ... thirteen minutes later, the deeps of the earth far down under the foundations of the city began to rumble and vibrate.'

That is part of an eye-witness account of what happened in San Francisco at 5.13 a.m. on the 18th of April, 1906. Even with the earth lurching, people dashed out into the streets and sniffed clouds of dust and saw bits of masonry crumbling. But then the city's gasworks blew up, and the fire began. It was the fire that consumed the city, and after seventy-two hours it had demolished 28,000 buildings in five hundred city blocks and left seven hundred dead.

Everybody has heard about the San Francisco earthquake and how the city is balanced precariously on a long geological fault—the San Andreas Fault—that starts up north way out to sea and goes rippling five hundred miles down to the Mojave Desert and across Mexico into the Caribbean. People have already forgotten, or had until last Tuesday, that there is no law of nature which says that American earthquakes have to happen only in and around San Francisco. Running off and across the long San Andreas Fault there are several others— the Nacimiento Fault, the Big Pine, the Garlock, the San Gabriel, the Mission Crest, the San Jacinto Fault—all of them long cracks in the underpinnings of the earth, so that you have a jagged break, two levels where a firm carpet ought to be. It

70

takes only a momentary shudder, some deep earth movement, to shift the broken levels, so that whatever is balanced on top of them topples for a while till it finds a new footing.

The earthquake that struck last Tuesday on the northern edge of Los Angeles was along the San Andreas Fault, though some bland experts say that was a mere coincidence, it could have been one of three others. This remark, coming on top of dramatic television films of the physical damage, has given a fillip, or a shudder of unholy glee, to the large family of death-wish addicts who itch to resolve all our troubles with the expectation of one big, clean catastrophe. The crudest of the type are the people who keep on predicting the end of the world, and give you the date, until it doesn't happen, and then go back to *Ecclesiastes* or the *Book of Leviticus* and say they must have got their signals wrong.

But the same deep yearning for the Day of Judgment seems to fetch other types, often highly intelligent, who by some emotional chemistry long for disaster. Only a month ago, an English friend of mine, a serious, kindly intellectual, got hold of me in London and shunted me into a corner and looked over both shoulders before confiding to me his delicious Doomsday bulletin. He had just been to a private showing of a film called *The City That Waits For Death*. 'Do you know,' he said in a very low, conspiratorial voice, 'that San Francisco is going to be hit by the most devastating earthquake in the next year or two, and do you know what the casualties will be?' He didn't wait for me to say 'No kidding?' He took a deep breath; 'Between two and three hundred thousand! Do you believe it?' No, I said.

He was startled. Hadn't I heard that the seismologists had worked it out and it was a practical certainty? All I know, I said, is that the chief seismologist up at Fordham University in New York has said that San Francisco is quite certainly going to suffer another, and possibly more devastating, earthquake in the next —— 'Yes, yes?'—my friend's face was one big sunrise of a smile. In the next—well, somewhere between the next forty and three hundred years. My friend's hopes collapsed.

This film appears only two years after a book called *The Last Days of the Late Great State of California*. It is a cunning, plausible bit of prophecy based on popular geology and a sort of numbers game. It was very soon a best-seller in Los Angeles and San Francisco. And it made enough people feel mighty uncomfortable for small groups of them to decamp from the State then and there. 'Is it true,' I was asked in letters from England and other countries, 'that the Californians are beginning to leave the State?' You should never talk about 'the Californians' without saying which Californians. For apart from the great body of citizens who are much like you and me, but happen to live in California, the State abounds with scores, perhaps hundreds, of odd religions and weird cults. There is no theory of life and death, health and ill-health, sexual vigour, predestination, reincarnation or whatever that is too simple or too stark to attract a fervent following.

You have to remember that Southern California, Los Angeles and its environs especially, had its population greatly boosted in the prosperous 1920s by retired farmers and other old folks from the Midwest who were sold small lots by jumping-jack real estate agents. They were told that they were going to a paradise where all their earthly infirmities would fall away like dead skins. And if their particular infirmity was stubborn, there were legions of miracle men, and women, whose acquaintance with various occult arts had made a monkey out of medicine as it is practised in such fuddy-duddy capitals as New York, Boston and Chicago. You can legalise almost any profession in Los Angeles, and apart from such abstruse religions as the Nuptial Ecclesia, the Self-Realization Fellowship, the Institute of the Cosmos and the 'I Am' cult, the newspapers bristle with ads that promise a new lease on life through black magic, or bizarre diets, or high colonic irrigation, or the thumping of the lower spine by ex-piano movers.

Of all the healers, the movers and shakers towards the Day of Judgment, Los Angeles has never had one more famous, and more idolised in her time, than the astounding Aimee Semple McPherson. She was, in the early Thirties, the world's leading evangelist. Her mother, a Canadian, begged the Lord for a girl who might grow to be a preacher. God obliged, and Aimee was born. She was converted by the Salvation Army, but then she took to the world and its pleasures and had to be converted all over again by a lay preacher, the Reverend Semple, who preached in 'special tongues'. They were unintelligible to everybody but the disciples, and Aimee was the top disciple and married him. They went to China, and the word got back that they were healing Orientals in freight-car loads. However, Mr Semple was bitten, it was said, by 'a heathen mosquito' and died. Aimee came home, married and divorced, and took up her first husband's mission by preaching, as he had, in 'tongues'.

The old and the lame, the halt and the gullible, legions of hopeful suitors (for she was a strikingly handsome woman) flocked to her and contributed their dollars and built her a temple costing—even then—a million and a half dollars. Here, in front of a huge pipe organ that would have impressed Gabriel, and a brass band, and a choir of gorgeous females, she preached the Four Square Gospel, based on the presumption that heaven has four walls, 'of pearl, gold, jewels, milk and honey'. In her golden days, she simply glared at the sick and aged, and they swore that she had cured them.

One day, she went for a swim in the ocean in a pea-green bathing suit and vanished. For thirty-two days and nights her flock kept up a vigil on the beach with prayers, wailing, trumpets, bonfires, dancing—and one sacrificial suicide. Then they gave up. She was dead, and there was an immense memorial service.

Next day, she stumbled into a small town in Mexico. She had been kidnapped, she said, but the Lord had saved her from any scratch or stain. Los Angeles was beginning to look odd even to Los Angelenos, and the city got after her in a series of barbarous quasi-legal moves. But she beat them all, went back to preaching and married again. The only time I saw her she stood as majestically as ever, a voluptuous creature with blonde bobbed hair, directing her angels to throw out a lifeline to a cluster of repentant sinners before it was too late. When I say the angels threw out a lifeline, I am not using a figure of speech. In this performance, lightning flashed, the organ belched and roared, twelve virgins in white nightgowns clung to a *papier-mâché* Rock of Ages while searchlights raked a cardboard sea. 'The Day of Judgment is at hand,' Aimee warned in her rolling contralto, 'but'—there was a roll of drums—'the sinners are saved!' The band broke out, and the American flag was hoisted and flapped in rhythm to a wind machine. And the congregation went into delirium.

Well, Los Angeles is forty years on in sophistication and a rock group has a new hit song, which it croons with no misgivings. It is, 'Where you goin' to go when there's no more San Francisco?' San Franciscans look on this new panic, and the accompanying jokes, as typical Southern Californian waggishness. But, after last Tuesday, there is a new exodus, of soberer types, enough of them to be interviewed for a television feature. They are looking at maps and geological sections and searching for a place, like old Brigham Young, where the Devil will not find them out. But one thing is fairly sure. The faith-healers, and black magicians, and the end-of-the-worlders, and even the chiropractors, will be doing a land-office business. By the way, the man who invented the scale by which we measure the severity of earthquakes is still with us. His name is Charles Francis Richter, and he lives cheerfully in—Southern California.

# The Last
# of the Romanoffs

*11 September 1971*

The President has devalued the dollar. A distinguished
ecologist has announced that practically everything we eat
contains some poison or other. The John F. Kennedy Center
for the Performing Arts has opened in Washington with a
blaze of celebrities and intending celebrities. But the most
important, certainly the most American, thing that has
happened in America is the death of a scoundrel.

I opened the paper and saw that he had gone, and I recalled
something I hadn't thought about since it happened. An
evening nearly forty years ago. Those were the days and
nights when in most cities if you went off to the movies, you
had to be careful to get into the right queue. There would be
a line that looked as if it led to the box office but more often
than not it wove round the theatre and wound up at a soup
stall, which had been set up to hand out a minimum meal to
some of the thirteen million unemployed. These lines of
listless people shuffled like castaways through all the cities of
America.

When one family in three or four didn't know where its
next meal was coming from, most Hollywood movies seemed
crass and trivial. The people who had a heart in those hard
times were called 'socially conscious' and wouldn't have been
seen dead at a Hollywood movie, at any of the movies which
we are now told constitute the golden age of American film-
making. But, I must sheepishly confess, I was not hungry, and
I was young and in a new country, and therefore I was callous.
So one evening—it must have been the winter of 1933—I

gave a wide berth to the breadline in Times Square and enlarged my acquaintance of American theatre by venturing into a realm of it that was a glorious discovery to me, though the old hands told me it was sick unto death. I mean American vaudeville, with its wonderful roster of character comedians— Lou Holtz and Willie Howard and Frank Fay and Herb Williams and Bert Lahr and Bert Wheeler—who were very soon to give way to the non-character comedian with a gag-writer and a wisecrack.

I forget which of these peerless comics I had gone to see, but I was no sooner in the theatre than I decided I was in the wrong place. The orchestra struck up the Russian national anthem, the old White Russian anthem, and a backdrop descended on which was emblazoned the imperial double-headed eagle, and a little squat man waddled out with a toothbrush moustache, jug ears, cutaway jacket and an uncomfortable high collar. Of course, he was a comedian. But then I realised, of course he was not. His jug ears were a natural misfortune, his cutaway and four-inch collar were no gag but a strenuous impersonation of elegance. He was announced by a thunderously amplified voice as the son of Alexander III, none other than His Imperial Highness the Prince Michael Alexandrovich Dmitry Obolensky Romanoff. There was little applause and much rustling curiosity, because the audience knew that he was not the last of the Romanoffs but the first—and certainly the last—of the Gergusons of Brooklyn to claim the imperial purple and the blood blue.

All I remember about the performance was that it was weirdly pathetic without meaning to be. He spoke in a rolling Oxford baritone, in an English much too grand for the King's English. He told about his experiences at court, and the audience tittered, the orchestra played again the last twelve bars of the anthem and he bowed himself out. He was, of course, a fraud and he had no performing talent. If he had been W. C. Fields pretending to be the King of England, the audience would have been in hysterics.

I forgot all about him for several years until I read a comic piece of Robert Benchley's about the death of Rasputin. Benchley wanted to put an end to the rumours, which were rampant in the Sunday newspapers, that Rasputin was alive and wickedly well in Argentina or Peru or some such place. Benchley's piece began with the memorable line: 'Let's have an end of all this shilly-shallying. *I* killed Rasputin.' Benchley insisted that it was done in the cellar of the Winter Palace by himself, Mike Romanoff 'and a Grand Duke whose name I have forgotten'. It began by passing to Rasputin a tray of *hors d'oeuvres*, each canapé of which consisted of a little mound of elk-poison ('Four elk had been killed in the out-of-town try out') and it ended with Benchley and Mike Romanoff replacing the block of ice over the hole in the frozen lake through which they'd pushed him.

From this it appeared that Prince Michael Romanoff had graduated from a fraud into a character and was out in Hollywood along with Benchley and other simpler rogues. In fact, he landed up there a year or so after his vaudeville flop and he turned up one day at a studio, and at the office of Nunnally Johnson, who—to Benchley's set—was known as 'Robert Benchley with a Georgia accent' but is known to the film histories as probably the most successful screen writer (from *The Grapes of Wrath* to *How to Marry a Millionaire*) there has ever been. Johnson is a very droll and kindly Southerner and he saw that the Prince (he announced himself as such) was not living on caviare and vodka. Johnson at the time was making a movie that required a big nightclub set. He suggested to the casting manager that he give the Prince a job, at the going rate of seventeen dollars a day, as a guest or a waiter. 'Go and ask him,' Johnson said, 'which he'd prefer to be.' The man came back a little shaken. The Prince was outraged. The Prince had assumed that a special part was being written in for him. He declined the offer and returned to his garret.

I think now of the last time I saw him. He was the owner and the imperious overseer (he was imperious though he was five feet three) of the most successful restaurant in Hollywood. It was called, with regal simplicity, Romanoff's. Over its entrance, and on its menus, was embossed a pair of capital 'R's' backed up against each other, and over them hung a crown. The place was jammed with his usual crowd, mobs of movie stars of great grandeur crowding the bar and waiting for tables. There was, facing the entrance, one empty banquette. When he came over to drop one of his resonant droll stories, I asked him why the banquette at my elbow was empty. 'Very simple,' he said, 'it is Friday night and it is reserved for ...' He lowered his voice and mentioned the name of an ageing English star who had taken to the bottle in the worst way and—in a familiar tragedy—was being bravely paced by his young wife, to the point where she too turned into an alcoholic. 'But do they ever manage to get in here?' I asked him. 'Very seldom,' he said, 'but, you know, there is— shall I say—little call for his services, and if he should turn up no harm is done to invest him with a little of his old—er— splendour.' I learned later that whenever the couple did show up, they could order the entire kitchen, and there was no check, no bill. I didn't know this when the Prince leaned over to me and said, 'You see, dear boy, I remember those days.'

I call him the Prince because he was either that or Mike, but never Harry Gerguson. His impersonation of a Russian prince over forty or fifty years was so convincing that if he had called himself Harry Gerguson, *that* would have seemed like an impersonation. I suppose it wasn't always so. In fact, he had tried on many characters before hitting on the one that fitted him more truly than the only genuine White Russian prince he ever met, a gentle, sweet man but—as Mike was the first to confess—'tall, yet mousy' by comparison.

Mike began, then, as Harry Gerguson of a poor Jewish family in Brooklyn. He started not even as a buttonmaker. He made button holes. To this day, nobody is sure whether he was born here or, as the immigration authorities maintained, in Lithuania and brought here at the age of six. For four years, anyway, he was in a series of orphanages from which he was tossed out as incorrigible. At the age of nineteen he somehow got to England. He must have had a marvellous ear. For his accent, his cultivated Southern English accent, was exact except for a consonant here and a vowel there which betrayed, as he said later, his Russian blood.

He came back here and proclaimed himself Count Gladstone. All that this proclaimed was his embarrassing ignorance of British nobility. 'Count,' he later said, 'was a frightful error. A gaffe, I do declare, a gaffe.' He was restless in the new knowledge that he couldn't possibly pretend to be of the English royal blood, so he settled for the Romanoffs and showed up in 1919 in Paris, which was rife then with bogus Russian princes. Nevertheless, having decided to be Prince Michael Romanoff, he maintained it through thick and thin. And there were plenty of thin times. He was incarcerated on Ellis Island. He escaped. He applied, as Prince Michael, for admission to Harvard and was given a warm welcome by the President of Harvard himself when he confessed that all his academic honours had been burned during the ordeal of his family in the Revolution. They found him out and he regally departed. He passed a rubber cheque or two and was deported to France, went to jail there for swindling, came back to America and with the help of sturdy friends like Robert Benchley and John Hay Whitney (later to be Eisenhower's Ambassador to Britain), he scraped up the money to start his Hollywood restaurant. He never looked back, and he died at the age of eighty-three.

It is impossible to understand the appeal of this charmer, and he had enormous charm, if you start to analyse him as a merely successful impostor. He was in his own person a marvellously sustained gag. He did not pretend to be Prince Michael Romanoff of Russia. He pretended, and managed, to be a great comic pretending to be Prince Michael Romanoff of Russia. This front appealed to Americans, who are ambivalent about the whole business of royalty and titles. It is a European delusion that Americans are simple-minded and idolatrous about such things. Some may be. Many more share the conviction of Thomas Jefferson that titles of nobility—which the Constitution forbids—are 'a very great vanity'. Most Americans, I believe, think of titles as decorative and also comic. All hail, then, a man who by caricature exposed the pretensions of nobility in countries which have long been republics. Mike Romanoff was a one-man satire on the whole French and Italian jet set. He simply decided to be a prince and chuckled up his enormous cuffs to see the descendants of genuine noble houses kow-tow and haggle for a choice reservation in his restaurant.

As Nunnally Johnson put it: 'A real prince is an accident. Mike made it by his own efforts. It only goes to show what a good American boy can do if only he applies himself.'

# The
# Acheson Plan

*16 October 1971*

On a fall evening, as the twilight came on, the control tower at Kennedy Airport stacked up some incoming jets to allow a flight of wild geese to go on their way unharmed to the South. As they passed over tidewater Maryland, an old man with a noble head and a bristling guardsman's moustache was sitting in his study on his Maryland farm. One minute he was a vigorous man, plagued, however, lately by a swollen eyeball. The next moment he slumped over, and at nightfall the news went out from Washington that Dean Acheson, Harry Truman's champion, friend and field-marshal, was dead. A thousand miles away, Mrs Truman got the word and said she would not give it, just then, to the old President, who is frail and pretty much over the hill. But she guessed that he would be 'very disturbed'.

For once, it is possible to avoid a cliché with conviction. Acheson's going does not mark the end of an era. The era he dominated ended long before he died, and it took some fortitude and much humour to live serenely through the years when everything you'd stood for was condemned or ridiculed and when the labours of the Truman Administration—from the end of the Second World War to the arrival in the White House of General Eisenhower—were put down by a young generation of historians as a calculated effort to police the world and so bring on all our present woes. It is never possible, either when you're looking back on history or living it, to say for sure that B happened on account of A simply because B followed A. But though schoolboys are taught this, or ought to

be, as the most gross error of elementary logic, it is unfortunately one of the axioms that most of us live by. Nobody
knows this better than politicians, and while they dread having
it used against them, they leap to use it against the other party.
Next year, we shall certainly be hearing from the Republicans
that they are and always have been the true party of peace.
Because, when America went into the First World War, and
into the Second World War, and into Korea, and into
Vietnam—there was a Democrat in the White House. Ergo,
the Democrats are the war party.

Dean Acheson was alive and well while a new generation
was becoming articulate, verbose anyway, and looking back in
anger to the Truman–Acheson years. I can't forget the first
time I felt the blast of this new indignation. Four or five years
ago I was up in Minnesota during its perishing winter, dashing
out of twelve below zero into the ninety-degree oven of a
university auditorium. I was to talk to an audience of a
thousand or more students. They were polite and even cordial
until I started to recall the years after the Second World War,
the threadbare years when Western Europe was an invalid
and a total dependant of the United States—an invalid greatly
alarmed by the Russian pressure first in northern Iran, then
down in the Mediterranean, then during one terrified summer
in Berlin. I was not proposing a thesis, or even thinking to
defend such things as the Marshall Plan or the North
American Treaty Alliance. I took for granted that everyone
knew that the Marshall Plan made possible the recovery of
Europe, that everyone could understand why old Ernest Bevin
had cried, 'We grabbed it with both hands.'

What I didn't know was that the vast majority of these
students had never heard of the Marshall Plan. The minority
that had were pretty cynical about it, as about the first
instalment of an American imperial plan. I realised, a little
late, that when the Russians had been huffing and puffing, and
the Marshall Plan was passed, these students were two years
old. And that therefore Azerbaijan, and the Siege of Berlin and

the Marshall Plan lay, for them, in that dead zone between what you can read in the books and what you have lived through. In the question-time after the talk, I was made to realise that most of them did not know, or did not believe, that the Soviet Union had ever been a powerful threat to Western Europe once the Second World War was over. It was a strange feeling to be told, in many heated little speeches from the floor masquerading as questions, that Truman and Acheson had been sleeping partners of the late Senator Joseph McCarthy, quick to see Communists under every bed and to respond in panic with billions for arms. I very much hope that Dean Acheson never found himself facing an audience that lumped him with McCarthy. For no American statesman or politician of our day went through a more demoralising time than Acheson did between about 1950 and 1953. For three or four pitiless years, Acheson—now known as 'the Commissar of the Cold War', a man with a built-in alarm bell at the mention of the Soviet Union—was pictured by McCarthy, and by most of the Republican rank and file, and most actively by one Richard M. Nixon, as something very close to a traitor, a 'coddler of Communists' in the State Department, a coward, and quite conceivably an underground agent of the Communists. During his last two years as Secretary of State, his public appearances were frequently hissed, he went in danger of physical harm, his telephone rang incessantly with threats and obscenities. I cannot forget the bawling, shabby scene at the Republican Convention in 1952 when somebody unfurled a banner inscribed with the legend, 'Acheson—Twenty Years of Treason', and there was a thunderclap of cheers.

It would have been easy, it would have been almost forgivable self-protection, for Acheson to throw a few lambs in the State Department to the slaughter house of Senator McCarthy. But he never did. And when Alger Hiss was found guilty of passing on secret papers to the Soviet Union, Acheson was on the touchiest ground of his public life. He had been a friend of Hiss, and at his next press conference he was asked how he felt about Hiss now. The Secretary had anticipated the question. He picked up the New Testament and said, 'You will find the answer in the gospel according to St Matthew.' Pressed to say that Hiss was well worth renouncing, he simply said, 'I will not turn my back on Alger Hiss.' That, of course, let off another national uproar.

I think first of those shameful days because I wondered at the time if Acheson could survive them without a breakdown. Somehow, under a strain that only his intimates agonised over, he managed. It is part of the common tragedy of the passing of time that those who know what such a man as Acheson did don't need to be reminded of it, and the rest are either too bored or sceptical to care. Nevertheless, we had better remind ourselves that whether or not our present troubles stem from Truman and Acheson, or from earlier or later times, Acheson was the man who, with one other man in the State Department, Will Clayton, conceived what I take to be the magnificent and munificent idea of the Marshall Plan, of the vast system of loans and gifts to battered old Europe that made possible not only her recovery but also—as Acheson was well aware—the healthy growth of a generation of young Europeans with lungs powerful enough to exercise in the withering denunciation of this Secretary who looked like a Spanish grandee and was, they swore, an American imperialist who had spawned the Marshall Plan as a fat insurance racket.

You may wonder why it was called the Marshall Plan. Well, in 1946 and 1947 it became frighteningly clear to most of us that the old Soviet ally had expansive ambitions of his own. In Acheson's words, which seemed mild enough at the time, 'The Soviet Union is embarking on an offensive against the United States and the West in Iran, in the Middle East, and especially in Greece and Turkey.' If Greece fell to the Communists, Acheson saw the same 'infection' spreading through Iran and the East into Africa and Asia Minor, and to Europe through Italy and France, 'already threatened by the strongest Communist parties in Western Europe'. Does this sound now over-simple? I can only tell you that it felt very real at the time.

This fear, which plagued the West, was met in the so-called Truman Doctrine, a grand and—we can now see—over-ambitious plan 'to support free peoples who are resisting attempted subjugation by armed minorities or by outside pressure'. While Congress was deciding to give arms and money to Greece and Turkey, Acheson began to have doubts about the sense of a piecemeal approach to particular crises. He sketched out the huge dimensions of a plan for the whole of Europe. He gave a preview of it, never noticed, in a speech down in Georgia in May 1947. The following month, General Marshall, the actual Secretary of State, was to give the main address at the Harvard commencement exercises. Acheson begged him to forget the speech he had written or, at least, to incorporate into it the main lines of the Acheson Plan for the recovery of Europe. General Marshall agreed, and performed. There was a curious blank pause, during which neither the British nor the American press took in the scope and daring of it. It was left to the BBC's Washington correspondent, Leonard Miall, to sense the novelty and the vast generosity of the plan, to wake up Ernest Bevin, the British Foreign Secretary, in the middle of the night, to catch his breath with the news and to cause a general, if delayed, outburst of spontaneous rejoicing in Europe.

When a man is saved from drowning by a hefty lifeguard, it is not surprising if in later years he reflects that while the lifeguard had plainly bulging muscles, he would probably have managed to swim ashore on his own anyway. That, after a decade or so was the reaction of Europeans too young at the time to know about, let alone acknowledge, the magnitude of the debt to America. The next generation assumed that throbbing factories, and supermarkets and frozen food, racy clothes and the national health service, a much admired theatre, a booming football business, holidays abroad and

85

general affluence were simply the passage of history, the natural expression of an old habit of pulling through.

But for those of us who were there, it is worth recalling an evening, twenty-four years ago, when Acheson, in a private session with some pretty flinty United States Senators, was trying to din into them the need, the inevitability, of his plan. 'Because,' he said, his eyes rolling and his face a lobster in anger, 'if you'd only go there, and see, and see the railroads smashed, their factories bombed out or crumbling, the food scant. They are prostrate. This thing must be done, simply to restore the fabric of European life.'

It was done. And in the long run, the children or grandchildren of his present detractors will know who was the American who did it. More than most Presidents and public magnificoes, he deserves, somewhere in Europe, a statue. Make it an equestrian statue, facing the East, with a cape rising in the wind, and his moustachios bristling, and the inscription underneath: 'Dean Gooderham Acheson, 1893–1971. To Restore the Fabric of Europe.'

# A 'Frontal Attack'
# on Cancer

*10 February 1972*

The late Alfred North Whitehead, the philosopher-mathematician, was one of those rather bewildered scholars who stumble about in a fog because they have their mental twenty-twenty vision focused sharply on a single problem in life. Like the rest of us, however, even a great philosopher must perform as an animal and a citizen. He must take a bath, even though Whitehead probably watched the water gurgle out counterclockwise and wished he were taking a bath on the other side of the Equator in order to watch it gurgle out in a clockwise direction. Surely even Whitehead had to pay his taxes? He forgot.

One day, he was visited by agents of what then was called the Bureau of Internal Revenue. They were respectful, for they had been well briefed about the enormous dimensions of Whitehead's brain. They pointed out to him that years had gone by since they had heard from him. He made a weary gesture. It had not, as he recalled, come to his attention. But, they said, we have sent you scores of letters, and you have not replied. He looked at them as they would have looked at him if he had told them about his theory of mathematics. 'But,' he said, 'I never write letters.' Never write letters? 'No, indeed,' he said, 'if I wrote letters, how could I possibly do my work?'

I felt an aching bond of sympathy for old Whitehead this week. I've just had a letter from a lady who apparently had written once to me, once to the BBC, then to an innocent and totally uninvolved member of the British Medical Association. In the latest letter she dropped blood-curdling hints that she was going to take this thing up with the Prime Minister, the FBI, President Nixon and Mao Tse-tung. I had done a broadcast in which *she* said I said that a positive cure for arteriosclerosis had been reported from Chicago that required only the simple digestion of large doses of bicarbonate of soda. I had said no such thing. But enough people apparently misheard me to rouse me, unlike old Whitehead, from the preoccupations of my trade to sit down and write over two hundred letters of apologetic explanation. But still the letters swirled in and formed three-foot drifts outside my door. In the end, I made the point over again in another broadcast.

Briefly, I had said that after many years of devoted research in many places, no sovereign remedy had been found for arteriosclerosis, but the Chicago study had ruefully concluded that the only known drug which might be useful was bicarbonate of soda as only one ingredient of a compound that had yet to be developed. This passing thought was only an item in a lament over the folly of any government's setting aside a large wad of money and announcing that it was to be used exclusively to wage a direct assault on some famous killing disease.

Recently, President Nixon announced such an appropriation in the great crusade to fight and conquer cancer. My point was a simple one that government departments, and well-endowed research institutes, tend to forget. It was sharpened for me by a distinguished friend of mine who has worked for the past few years as a scientific adviser to the government and had warned two Presidents, to no avail, of the cruel dangers of ever saying this money, or these men, or this job of research, is to be aimed at a single target. The point is, that very rarely have the giant steps in the conquest of a given disease been taken in the direction of that disease. Let us get down to cases, to a famous one, but one that is by no means unique.

In 1966, Charles Huggins, the director of a laboratory—and notice that it is called the Laboratory for Cancer

88

Research—at the University of Chicago, was awarded the Nobel Prize for physiology and medicine. He had discovered a way of controlling cancer of the prostate in humans. It was a richly deserved honour, and I'm pretty sure that he had a telegram of congratulation from President Johnson. It must have confirmed Mr Johnson in his belief, which he announced the same year to all the health agencies of the United States, that 'Too much emphasis is being placed on basic research at the expense of immediate medical problems.' That sounds sensible and highly practical. It is, on the contrary, senseless, misleading at best, and wildly impractical.

Let us take a look at a series of events, quite irrelevant to the conquest of cancer, that led to Dr Huggins's Nobel award. We have to go back to the eighteenth century and a Scottish physiologist named John Hunter. He was interested in the physiology of bulls, though nobody had given him a grant to tell us how to get stronger, more bullish bulls. He discovered a very simple thing, which, however, no one had noticed before him. If you castrate a bull, its prostate gland becomes small and flabby. Astounding. The discovery lay untouched for another century, when a Russian found out that the same thing happens to men. Just over eighty years ago, an Englishman, J. Griffiths (you won't find him in the encyclopedias or the Nobel roll of honour), was pursuing a peculiar interest. He watched, from year to year, the physiological changes that the passage of the seasons causes in moles and hedgehogs. And he came to notice that *their* prostate changes size in winter and summer. Now we go forward to 1926, when two physiologists in Paris found they could decrease the size and activity of the prostate gland in moles by injecting them with female hormones.

Patience! We are nearly there, although none of these scientists I've listed had the remotest notion where his peculiar obsession was leading. Meanwhile, two Germans, way out in left field, and following a quite different bent, discovered a substance called phosphotase, an enzyme which exists in the intestinal lining of the human. Then a Welshman and another German discovered there were two sorts of phosphotase, and that one of them is found in the secretions from the human prostate. In 1938, in the United States, a man and his wife who were studying cancer of the prostate discovered that the blood of such victims has a surplus of phosphotase. This provided a knotty puzzle to the researchers interested both in cancer and in the composition of the blood stream of cancer patients. For this man and wife proved that cancerous cells in the prostate flood the blood stream with phosphotase.

So, at last, we come to Dr Huggins. In 1940, he announced that the prostate gland cannot function without the production of male sex hormones. He was working on dogs, and on Sunday mornings he went off to the Chicago pound, where he was allowed to examine stray dogs and go to work on the ones that were old enough to have tumours. By tinkering with their hormones, he was able to control their tumours, and he took a big leap into a true diagnosis and a treatment for cancer of the prostate in men. Twenty-six years later he got the Nobel Prize. What—throughout that quarter century—were they waiting for? They were waiting for all sorts of other tests, and proofs, and disproofs, and the confirmation of Dr Huggins's discovery in other labs far from Chicago.

An English zoologist put the thing in a nutshell in the 1950s when he said, 'What politician, what central planner, interested in the cure of cancer, would have supported Griffiths in 1889 in his studies of the seasonal cycle of the hedgehog?' And I'm saying that if a young scientist had gone to President Johnson any time before 1966 and said, 'I'd like a large grant to further my fascinating work on what happens to moles in the spring,' he'd have been tossed out of the White House.

The Chicago study that reported on arteriosclerosis was saying, not in despair but by way of a warning to people eager for a quick cure, that so far, in all their *direct* research on the disease, the only chemical that seemed to offer a hope of being useful, in some as yet undiscovered compound, was sodium bicarbonate. That, they were saying, is the present pathetic state of our research.

This very day, I have had in the mail four separate appeals for contributions to cancer research, three of them boosted with reminders of President Nixon's appeal to apply massive money and massive brains in, I think he called it, 'a frontal assault' on the dread disease. It is the kind of crusade that makes first-rate researchers groan. I have a great friend who, during the Second World War, was approached by the military and asked to follow a particular line of research. He was a botanist with splendid credentials, a modest man and an exact and patient scientist. They kept coming back to him at six-month intervals and saying, 'Well, fella, any results?' Then they came back at three-month intervals. This drove him up the wall. Finally he said, 'Look, when you're doing basic research, you haven't a clue where it's going to take you. I may get the result you want tomorrow, or next year, or never. I may get a result you don't want.' They wrote him off as a sluggard. He went on doing his own research, on seaweed. And when Sir Alexander Fleming stumbled on his great discovery of penicillin, which occurred by accident while he was studying moulds, this fellow too was promptly designated as a mould chemist and offered fancy jobs from Harvard to Berkeley. He turned them down and stayed with his seaweed. Who knows? One day, he may be seen to be the first link in the conquest of—I'd better not say what, or people will be begging me for batches of seaweed.

The hard rule in these things, and very hard indeed for Presidential hopefuls in an election year, seems to be trust to the good patient ones, and the remote possibilities of basic research, and stop kidding the people with the promise that two billion dollars set aside for cancer or bunions is going to cure either of them.

# The
# Charm of China

*26 February 1972*

A journalist I knew, a man of considerable talent and a mammoth ego, once said in a rueful moment that the secret aim of every journalist is not to get one of his stories on the front page but to get himself on the front page as a news story in his own right. 'The only time it will happen to me,' he said, 'is the day after I die.' His name was Randolph Churchill. Alas, he died the day of Robert Kennedy's assassination, and he never made it.

A day or two ago, I was pretty sure that this talk would be given over entirely to a journalist who quite possibly possessed the most colossal ego of modern times. But you had to try to peer through the dazzling and majestic view he held of himself to see the streak of original talent which made him transform daily journalism in our time. Not necessarily for the good of any of us. However, he died the day that President Nixon arrived in Peking. And the Presidential visit, we are being told, is of such vast historical significance that I'm afraid we shall have to forgo an elegy—on Walter Winchell.

We have heard and read so much about the scale of President Nixon's 'historic breakthrough' that it mightn't be a bad idea to say at the start what we might fairly hope to gain from the trip and what we shouldn't deceive ourselves into expecting. I spent an evening last week with an old friend who was in China throughout most of the Second World War and who has recently been back there. He told me about the China he first knew: the dirt and disease, the children with running sores, the scrimping life of the peasants, their rough treatment of each other, bordering on brutality, when anything went wrong. He tells me now that the Chinese Revolution, however ruthlessly it was accomplished, has plainly achieved a great change in the life of ordinary people, and a change by any material standard very much for the better. We should, I think, wish them well of it while at the same time not for a minute expecting the Chinese rulers to lie down with Mr Nixon to enjoy the big sleep of perpetual peace.

We were prepared for the President's journey with three evenings on television of—I don't know what to call them, except Intourist travelogues about the new China, showing us the charm, the domestic simplicity, the abounding joy and essential innocence of life among the 800 million people. We were told that the camera crew that recorded this Utopia had been given complete freedom to photograph what they chose. I must say that if they had all that freedom, they must have been going round in very small circles.

Because, whenever any question came up about home life, working conditions, the economy, anything, we kept seeing the identical quartet: a jolly man on the left, a handsome gaunt man next to him, and two amiable faceless pals who nodded eager agreement at everything the official spokesman had to say. One of the things he said, with beaming enthusiasm, was that whereas in the bad old days the workers sweated twelve hours a day, now they worked only seven hours. And what did they do with the other five? He said, believe me, that they used them 'to study the thoughts of Chairman Mao'. Personally, I found this about as believable as a Chinese interview with, say, George Best and an English Cup Final team in which the players lined up and said that whereas in the bad old days first-class footballers got twelve pounds a week, they now got a hundred pounds a week, which left them eighty-eight pounds to spend in buying up records of Sir Edward Elgar's 'Cockaigne Overture' as conducted by Prime Minister Edward Heath.

We saw shots of the great square of Peking, devoid of its

former splendid architectural monuments (no comment) but also as heavily populated as the Sahara Desert. We saw people catching buses, people threshing rice, children on bicycles, all carrying in their hands small red books—the sacred book— *The Thoughts of Chairman Mao*. There was even one sequence in which surgeons about to undertake a major operation advanced on the patient to perform the singular feat of saving his life with one hand while clutching, in the other hand, the little red book.

I don't wish to belittle—or, as we now say, downgrade— the testimony of recent foreign visitors to China to the effect that the Chinese are in all walks of life noticeably courteous, hospitable and gentle. (In all walks of life, that is, which we are allowed to see.) Nor would I want to imply that because we saw nothing but gentle and genial Chinese, they are in reality monsters. But if the official films about Chinese life are as Disneylike as the ones we saw, then there must be a great deal to hide. The official commentator did get off the remark, the rather terrifying remark (which the censor must have passed), that more than ninety per cent of the literature available to the Chinese is either by or about Chairman Mao Tse-tung.

You have only to ponder this statistic for an instant to infer what it implies: a government so authoritarian, a dictatorship with a grip so vise-like, that even ordinary human curiosity, let alone protest, is effectively suppressed. Transfer the statistic to our own countries. Imagine the state of submission to which the ordinary, and the extraordinary, Englishman had been brought if it could be truthfully said that ninety per cent of everything printed or circulated in England was written by or about Mr Wilson, during his regime, or Mr Heath, during his. Or that in the United States, ninety per cent of everything published was either the collected speeches of Mr Nixon or fawning profiles of him.

In the most iron days of Stalin's rule, nothing like it could be said about Russia. They had, even then, their own comic weeklies poking fun at the frailties or cunning of local commissars. And they have gone on printing and circulating Dickens and P. G. Wodehouse as part of an official campaign to show—no mention of the date— how the working people of Britain are ground down, and how in the case of Mr Wodehouse, the asinine types do the grinding. Mr Wodehouse, by the way, told me a year or two ago that the sales of his novels were most brisk behind the Iron Curtain, 'Because, don't you see, their peoples are most eager to be in touch with the psychology of the types, Bertie Wooster and Jeeves, for instance, who run the Western world.'

Imagine a child of yours, especially a bright child, who has never heard, has no way of hearing, of Shakespeare, of Confucius, of the House of Commons, the United States Supreme Court, trial by jury, opposing political parties, a free election, an indignation meeting, conscientious objectors, a coal strike, or ever sees a caricature of any of his rulers. What we saw of the Chinese children—and I have to believe that the producers didn't think twice about this one—was a single group of eight-year-olds performing a dance in which they stabbed the air with fixed bayonets.

In short, what we saw was a combination, or splicing together, of the Intourist films the Russians put out in the 1930s with disturbing glimpses of the Nazi Youth performances of the same time. It can only mean what I am sure the films were never meant to suggest, that the rulers themselves, Mr Nixon's gracious hosts, are very tough gents indeed. And it seems to me naive to imagine that Mr Nixon, taking tea with Mao or Chou En-lai, can possibly negotiate the realities between a turbulent democracy (ours) and a dictatorship so total that its people have been planed down into cheerful automata.

We should also remember that no summit meeting in the past quarter century has ever achieved an impressive law or treaty. As for the institution of summitry itself, I recommend to you a sentence written centuries ago by one of the most astute of political commentators, by none other than

95

Machiavelli: 'It is an error for princes to come together in their persons to consummate what their envoys have failed to do.' This axiom, I believe, still holds. All the effective and helpful agreements between the superpowers since the Second World War—from the Berlin Agreement to the Nuclear Test Ban and the Strategic Arms Limitation Talks—have been achieved by comparatively anonymous diplomats working and arguing together in private for months and even years.

My own feeling, which nobody is required to share, is that the rulers of China are playing for time, and it is their time not ours. In the meantime, the best—indeed, the essential—thing to hope, as the Chinese begin to develop their nuclear offensive power, is that our diplomats, and the Russians too, will convince them that nuclear might has already passed beyond the point where any nation, even one so enormous as China, can possibly hope to win.

The late Walter Lippmann, in one of his rare appearances on television—I believe it was his last— was asked at the end by a student what did he consider to be the worst catastrophe that could happen to the world. The clock ticked audibly as he thought for the longest time. Then he said, very slowly and emphatically: 'China—on the loose.'

To end this ghoulish bulletin, I can think of something worse: the possibility that China and the Soviet Union, deciding in a year or two that they have more to lose by being at odds than being together, might conclude a pact as unthinkable as the Hitler-Stalin pact of August 1939, which guaranteed the Second World War, as this second get-together would herald the end, or at best the last stand, of the West.

# Angela Davis
# *v.* the Establishment

It will not, I hope, sound patronising if I say that working with the young, as I am doing these days, is a stimulating thing and full of surprises. By the young I do not mean toddlers or even university students. I speak of a television camera crew mostly in their late twenties. The director is English, twenty-eight, has eyelashes like bee's wings, a button nose and looks about twelve. In the course of attempting a preposterous undertaking—to do a television history of the United States in thirteen hours—nothing has been healthier for me than to have what I might call my tutored assumptions, about various bits of American history, rudely shaken by my director's untutored assumptions. It makes you take nothing for granted in the audience, even the American audience, that will eventually see this opus.

For instance, when we started to do a programme on the history of immigration into America, this young director came to me with a shadow on a face that is normally as bright and innocent as a cherry. He was worried about our ability to convey, in the 1970s, the babble of languages and accents that once flowed through Ellis Island and then out onto the streets of the Lower East Side. 'Are there,' he wondered, 'still people left in New York who talk English in what I'd call a broken accent?' Well, we had our troubles but this was not one of them. The first few cabs we took downtown were driven by men named respectively, Pandel Savic, Yehudi Sabin, Jesus Perez and Paul Darvas, with accents to match.

A week later, we were out on Long Island filming in the old

97

home of former President Theodore Roosevelt. In the script I sketched out, I made no bones about regarding Teddy Roosevelt—certainly in his early career as a police commissioner and a Governor—as a hero. He came crashing into politics in a corrupt time and fought the immigration inspectors, the bribed police, the bankers and the slum landlords. If ever there was a spokesman for the poor dumb victims of these gougers—he was it. However, when my director read over what I'd written, he was puzzled to the point of embarrassment. 'Do I understand,' he said, 'that Teddy Roosevelt was *not* a Democrat?' 'On the contrary,' I said, 'he and Lincoln are the two great Republican Presidents.' 'But, I thought,' he said, 'that Republicans were the bad guys, the Establishment, and the Democrats were always the good guys, the reformers?' 'Not in Teddy's time,' I said: 'the Democrats were the machine politicians, the well-entrenched and crummy Establishment of the cities. The Republicans in Teddy Roosevelt's time were the great progressives.'

At the moment we are busy recalling and filming a period through which I lived as a goggle-eyed boy. But so far as my director is concerned, it might just as well be the period of Ethelred the Unready. Worse. Ethelred the Unready is in the schoolbooks. Whereas the era of the Blue Eagle of the NRA is not quite there. But pretty soon the director had read up everything on the 1920s and '30s. Now, he has a new problem. Though he feels comfortably wired for sound from Jefferson to the Reverend Martin Luther King, he wonders how we can film the last programme, on America today: how, that is, to strike a fair balance between the facts that will go into the history books and the 'facts' as they are seen on television. How do you mean, I said.

'Well,' he said, 'take Angela Davis.' (It is an instant proof of the power of television that I do not need to explain to anybody listening, in Australia or India or Glasgow, who Angela Davis is.) Why, I said, playing Socrates, take Angela Davis? 'I understand,' he replied, 'that the judge chosen to run her trial is some sort of a hick, if not worse.' How so?

He then told me that the other weekend he'd been up in Cambridge, Massachusetts and while he was strolling across Harvard yard a girl student came up to him and held out a button for him to wear on his lapel. It said, 'Free Angela Davis Now!' He faltered for a moment—she was a pretty girl—and he said 'I really don't think I could until I know more about the case and came out agreeing with you.' 'But, you *know*,' the girl insisted 'that she's innocent and won't get a fair trial anyway.'

'But I *don't* know,' he said, 'tell me the facts that I ought to know.' Through a series of vocal spasms, involving words like 'like' and 'you know' and 'I mean' she herself revealed the loosest grasp of the events that led to Angela Davis's arrest, or the charges she faces, and the legal plausibility of those charges. 'But,' he said, 'she is charged, isn't she, with murder, kidnapping and criminal conspiracy, and with buying the guns that were used to kill, for instance, a judge in his own courtroom? Don't you think we'd better wait and see whether or not the charges stand up? You may admire her for her ideas, but she's getting a trial, isn't she?' The girl snorted it was a frame-up and went off in search of a true believer.

You can see that he's a pedant. I depressed him further by telling him that the teenage son of an English friend of mine had just been signed up by a teenage girl to join the Golders Green (London) Junior Committee to Free Angela Davis. Golders Green?!! Yes, I said, and I don't doubt there are chapters of the Free Angela Davis movement in Bombay and Berlin and Stockholm.

We reluctantly decided that this was probably so, because of the thing that had worried him about filming any part of history today: the 'facts' that count for the vast majority of people are the facts on television. And the indisputable facts are that Miss Davis is black, beautiful and very bright. Therefore, it is hard not to declare, she must be innocent. Or, as the persistent button carrier in Cambridge, Mass. put it, 'She's up against the Establishment, she can't win.'

Well, two years ago, we were all assured by the President of Yale University that a black boy couldn't get a fair trial in New Haven, Connecticut. Fair or not, he got his trial and was declared innocent. And last Monday, two black brothers who were charged with killing a white prison guard over two years ago—the famous Soledad Brothers, also the heroes of a world-wide cult—were set free by an all-white jury in San Francisco. Miss Davis, now on trial in San Jose, California, called the verdict 'beautiful'. We must wait to know whether the verdict in her case will be—according to one's prior feelings about Miss Davis—'beautiful' or 'political'.

At this point, we ought to get down to the nub of the minority prejudice in her favour: which is that she is a black girl and a Marxist, and without doubt subject to widespread prejudice on those counts alone. But also, that the judge in her case is an ignorant, rural pillar—again—of 'the Establishment' Let's take a look at him.

His name is Richard Arnason. He was the sixth judge to preside over the pre-trial hearings. The first five bogged down, for one reason or another. Arnason got the federal courts to give jurisdiction to the State of California, and he had the case brought to San Jose, where he believed Miss Davis might get a fairer trial than in the small town to the north where the shoot-out took place, and where the judge was killed.

A few weeks ago, the State of California abolished the death penalty, and Judge Arnason then set Miss Davis free on bail. The original uproar about his assignment to the case has died down, except among the far-flung Free Angela Davis advocates who say he is a country judge (which is true) and unfamiliar with the racial turmoil of the cities.

He had practised for some time in a white suburb across the San Francisco bay. But he was born on the prairie, in North Dakota, one of ten children brought up on a farm. He married a hometown girl, has four children, is a baseball maniac and has little taste for politics. He has been under the worst forms of pressure: the pressure of abuse and bigotry— black, white and international. He says he's not sure this is a bad thing. 'Sometimes,' he says, 'we do our best work under pressure.' As for his fitness, the burden of his own prejudices, he says it is his duty to hear every scrap of testimony that can possibly turn into evidence (he compelled the federal courts to accept as relevant the testimony of a black convict who could barely write but had painfully scrawled out a deposition). As for the Establishment, justice, political bias and all that, he says firmly: 'The only person I have to satisfy is myself.'

I don't know whether this prairie boy is the ideal disinterested judge for a case involving such violence, trickery and world-wide indignation. For the time being, maybe, we ought to stay with him. What the Free Angela Davis groups most certainly do not know is that in this country, the wisest judges are not always those who have been civilised by cities. Some of the most profound judgments on what we have come to call 'the human condition' were made in the most uncouth places in the lawless days of the West by men who had never been out of Dodge City or even of the Nevada desert.

In a railroad case in the 1870s, it was a Western judge in Virginia City who reminded a jury recruited from shacks in the sagebrush that judges are not the best judges of the facts. Listen to this greenhorn: 'In all delicate cases that call for judgment more than expert knowledge, we summon twelve men of the average of the community, comprising men of education and men of little education, men of learning and men whose learning consists only in what they have themselves seen and heard: the merchant, the mechanic, the farmer, the labourer. These sit together, consult, apply their separate experience of the affairs of life to the facts proven, and draw a conclusion. The average judgment thus given, it is the great effort of the law to obtain.'

I remember from my own time out West a judge who never left Reno, Nevada, and who, if he'd ever been involved in a case with a famous defendant, would have attracted almost automatic scorn and contempt. For everybody knows that Reno is the ancient capital of the 'quickie' divorce, and surely the Establishment could have no more cynical stand-in than a judge content to spend a lifetime brushing off quick divorce cases. He was, by the way, also a country judge. Very much of the type of Judge Arnason. One time he felt himself called on to say a final word or two to a young, idealistic bride who was more ashamed than saddened to find her marriage so soon on the rocks. Divorce, she was afraid, would stigmatise her for life as a fast woman. This is what he said to her: 'A young bride will find marriage very much like a flight in an untested airplane. No matter how much flying has been done before, no matter how many successful flights have been made by just this type of machine, the new and untested one is full of danger . . . the great majority of all marriages are failures. Not all of the failures end in the divorce court, but two-thirds of all marriages should do so. If the marriage of two hearts that beat as one is a sacred thing, then by the same token a divorce where love is dead is a holy thing. It is a kind of spiritual surgery, and the only cure for broken and embittered homes.'

I don't wish to balance things in favour of Miss Davis's judge, except to throw in a cautionary note about the great range of wise and stupid people who make up 'the Establishment'. I feel with my young director, when he was urged to wear a button, that the country judge and the jury should for the time being be given the benefit of the doubt. 'Don't you think,' as he said, 'we'd better wait and see whether or not the charges stand up?'

# Watergate:
## Act One

### 16 September 1972

I am always reluctant to explain anything as an expression of national character, because it is so easy and so often wrong. But one thing you have to say about Americans: they love drama, especially in its undiluted form of melodrama. They've had so much of it down their history that whenever life seems to be stretching ahead as a grey, predictable routine, they get restless. The wonder is that in the nearly two hundred years of the Republic, they have never succumbed to the thrill of a dictatorship. Somehow, the loud, broiling mixture of nations and races has bubbled up into an explosion only once, into a Civil War, but that was practically an Anglo-Saxon blow-up. It took another twenty years for the population to swell to twice its size from the tidal influx of the peoples of Central and Southern Europe.

If there is a tendency to be bored with what is predictable, there is along with it a secret suspicion that things won't stay that way, that the grey skies will suddenly unloose a thunderbolt. I should like to be able to report one, because we are now launched on the very grey seas of a Presidential campaign that must be the most lack-lustre of recent history. People talk about the Democrats as of a battered old friend with only so long to live, and of the Republicans as the pushy old brother who has had a rejuvenating shot and is about to take over the business. Nothing that has happened in the past week or two, since Senator McGovern got out on the stump, has changed the feeling among politicians old and young, among the veterans and the tyros, that the Democrats are going to take something like the beating that the Republicans took from Franklin Roosevelt in the election of 1936.

So why talk about it? Well, in any such foregone conclusion it is the loser who gets desperate to reverse it, which means that the Democrats are scratching around hoping to come on the time-bomb of a big scandal. They think they have found one, though it is no bigger than a Molotov cocktail. It first appeared in the inside pages of the newspapers and is now familiarly called 'the Watergate caper'.

On the 17th of June last, at 2.30 in the morning, five men were captured burgling, or raiding with intent to burgle, the offices of the Democratic National Committee in a big apartment building that overlooks the Potomac River in Washington and is known as the Watergate. They were caught with cameras and electronic bugging equipment. The leader of the raid is a former employee of the government's Central Intelligence Agency. He was born in Cuba, of an American father and a Cuban mother, had lived for a long time in this country but was in Cuba when Castro came to power. He was an ardent anti-Castro man, was known to be so, and he escaped to the United States. When the United States sponsored the abortive Bay of Pigs invasion, this man acted, on behalf of the CIA, as paymaster for the invaders. Three of his accomplices in the Watergate raid were also anti-Castro men, and the only motive for the escapade that the leader will disclose just now is his belief that 'The election of McGovern would be the beginning of a trend that would lead to Socialism or Communism or whatever you want to call it.' Another of the arrested men hinted darkly that they were performing a patriotic act to prevent a Castro take-over of the United States.

So far this sounds like something dreamed up by television addicts exposed for too long to the sort of show called 'The Invaders', 'The Collaborators', 'The Undertakers'. It is certainly a pathetic strike for the Democrats to mine and surely offers no more ammunition for an election scandal than, say, dragging up as imminent threats to the national security the names of those two islands off the mainland of China which Kennedy and Nixon spent most of their television debates arguing about. (Is there anyone in the class who now believes, or can remember when anyone else believed, that the United States had a sacred obligation to defend those islands? Their names, for the collectors of trivia, are Quemoy and Matsu.)

Well, the Watergate raid was a bizarre exploit, but if it had stopped at the wild attempt of a few anti-Castro partisans to prevent the United States plunging into Communism, via the route of a McGovern election, it could have been consigned at once to the comic strips. But now there is a little matter of a missing $114,000. Candidates for the Presidency are required to publish the sources of their campaign funds, and it seems the Republicans have failed to report $114,000. It is the precise amount which the Democratic National Committee now says the Republicans used to finance the raid on its offices. The Democrats have made this accusation in a lawsuit they have filed for invasion of privacy. Moreover, they have named names, some of them uncomfortably close to the White House. They go so far as to allege—and I must say they've been helped by a couple of Washington newspaper reporters who smelled more than a burglary way back there in June—that President Nixon's former Secretary of Commerce, and now the finance chairman of something called the Committee to Re-elect the President, gave the unreported $114,000 to a former White House aide who became the paymaster, so to speak, for the Watergate raid as its leader had once been the paymaster for the Bay of Pigs raid. So what happened to the $114,000? The leader of the raid apparently passed cheques for that amount through an account his real estate company keeps in a Miami bank.

He must have had it from somewhere. The Democrats charge that he got it from two Nixon men, unidentified, to finance an 'espionage squad' set up to break into the Democrats' offices, to photograph and steal documents and plant wire-taps and eavesdropping devices. The complaint goes on to say that on the day the five men were caught, two other burglars were tipped off by a lookout and escaped and that these two lucky ones were both members of that committee for the re-election of the President. By the way, the finance chairman of the Nixon campaign, who is accused of actually handing over the $114,000, has refused to appear before the House Banking Committee, which is looking into this weird escapade. His refusal is based on the grounds that the FBI is conducting an investigation, and that as a member of the Presidential staff, the executive branch of government, he might be called on to reveal Presidential secrets. The chairman of the Banking Committee says his refusal only 'serves to increase suspicions that there is a great deal to cover up in this case'.

The Republicans, not least the accused men who are said to be close to the White House, dismiss these charges as scurrilous manoeuvres, lies invented for 'a base political purpose'. Meanwhile, all the published pictures of Mr Nixon show him untroubled and radiant in the knowledge of his whopping lead over Senator McGovern in the polls, even though the Watergate enigma is being unwrapped to reveal other riddles not visibly invented by the Democrats. For instance, the House Banking Committee received last week from its investigating staff a confidential report, which stayed confidential for about two hours. It says that last spring in Mexico a suitcase was stuffed with $700,000 and flown to Washington in the private plane of an oil company as a secret contribution to the President's campaign fund. It arrived two days before the new law went into effect requiring candidates to disclose the source of their campaign contributions. If this money came from foreign nationals, it violated laws already in being. And there's another court case, filed by a citizens' group called Common Cause, which is trying to compel the President's campaign organisation to comply with the Federal Corrupt Practices Act by explaining where it got $10,000,000 of campaign funds just before the new disclosure act became law.

What is the President doing about all this? Whenever something comes up that seems to embarrass his administration, it has been his habit, and a very successful one, to look the other way and point with pride to another subject, to some other policy that is doing very well. For example, he named a man to be Attorney General who was then seen to be involved in quashing an anti-trust suit against a big corporation very friendly to Mr Nixon. You might have guessed then that the man hadn't a prayer of becoming the government's chief prosecutor, a job which, like that of a Supreme Court justice, calls for the spotlessness of Caesar's wife. There was a long fight in the appropriate Senate committee over confirming him. Mr Nixon took no part in it. He was busy extolling the splendid fruit of his visits to China and Russia. And the man was confirmed.

As for the Watergate case, this very man—the new Attorney General—and the President got the FBI onto it, the five men were caught and indicted, Mr Nixon congratulated the FBI for acting 'promptly and thoroughly' and assured us that the case was solved. Mr Nixon and the White House men closest to him do seem to be bending over backwards and sideways to see that nobody close to the White House is linked with the arrested five. The Democrats are doing everything in their power to prove several such links. They are being powerfully, if indirectly, supported by the *Washington Post*, the original newspaper detective on this case, and by the *New York Times*, which is swollen by the most elaborate coverage of the affair and which, the other day, had an editorial entitled 'The Smoke is Rising'. The White House decided to fight smoke with smoke. The man accused in the Democrats' lawsuit—Mr Nixon's chief fund raiser—has himself brought suit against his chief accuser (the former chairman of the Democratic National Committee whose offices were raided). This countersuit says that the Democrats' suit is 'unlawful and political in nature'.

Is this already confusing? Do I sense the first polite suppression of a yawn? If so, your instinct is a healthy one and may soon be shared by the American people. The elephantine progress of all suits and countersuits through the long and winding corridors of the American courts will, I should guess, guarantee that nothing at all will be proved or settled before the election. By then, the public will be too bored to care. And, as I say, the American people detest boredom. I should like to be able to recall that the late Senator Joseph McCarthy was finally routed because he roused the American people to an outburst of moral indignation. Not so. He did something worse. He ultimately bored the Senate, and it buried him.

# Justice Holmes
# and the Doffed Bikini

## 7 *October 1972*

One day last summer, a young woman sunning on a public beach decided to take off her bikini and lie naked on the sand. Pretty soon, the families lolling nearby came awake. Husbands began to dive for their cameras and in no time wives were diving for their husbands. One husband, at the instigation of his wife, called the police. The young woman was arrested and last week she appeared before a judge.

That's all. Or, that *would* have been all a few years ago. But the young woman was furious over her arrest. She is a product of the 1970s. She is therefore not a law-breaker but an evangelist. She maintained, as a daring and original proposition, that the naked human body is decent and that she was causing no harm, only going about her decent business of sunning in the nude.

Her lawyer asked to have the case dismissed on the legal ground that she had a Constitutional right to go naked, the implication being that her arrest violated the First Amendment to the Constitution which says, among other things, that Congress shall make no law—nor by extension shall the States—'abridging the freedom of speech or the right of the people peaceably to assemble'. The judge asked her a rhetorical question to which no answer was reported. What would she think if people chose to go naked in the subway?

There will be many people, in countries that don't have a written Bill of Rights and so cannot keep pointing to their private interpretation of what the original authors made public—there must be many of you who find this case hard to credit. But the burden of it is almost as constant as a ballad refrain in the public outcries of radicals and even of liberals who ought to know better. It's the fairly new assertion that anything you feel like doing in public, short of assault or robbery, is an actual right of citizenship.

When the first play was shown in New York in which the characters mimicked sexual intercourse, the defence maintained that their performance was a form of free speech sanctioned by the Constitution. Possibly the thought of James Madison and John Jay and George Mason and Jefferson and the rest whirling in their graves with disbelief was too much for the court. Anyway, the claim of free speech was not allowed, and the play had to close. The verdict sparked a manifesto from a group of playwrights who leaped to the barricades to defend a fellow worker without ever defining what they were supposed to be defending: namely, how limited is the right of free speech? (By the way, since then New York, San Francisco and other cities have sprouted a rash of little theatres and back alley 'massage' parlours that advertise 'live sex' and perform it and go untroubled by the courts, which apparently have given up on the whole question.)

The courts have found obscenity impossible to pin down as a punishable offence and have turned in great relief to asking how free can speech get before it threatens society by inciting to riot? They have a pat and famous answer already at hand, in Justice Oliver Wendell Holmes's assertion that there is no right to shout 'Fire!' in a crowded theatre unless there is a fire.

I have just come on a passage from the same great judge which he delivered to the New York State Bar Association seventy-three years ago. And I think—to coin a well-worn word—it is 'relevant' today. He's talking about how much strain you can put on the word 'right', when you say that you're exercising one.

For those who never had the pleasure of knowing the majestic old Yankee, one of the two or three greatest jurists of his time, let me say that he was not so wedded to the sacredness of precedent as some of his English colleagues. In fact, he often scolded them for citing a precedent and saying 'Well, that's the law,' and then delivering a final judgment, however greatly or subtly the social conditions of the time had changed.

Talking about the jury system, for example, Holmes says: 'I have not found juries specially inspired for the discovery of truth. I have not found them freer from prejudice than an ordinary judge would be.' But—this is precisely why in certain cases he believed in juries—'because of one of their gravest defects from the point of view of their theoretical function, namely that they will introduce into their verdict a certain amount, a very large amount as far as I have observed, of popular prejudice and thus keep the administration of the law in accord with the wishes and feelings of the community.'

Well, it may be, in the matter of the young woman doffing her bikini, that the wishes and feelings of the community will come to be on her side in some early future, and that public nakedness will be legally OK. But when people assert a right, they have to watch out that they don't do what Justice Holmes described as 'letting the word stand for some great external principle. Right itself,' he says, 'is a vague generalisation. Different rights are of different extent, and have different histories, and it does not follow that because one right is absolute, another is.' He then picks out a couple of rights that we might think, even today, are absolute: the right to sell your own property, and the right to make out a character reference for somebody who's about to employ a person who has worked for you.

Says Holmes: 'Under the statutes, the right to sell property is about as absolute as any I can think of.' But suppose your intention is to get the jump on your creditors. Would the right not be modified by 'the motive of deceit'?

And about vouching for somebody's character, he says, 'A man may write down actual untruths in a character reference volunteered in good faith out of love.' But would the same 'right' extend to 'statements volunteered simply out of hate for the man'?

In recent years, no part of the First Amendment has been more frequently claimed as absolute protection of free speech than that which gives the people the right 'peaceably to assemble'. It has been triumphantly claimed by street marchers taunting the police and fighting them, by students storming and breaking up university offices, even by random mobs setting fire to things. In all the subsequent court hearings that I have followed, the magistrate or the judge never seems to remember the qualifying adverb that the Founding Fathers, after a long debate, were careful to put in: peaceably—the right 'peaceably to assemble'. Of course, there were in the 1960s, and are still today, outrageous cases of court injunctions and police prohibitions of parades and protests *before* the event, before they'd assembled either peaceably or unpeaceably.

But now listen to this tricky test of free speech. In upstate New York, a judge has asked a sitting grand jury to investigate a book of nursery rhymes, or rather a book of satirical, mock nursery rhymes. The judge did this on quite positive grounds. He said, 'This book of so-called nursery rhymes advocates the commission of certain crimes.' And he read aloud one of them. This is it:

> Jack be nimble,
> Jack be quick,
> Snap the blade
> And give it a flick,
> Grab the purse,
> It's easily done,
> Then just for kicks,
> Just for fun,
> Plunge the knife
> And cut and run.

It may seem that the judge was pre-judging the case by telling the jury what to find. But I ought to stress that this was not a trial but a hearing before a grand jury, whose job is no more and no less than that of a magistrates' hearing: to decide if there's a case, if the charges brought before the grand jury warrant a trial. It's important to say this especially for countries, like Britain, which abolished the grand jury system. It started, by the way, in England, in the Middle Ages, when there were few settled courts. So that judges rode off on circuit to hear cases in towns with which they were unfamiliar. They called in, so to speak, the neighbours—sixteen people who might know the defendant and could say, from their knowledge of him and the place he lived in, whether the charge was ridiculous or plausible. Sometime in the 1910s Lord Birkenhead, later the Lord Chancellor of Great Britain, wrote a scathing and characteristically ironical piece about the likelihood of sixteen people drawn from a city with a population of seven millions knowing more about a defendant than the ordinary competent magistrate. The grand jury system was already declining, and in 1933 it was formally abolished. It continues in the United States with great vigour, and if it has a fault—two faults—they are: that too often, the grand jury becomes the creature of the prosecutor; and that the press, champing under the restraint of not being able to report what is a secret hearing, explodes at the end, whenever an indictment is handed down, with a streaming headline: 'George Spelvin Indicted!' I'm sorry to say that, from the results of a recent galloping poll of my own, most Americans tend to confuse the word 'indictment' with the word 'conviction'. And when the indicted man comes to trial, too many Americans think of him as a guilty man who is going to have to prove his innocence.

Well, back to the mock nursery rhymes. All is not lost for the saucy author. But the judge did declare as a peril what Justice Holmes might have introduced as a warning. The book is called *The Inner City Mother Goose*. It was written by the author of thirty-five straightforward children's books, and it seems that this one was written as a bitter warning to parents.

Unfortunately, it's in school libraries. And whereas adults may take it as a satire on the problems of the cities, it's possible that some children may take it as a book of recipes.

I'd like to add a final note to the ringing announcement of the bikini-doffer that the naked human body is decent. The word 'decent' is another victim of the habit, common both to politicians and their enemies, of using noble or impressive words not for thinking with but for raising, like those boards they hold up before television audiences, as invitations to applause. Vice President Spiro Agnew simply proclaims that something is indecent, and the cheers ring out on the Right. A girl takes her clothes off and says the human body is decent, and there is an ovation from the Left. The word 'decent' means 'becoming', and the question surely is, becoming to whom and in what place? It was Bernard Shaw, I think, who defined evil as 'matter out of place'.

Anyway, the plea of the actors prosecuted for mimicking sexual intercourse was that it was natural. So, of course, is diarrhoea. But, on the stage, is it becoming? My own view is that of the late Mrs Patrick Campbell who didn't mind what people did in private 'so long as they don't do it on the streets and frighten the horses'. At any rate, I think the judges could make a sensible clearing through the verbal undergrowth of such words as 'rights' and 'decency' if they went back and considered the original meaning of the word 'indecency' as whatever is unbecoming to a certain person, place or time.

# Give Thanks,
# For What?

A week ago I was on one of the islands that the English had a rough time settling, because it is whipped at all times by high winds around a rocky and treacherous coastline. It is made of coral, which is not hospitable to swarming algae. So the sea around it does not present the usual blue-grey goulash that slops up against the islands of the North Atlantic. It is clear water, and even on overcast days it's of a light and shimmering aquamarine or turquoise colour. This beautiful sheen disguises the many perils of the rocks and helps you to forget the winds and the fact that in the late summer the island is in the path of the hurricanes that are brewed in the tropical Caribbean. I am talking about Bermuda, which Shakespeare vividly and accurately called 'the vexed Bermouthes'.

Well, I was rambling over the hills and dales of a hundred odd acres of this island thoughtfully set aside for the pursuit of a little white ball with a liquid centre. I was accompanied by one of the most celebrated brooders in America, a man who denies himself the pleasure of chasing the ball for about 363 days in the year because, like the unflagging Calvinist he is, he feels a prior obligation to his job as a journalist of the most awesome kind: a daily preacher whose duty is, in the good old phrase, to 'comfort the afflicted and afflict the comfortable'. I cannot think of any more forgivable auspices under which to play any game whatsoever. Playing a round of golf with this man is as comfortable as drinking double martinis with Billy Graham.

His routine of self-sacrifice would not be praiseworthy in a golfing duffer. In fact, to most of us, wrestling with the problems of inflation or foreign policy is a good deal easier than guiding the damn ball into a hole 425 yards away. But this old Scot (and the fact that he has spent the last fifty years in this country has not pacified his conscience in the least, he is still the dour little—well, large—preacher from Clydeside)—this old Scot was once, I believe, the junior golf champion of Ohio. He was, in other words, at one time that forever forbidding figure, a scratch player. (For the uninitiated, may I say that golf is one game in which you do not start from scratch.) James Reston began on the sports desk of the Associated Press. In his late twenties he heard the call of John Calvin or John Knox or John the Baptist, it doesn't matter which, and turned to politics during the London blitz, and then to Washington. Since when he has been urging us, on a syndicated basis, what to believe about Europe, the Soviet Union, Cuba, China and all fifty of the United States.

If all Mr Reston's powerful sermons were lost, he would still be a large footnote in history. Because, on his visit to China (it was typical of him that he got there before Mr Nixon) he came down with appendicitis and had the useless organ removed by a top team of Chinese surgeons (they may be seven thousand miles away but they know that you don't leave the appendix of the chief columnist and Vice President of the *New York Times* to a horse doctor). While he was under the anaesthetic influence of acupuncture, he wrote it up, and when he could amble around, he and his wife were allowed to watch several operations, during which—so he claimed—the patient who'd just had a brain or a lung removed said, like the boy in *Pickwick*, that he 'wouldn't lie there to be made game of, and he'd tell his mother if they didn't begin'.

So Mr Reston returned with the glad tidings of the wise men from the East who stick needles in you and lo, you feel no pain and, practically before the bandages are wrapped, you get up from your bed and walk. The news of this miracle was syndicated in papers around the world, and in this country we are now in the full flush of the belief, or the fashion, or the superstition, that there is no human ill that cannot be cured in a trice by a Chinese sinking in a needle. Many an American doctor, and non-doctor, is already preparing to moonlight with acupuncture and pick up a little pin-money, so to speak, on the side.

I've built up Mr Reston's considerable credentials as a seer and prophet—not beyond his due—because I wanted to assure you that I don't spend my time loping around a golf course with heedless bums. We would fall silent occasionally to ponder the nasty stance required to pitch to a pulpit green from squirty crabgrass. But we would then get down to the business in hand and fall in together (as, we are told, the British Ambassador and the Emperor Franz Josef used to do while in pursuit of the stag in the old days) and ponder tremendous matters. Even when Mr Reston is pursuing the little white ball, he is pursued in turn by a deadline.

Much on his mind, that beautiful afternoon, was a column he had to write on the eve of Thanksgiving. What, he wanted to know, had we cause to be thankful for? It was a problem. He stood to the ball, reminding himself to imitate the immortal Bobby Jones, whose swing was said to have 'the drowsy beauty of a summer's day'. Reston then unloosed the tornado of his caddie swing, which has all the drowsy beauty of a pneumatic drill. Well? he said. 'Come to think of it,' I said, 'I can't think of anything we can be grateful for.' I moved over to my ball and performed my own ritual swing, which I have often thought bears a striking resemblance to Tom Weiskopf in the take-away and to Henry Cotton in the finish. A recent series of stop-action pictures, however, shows a man who, at the top of the backswing, is either taking off a sweater or putting on a lifebuoy.

'Come now,' said Reston, fluffing a three-foot putt, 'there's a lot of things to be thankful for.' Name one, I said, and dispatched the thing ten feet into the back of the cup. Well, he said, and he now had his pipe out, which is always an impressive accompaniment to a stalling mind. Come on, come on. 'Why, sure,' he said, ambling off down the next fairway like Barnacle Bill the sailor. All I could think of was the demonstrable fact that Mr Nixon, like him or loathe him, had done something that no Eisenhower, Kennedy or Johnson had done before him. He had not conquered inflation but he had held it remarkably in check. The economists knew it, and praised him. The bankers knew it, and rejoiced. Even the liberals knew it, and grunted reluctant approval. More important, the housewives knew it, and they had voted for him.

I was giving Reston time to digest his column. He brooded some more and put two balls in the drink of a long water-hole. Which is ridiculous in a former scratch player, though playing twice a year does not tend to maintain the handicap at a single figure. Then I teed up majestically, thought about Thanksgiving, and with incredible accuracy placed two balls in exactly the same grave as his. After that, we jokingly decided it was only a game and, anyway, we were still wondering what to thank the Lord for.

Mr Reston's column appeared duly on the eve of Thanksgiving and it betrayed no smitch of strain, no hint of the writhings that had seized him as he peered all over the rolling course looking for blessings to count. He put up a brave show. There may be five millions unemployed, but there are eighty-two millions in jobs. More than half of all American families, families not individuals, have an annual income of roughly twelve thousand dollars. Vietnam, they say, is close to a cease-fire. The campuses have cooled. There is, he believes, 'a calmer atmosphere between the races and the generations'. America may be relatively less powerful than she was but there is 'less danger and fear of a major clash between the nuclear powers than at any other time since the start of the Cold War'. Mr Nixon, he believes, has at least 'bought time to arrange a kind of truce between the Communist and the Western worlds'.

In the main, I believe that this is, with one big reservation, fair enough. Nobody ever expected a Republican President to introduce compulsory price and wage control in peacetime, but it seemed to work. A Democrat and an economist, who takes a generally dim view of Mr Nixon, has just written: 'He hasn't mastered it, but it's working, and that's something when you look at South America (Chile has reduced its inflation in the past year from a hundred per cent to eighteen per cent). And in Europe, the British inflation is disastrously out of hand.'

Also, one has to grant, if there had been a Democrat in the White House, the liberal press would be sounding hosannas for the courage of the visits to Moscow and Peking and the shrewd recognition that they both need money and trade and good crops more than they need arms. (The Russians are doing very well building their own mammoth navy, thank you, and the Chinese move on deferentially, with charming smiles, toward their own nuclear capability.)

My reservation is about the calm between the races and the generations. I devoutly hope it is so. But I cannot see how the widening gap between the prosperous majority and the poor and bitter minority will keep the minority from protest. All the groups that raised Cain in 1968 are still there. The colleges may appear to be beginning to share authority with the students, if that's a good thing. True, a black boy has a better chance of going to college here than practically any boy in Western Europe. Yet, one black boy in three between the ages of sixteen and twenty-two has no job and very little prospect of ever getting one. The cities groan quietly, and the President promises not to soften them by 'throwing dollars at problems'. The powerful malcontents—the young, the black, the radicals, the Mexican-Americans—who were told to work within the system tried it with McGovern and it got them a stone. We may have cause to give thanks, but we should leave as an open question whether militant America is calming down once for all or whether it is pausing. Anyone who has ever been in the eye of a hurricane knows the blessed feeling of relief when the damage is done, and the clouds are scudding, and the blue is breaking through, just before everything goes leaden and hissing again, and the fury is let loose from the other side.

This is just to say that I think there's a danger in the present lull of overlooking the hazard in front of our eyes. As Reston and I teed up on that long water-hole (we had to carry about 160 yards before the dry land) the caddie said, 'Forget the water, just pretend it's all smooth grass.' It would be nice to do this, looking out across the United States and seeing only the green haven beyond the drink. We shouldn't forget, though, that both of us, disdaining the briny deep in front of us, drowned in it—twice.

# A Reactionary at Six PM

*10 February 1973*

The clock struck six the other evening, or would have if I had a striking clock. The days are stretching out again and I was batting away at my typewriter peering closer and closer till my nose, a formidable organ, was in danger of entrapment, as the lawyers say, in the keys. In other words, I wasn't seeing very well. The twilight falls very fast in New York. We are, after all, at the precise latitude of Corfu, where old Kaiser Wilhelm in exile felt sufficiently removed from the mists and rheums of Northern Europe to get himself a large armchair shaped like a saddle and feel he was riding the Texas plains.

Well, as I was saying, it was six o'clock under a darkling sky. I looked up and Central Park was ablaze with hundreds of the new sodium lights that were installed by Mayor John Lindsay to discourage muggers and their like. (This may be Mr Lindsay's single contribution to city government.) The night strollers were long ago discouraged from their strolling by the muggers themselves. But since there are fewer potential victims, there are fewer warriors. The lights are beautiful and give the impression, on a clear night, of a shower of frozen fireworks. I was looking down on them and thinking what an agreeable, even an endearing, town this used to be, when an electric bell drilled through my reverie and brought me to with a bang.

It was the front door bell, and who should be there but my oldest friend, in both senses, just back from a visit to England. He is an Englishman, once a big shot in the BBC, before that a warden of an English prison, and before that a soldier who at the age of seventeen found himself in the Italian campaign, wounded and the winner of the Military Cross. He comes on like a panther and looks like a once superb light-heavyweight not gone to fat but gone to bone: lean and spare and twinkling, in his early fifties. The fact that he is moving into his mid-seventies is simply a puzzle of the calendar. He is what they used to call saturnine, much given to bearing the woes of the world, a scarred veteran of the liberal wars. He has tried awfully hard in the past few years to stretch his liberal tolerance to anybody, white or black or brown, who chooses to shoot his face off—stopping short only of endorsing any libertarian who in the act of expressing himself shoots off somebody else's face.

He was glad to be back from England though he is overcome in old age with attacks of nostalgic double-vision. These fits of longing can evidently be cured by quick trips to England. He had with him a copy of a London paper. Buried away inside it, in a tiny paragraph, was an item about a girl raped in some London suburb. There was another miniscule report about a whopping embezzlement. Eight lines in another place took care of the fact that somebody had been stopped at London airport with £50,000 worth of heroin in his briefcase. He pointed out these items not so much to deplore them as to marvel at their brief, crisp coverage.

Any of these happenings—the heroin cache especially—would have gone into headlines here, as indeed does every hold-up in the South Bronx or abandoned body in Oklahoma. Something struck me then that had never struck me before.

Each European country compares itself, for good or ill but mostly for good, with all the United States, which is really fifty countries. Country v. country. This one-to-one comparison is the basis of the European complaint about the far-flung violence of American life.

But suppose—the day may not be far off—when the Common Market gets really under way as a tight federation of states. Go further. Pretend for a moment that Britain is only one of the United States of Europe. Suppose that there were one, two or three federal television networks, as there are here, so that every morning you had newspapers, and every evening television networks, that felt an obligation to report the worst that was happening everywhere. Your half-hour television evening news round-ups would then carry on-the-spot reports of not only a murder in Chelsea and a disappearance in Dorset but also a kidnapping in Berlin, a strike in Stockholm, a fire in a hotel in Lyons, a power failure in Oslo, a protest march in Brussels, a bank robbery in Geneva, a drug arrest in Amsterdam, a shoot-out in Madrid. It would make—as our evening round-ups do—a melancholy if gaudy record.

Maybe things are worse than they used to be, and maybe not. But we are covering here all the crime and labour strife and citizen protests to which lines can be rigged and camera crews sent and reporters tapped, across a country, which is also a continent, three thousand miles wide. It gave us pause. Then my friend came on a piece about how England was dealing with what the paper called 'a wave of muggings'. Very simple. Three- to five-year jail terms, even for teenagers. Wow, I said. Can you imagine, my friend said, if they started handing out sentences like that over here? I could imagine. A colossal storm in the liberal press, marches outside the courts, a hullabaloo in Congress such as the one that has greeted Governor Rockefeller's call for a bill, in the New York legislature, that would impose a life sentence on heroin and other hard-drug pushers.

The uproar over this draconian measure has been such that it's very doubtful whether it will go through. My friend, since he was fresh from England, caught the Governor's proposal for the first time when he watched him on television. 'Quite right, too,' he said, 'if there's nothing more unspeakable than the lifetime's corruption of the young, then the criminals should pay for it with a life in jail.' Then he remembered his crusading liberal years and he blushed. We tended to jump at the Governor's attempt to make the punishment fit the unspeakable crime until the legislators began to ask nasty practical questions. Who is a pusher? Legally, it might be one teenager who had a pinch of cocaine and egged his pal on to try it out. And he'd be in jail for life. How large a dose of a hard drug corrupts? What are the protections a defendant could depend on against being planted with a drug by a mean neighbour or a crooked cop? The more we looked into this admirable bill, the bigger loopholes it grew.

My friend and I looked over several other rumpus-causing items. Two in particular that could be guaranteed to provoke strong—and, of course, noble—emotions. One was President Nixon's cutting back the Lyndon Johnson poverty programmes while he's increasing the military budget. Outrageous! Another was a report that in several states there were lobbyists working effectively to kill the proposed new Constitutional amendment giving equal rights to women. Disgraceful!

First, the military budget. Mr Nixon is actually reducing the armed forces by 55,000 men, fifty-six ships and two bomber squadrons. Yet he wants 4.2 billion dollars *more* than last year. Why? Well, he has finally given the liberals and the loving mothers what they've been crying for for years. He has ended conscription, and we are to have a volunteer army. Splendid. However, men who choose to go into the Army don't come at the bargain prices of men who have to go as a legal duty. They have to be coaxed and seduced by such military novelties as separate rooms, more time off, television sets, more pool tables, and attractive pay. These inducements are what will cost us another four billion dollars in the military budget.

The proposed constitutional amendment, which will be the sixteenth since the original Bill of Rights, says simply: 'Equality of rights under the law shall not be denied or abridged by the United States or by any State on account of sex.' Excellent, and about time too. Is it possible that the American Constitution has lived so long without considering women to be the legal equals of men? Well, the answer is no, it is not possible. It is not, in fact, so. The Fourteenth Amendment, ratified in 1868, says plainly: 'All persons born or naturalised in the United States, and subject to the jurisdiction thereof, are citizens of the United States and of the State wherein they reside. No State shall ... deny to any person within its jurisdiction the equal protection of the laws.' Notice, it says 'person' (not man), on the plain understanding that women, too, are persons. Indeed, women have lately been insisting on being identified as nothing else. An absurd habit is coming in of calling a woman who takes the chair at a meeting a 'chairperson'. This is meant to stress the fact that she's not a man. But 'chairperson' is only used of a chairwoman. The Congress and the States anticipated this absurdity and prescribed that no 'person' should be denied 'the equal protection of the laws'. It seems to me that the new, and so-called, Equal Rights Amendment, is built into the Fourteenth.

But I must be wrong, or there wouldn't be the tremendous to-do about having a new statement of it. However, we are a long way from passing it. When Congress writes a constitutional amendment, three-quarters of the state legislatures must ratify it before it becomes law. So far, twenty-five have done so. We need thirteen more, and some of them are being very tough. Oklahoma turned it down on the grounds that the Bible, written centuries before 1868, doesn't say women are men's equals. But in the other twelve states where the battle is still joined it's not the Bible that's the issue. Organised labour is working against the amendment from the fear that women may demand equal rights, and pay and privileges, as bricklayers, railroad engineers, electricians, shop stewards. Other states are giving careful heed to a militant lobby of women concerned to preserve some *inequalities*: they don't want to see an end to laws that compel an errant husband to support his ex-wife and their children. And even though the draft has been repealed, there's an alarming appeal packed in the cry of a lady who has appeared as a witness before several legislatures warning that 'Mothers would be subject to the same draft as fathers. Can you see women going into combat carrying forty-pound packs?' Well, can you? Anything is possible in a country where nearly half the Congress is made up of lawyers. Wouldn't it be an interesting twist if five, ten, years from now worthy women were in the Marines and worthless men were getting alimony? It is possible, I think, that the amendment may be defeated not by male chauvinists but by female chauvinists with expectations of old-fashioned gallantry. A tradition that may be curable but not legally definable.

No noble crusade is simple once it starts to get drafted into law. My old friend and I simply and shamefully copped out. I recalled what E. B. White once called the most beautiful sound at twilight: the tinkle of ice.

# Watergate:
# Act Two

*12 May 1973*

On the floor of the Senate the other day, Senator William Proxmire, a liberal Democrat from Wisconsin, had this to say: 'When former White House counsel John Dean is reported throughout the country to have privately told investigators that the President was directly involved in a Watergate cover-up, President Nixon is being tried, sentenced and executed by rumour and allegation ... I find this kind of persecution and condemnation, without trial, McCarthyism at its worst.'

Well, by now we've had time to look back over the whole business and consider where we got all our juiciest information from. And the fact is that practically all the malodorous details have come from leaks. The *Washington Post* is to be highly praised for the detective work of two reporters, Woodward and Bernstein, who have been on the Watergate case exclusively for the best part of a year. They didn't get their information from public sources, which are poor guides in any case of graft or scandal, since the criminals are usually careful not to leave any public record at all. The documents in the Watergate case, such as they are, are in the White House or the personal files of the suspects. Forty pages were actually taken out of the White House by the man who has been the big leak in the case: the President's White House counsel, John Dean, who got the sack and promptly gave the shakes to Heaven knows how many men in the White House by announcing that he was not going to be made a scapegoat and was in the mood to tell all. Mr Dean took those documents from his office in the White House without checking on the ethics of so doing and locked them away in a safe-deposit box in a Virginia bank. Then he gave the keys to a federal judge. We simply don't know what's in that box, though in the atmosphere of Watergate, no smell goes unidentified for long. An investigator from the Justice Department has just boasted that he knows what is in the Dean documents and that they are related to national security. If so, Mr Dean might find himself in the same hole as Daniel Ellsberg, who took those papers out of the Pentagon.

Meanwhile, one name leads to another, and the *Washington Post* has gone on piling up accusations made by the likes of John Dean. Hardly a day goes by when we don't read what some witness had told the grand jury investigating the case on the previous day. I had better remind you here that a grand jury is an official legal and *secret* preliminary hearing in what might turn into a criminal case. Nobody comes to trial on a criminal charge in a federal court unless he has gone before a grand jury, which is there to say whether or not there is a case. The transcript of grand jury hearings is sealed and may only be quoted at the subsequent trial to show perjury or some other legal discrepancy.

Yet we've been reading what various key witnesses are *said* to have testified before the Watergate grand jury almost as if the court reporter's shorthand notes had been made available to reporters. How does this come about? Obviously somebody has been feeding summaries or bits of testimony to the unflagging ditch-diggers of the *Washington Post*. Now, quite apart from the dubious ethics of publishing what is legally sealed as strictly secret material, there is a great hazard in putting into print what somebody told you somebody else had said in a grand jury room. It is surely no excuse that in the Watergate case an overwhelming amount of the stuff printed by way of allegation is turning out to be true. The *Washington Post* was the first to say that the former Attorney General, John Mitchell, one of the proudest of Mr Nixon's Cabinet appointments, was implicated. It gave names and places and dates. Last Thursday, Mr Mitchell, who appeared twice before the grand jury, was indicted. And so was another former Nixon Cabinet officer, Maurice Stans, the man who was the finance chairman of the committee to re-elect Mr Nixon. He came into the story last September as the man the Democrats accused of passing $114,000 to a White House aide to pay for the Watergate raid.

Mr Mitchell and Mr Stans will be brought to a federal court and if they are found guilty they will face a sentence of ten years in prison and fines of about $15,000. *If*—that is the word that ought to be stressed. It is a word that drowns in the flood of allegations from the newspapers. And the *Washington Post* evidently felt on safe ground in, so to speak, indicting the men before the grand jury did.

The most serious charge of all is one attributed to John Dean. He has said that President Nixon was not only involved in covering up the Watergate escapade but actually congratulated him on 'the fine job' he'd done. This is extremely serious, since it immediately implies that the President too had lied and thereby obstructed justice. Yet both the Justice Department and a Senate Committee that has taken up the case have told the *New York Times* that John Dean has no evidence at all to suggest that the President knew anything about Watergate or about the seventeen men now suspect, or that he took any part in the cover-up.

It is on the basis of the newspaper reporting, and the leaked grand jury testimony, that over half the American people, according to the Gallup poll, now believe that the President *was* involved. I'm afraid that what is more certainly involved is that common form of wishful thinking we call hate. The people, and they are often of high intelligence, who hate Richard Nixon are panting to see him proved guilty. He is going to have to prove his innocence, and in the meantime, more than half the people think him guilty.

The flurry of charges is so serious that we should all take a deep breath, wait for all the indictments, wait for Senator

Ervin's committee findings, wait for the trials, and then come to a conclusion. This self-restraint is long overdue. It is not, I admit, a good recipe for selling newspapers.

## 19 May 1973

There seems to have been a momentary lull in the Watergate case. But now we are about to settle down to what is being called the Sam Ervin Show. This is the investigation of Watergate by a select committee of the Senate, and its chairman is the engaging but formidable figure of Senator Sam Ervin of North Carolina. He is seventy-six years old, an old-time—almost a professional—Southerner, who is a one-man anthology of Biblical tags and Southern folk wisdom and has a face as homely as a turnip. He appears to be God-sent as a Daniel come to judgment on the wheeler-dealers and power maniacs who seem to have constituted President Nixon's White House staff. He will carry all the more weight with the American people because he is of the earth earthy and yet retains the instinctive courtesy of an old-fashioned Southerner. But, for all his air of being a country lawyer, just folks, he is a graduate of the Harvard Law School and the Senate's expert on constitutional law.

Senator Ervin called his committee into being because he suspected that the real story of Watergate lay in the White House. He announced that he meant to summon, if necessary to subpoena, White House aides to testify. He was immediately rebuffed by Mr Nixon, who said he would order his aides not to appear, on the constitutional ground that they shared the President's own immunity from questioning by a Congressional committee. Since the beginning of the Republic, since the emergence anyway of investigating committees, indignant Congressmen have tried to fetch Presidents up onto Capitol Hill to testify. Jefferson was the first to tell them that he had separate powers, and private information, which they had no constitutional right to probe into. (In a famous case of treason, however, he finally came through with the documents.) Only a little more than twenty years ago, a House committee tried to serve a subpoena on Harry Truman, and he told them first to read the Constitution and then to go fly a kite. But long ago, and in recent times, close Presidential advisers, Cabinet officers and such, have been called like any other citizen.

Senator Ervin was not to be put off by the President's claim of 'executive privilege' for his aides. The Senator threw a press conference and quoted a line from Shakespeare: "'What meat doth this Caesar eat that he grows so great?" And I say to you, what meat do these White House aides eat that they grow so great? We abolished titles of nobility in the long ago, and if these men refuse to come down here, I shall instruct the sergeant-at-arms of the Senate to go to the White House and fetch 'em. They are as subject to questioning as any other citizen. The President calls it executive privilege. I call it executive poppycock.'

The hidden irony in the President's refusal to let his men appear springs from his argument that the White House had done a thorough investigation of its own and found that nobody in the White House was implicated in Watergate. And you know who was given the job of thorough investigator? None other than John Dean.

It is a relief to be able to quote an outside comment on Watergate that is stunning, not to say delightful, in its originality. It never occurred to the *Washington Post*. It comes from Moscow. It is that Watergate is a 'conspiracy' by 'reactionary American elements' who want to re-freeze the melting Cold War and arrest good relations between the Communist and the Western worlds. Most of us are so used to having Moscow identify bankers and Republicans as 'reactionary elements' that it's a refreshing shock to hear that the new reactionaries are liberals and Democrats, the very people who were far ahead of Mr Nixon in pleading for warmer relations with the Soviet Union. But it has become practically compulsory in the Communist countries to like Mr

Nixon—once the arch-Communist hunter. A Polish broadcaster called him 'the best possible American President'.

Mr Brezhnev has recently been opposed by 'elements' in Russia who are against melting the Cold War. So, we are told (though perhaps it is only hearsay) that he has melted, or liquidated, them. Certainly, Watergate must be an immense puzzle to the Russians. Mr Brezhnev must be stumped to know why, as Art Buchwald put it, Mr Nixon doesn't simply liquidate the investigators, get the Army to arrest Congress, and put those nosey newspapermen in insane asylums.

### *26 May 1973*

The President is still asking us to believe that he knew nothing of the desperate and cunning means employed—with vast secret contributions—to re-elect him. More and more it looks as if this was done by the top echelon of the White House staff, the men he sees night and day to determine policy domestic and foreign. Every President has such a ring around him, and it was long ago called the 'kitchen Cabinet'.

Kennedy's kitchen Cabinet, for instance, consisted half of the so-called Irish Mafia (young Boston politicians he'd known most of his political life) and half of what you might call the Graduate School: Harvard (mostly) ex-professors of the stamp of Walt Rostow and Arthur Schlesinger, Jr. What Kennedy never had around him—nor Eisenhower, nor Truman, nor Johnson—were public relations men, advertising experts, real estate agents. This is the novelty that might bring Mr Nixon down. He has surrounded himself with high-pressure fixers of doubtful ethics whose instinct was to form a Politburo inside the White House, apparently contemptuous of Congress and ignorant, or contemptuous, of the Constitution. If it is to be saved, it seems it will be done by the press, which unfortunately has resorted to many surreptitious goings-on of its own. But by now we tend to shrug and say: Well, you know what they say about—catch a thief.

The Senate investigating committee is going into recess for a couple of weeks. We may use the interval to exercise a bout of compassion for any public man in a democracy who has made a bad slip, told a lie or been grossly indiscreet. A lot of us, I imagine, are all the happier, in the murky light of Watergate, not to be in public life. If we remember the memorable aphorism of an Irish-American girl who, looking over some revealed hanky-panky of a local politician, sighed, 'The whole truth about any of us would shock all the rest of us.'

## 28 July 1973

By now we are almost inured to the secret horrors that keep crawling out of the White House woodwork. But we have just been shaken by another horror, revealed by another Senate committee, which is causing some Senators and Congressmen to talk about the possibility of impeaching the President on an issue quite different from Watergate.

The Senate Armed Services Committee began, last autumn, to look into a rumour about 'unauthorised' bombings in Cambodia. Sometime in January a letter came into the hands of a Senator from Iowa. It was from a former Air Force major, and it provoked the autumn hearings. The major said he had taken part in falsifying some official documents, presumably issued by the Pentagon, and in destroying other documents, all of which had to do with bombing missions into Cambodia between the springs of 1969 and 1970. During that time, President Nixon put out a flat public statement announcing that the United States was not engaging in any military action in Cambodia and was concerned to honour it as neutral ground. On the contrary, wrote the major, he had been active in innumerable B-52 raids into Cambodia and he had been ordered to 'fake the reports' to say that his missions were into North Vietnam. The major came before the Armed Services Committee early last week and gave his story in the flesh.

133

And, behold, the Pentagon gave in and admitted that it had kept secret 3,630 bombing raids over Cambodia, and that they had been authorised by the President. They evidently didn't succeed in destroying the Vietcong in their havens, so the Pentagon adopted something it blandly called 'double-entry bookkeeping', a method of falsifying or suppressing the news of these raids so as to deceive, in the first place, its own people who were responsible for official reports of military action. The Pentagon also repented to the extent of admitting that in 1971, and early this year, it had sent to the Armed Services Committee two classified documents that contained the faked reports and made no mention of the Cambodia raids, which were going on almost every night. The Committee therefore had inferred that the United States was respecting the President's assurances of neutrality. He gave these assurances in a speech to the people on the 30th of April, 1970. In fact, on that day, the United States was almost at the end of 3,000 bombing missions undertaken to pry the enemy out of his sanctuary in 'the territory of a neutral nation'.

One Senator, Stuart Symington of Missouri, said that the issue of falsification extended to the money Congress had appropriated for the national defence. He put the cost of the secret Cambodia bombings at $145 million. 'By giving us false information,' he said, 'they' (meaning the Pentagon and the President) 'never gave us a chance to authorise the money for the use they made of it. They eliminated the Congress from any decision. This is clearly unconstitutional.'

The appeal to the Constitution was made in saltier terms last week by the man who spilled the beans: the retired Air Force major. At one point, while he was telling his wretched story, a Senator from South Carolina who is an impenitent war hawk doubted the major's loyalty to the United States. The major was briefly amazed. 'Sir,' he snapped, 'I didn't take an oath to support the military, I took an oath to support the Constitution.' So, of course, did President Nixon on those

January days of 1969 and 1973 when he was inaugurated for his first and second terms.

## 16 August 1973

The President went on the air this week to make his first public statement about Watergate in nearly three months. He flexed his jaw muscles and looked us square in the eye. For a time he seemed to say no more than he'd said before. He knew nothing of the Watergate break-in. He knew nothing of the cover-up. The new, alarming note was his admission that reports on the scandal had been given to him continuously for nine months by his closest advisers. And they were all wrong. He said the whole business should be left to the courts. In this, at least, he is right.

A Federal District judge will hear next week the arguments on whether or not the President should release to the courts the tapes of the White House conversations that relate to Watergate. I don't think there's any question that the losing party will at once carry an appeal to the United States Supreme Court.

The District Court now has before it two briefs. One from Archibald Cox, the special prosecutor for the government, maintaining that the President has no special power or privilege to deny the court the tape recordings. Another brief, from the President himself, maintains the opposite.

The President concedes that the effort of Mr Cox is 'a well-intentioned effort to obtain evidence for criminal prosecutions' but that it also 'represents a serious threat to the nature of the Presidency as it was created by the Constitution'. The Presidency was set up as a separate, but co-ordinate, branch of the government: the Presidency, the Congress and the Judiciary. He admits he is not above the law but—and this is the pungent and novel argument—he is not subject to the orders of any court or even to a criminal charge *until* he has been successfully impeached by the Congress and lost his office, or he has retired and been beaten in an election. In other words, he is immune from a court order or an indictment until he returns to private life. And an important element of this immunity is his right (which even his enemies grant him) to keep secret the conversations and records of debates inside the White House that have to do with national security and foreign policy. No President releases his internal correspondence, his notes to aides, or the substance of arguments and discussions he held at Cabinet or other advisory meetings. Not while he is still in the White House.

The trouble here is one of Mr Nixon's own making. He is the only President known to have secretly ordered all conversations, in the three main rooms of the White House, to be tape-recorded without the knowledge of the other parties who came in to see him. If he had not done this, there would be no tapes, and the Congress could howl till Doomsday with no hope of getting any more from the President than his own memory of what had been said and what had not.

The opposing brief of Prosecutor Cox is a blockbuster of legal dogmatism. The President, it says, 'has an enforceable legal duty not to withold material evidence from a grand jury'. Mr Cox shrewdly boosted this argument by quoting from a textbook written by one of the lawyers who helped to write the President's brief: 'The courts should determine the validity of a claim to executive privilege ... scholars have found little support for basing executive privilege on the [Constitution's] separation of powers.' Mr Cox then sank the knife in this wound by saying, 'The grand jury is seeking evidence of criminal conduct that the President happens to have in his custody, largely by his own personal choice.' Mr Cox magnanimously grants that 'A settled rule of evidence protects a broad range of Presidential papers and conversations' but 'The present case falls outside the rule of this well-established privilege.' In case Mr Nixon has not yet got the message, Mr Cox recalls a promise of the President himself, given in a public statement last May, that 'Executive privilege will not be invoked as to any testimony concerning possible criminal conduct.'

Surely that was a fatal promise? Certainly it must now haunt the President as a rash one. For it was given just before an old Presidential aide, in an offhand bit of testimony before Senator Ervin's committee, mentioned Mr Nixon's taping habits. 'What tapes?' asked the puzzled Senator Ervin. Why, the recordings the President kept of all the conversations that ever happened in those three rooms of the White House! The man looked as blank and innocent as if the Senator had asked him: What is a telephone?

# Intermission:
# The Agnew Wake

### *19 October 1973*

I suppose that Wednesday, the 10th of October, 1973, will go into the history books. It was the day when, for the first time in the life of the Republic, a Vice President resigned rather than dispute a list of criminal charges brought against him by the government. But what happened two nights later, the ceremony which installed a new Vice President, may well become more memorable to people who saw it. And not for admirable reasons either. For what most of us had expected to be a grave and rather humble occasion turned into Oscar night at the White House.

First, however, I ought to say something about the strange fact that until five years ago there was no constitutional procedure for replacing a Vice President. This is very odd in a nation whose inventors were almost clairvoyant in foreseeing every sort of twist and turn that might happen to the government and all its branches.

The Twenty-fifth Amendment to the Constitution, on which the President had to act, was passed by Congress only so late as 1965. And it was not ratified, by the necessary three-quarters of the fifty State legislatures, until February 1967. Before then, there was no provision for replacing a Vice President. Truman went without one for the more than three years of the dead Roosevelt's unfinished term. Lyndon Johnson likewise went a year before he ran for President on his own account and so was able to have a running mate in the election of 1964.

What prompted the Twenty-fifth Amendment, which

carries the title 'Presidential Disability and Succession,' was the thought that President Kennedy might have survived the Dallas shooting as a vegetable. The amendment was concerned with seeing that the Vice President should move up into the Presidency whenever a President was physically or mentally unfit to carry on. Eight times a President has died in office, and then, of course, the succession was automatic. But the amendment also had in mind the two serious illnesses of President Eisenhower. It also meant to anticipate and avoid the alarming lapse of Presidential power that occurred when President Wilson was so crippled by a stroke that for seventeen months he languished in a shaded room, and there was no effective President.

The main clauses of the amendment say that when a President is disabled, but sentient, he shall send to the Senate and the House a written declaration that he is 'unable to discharge the powers and duties of his office'. But suppose he has enough of his wits not to want to do this? The drafters foresaw that awkward—George III—situation in which a President might be out of his mind and refuse to budge. In that case, the Vice President and a majority of the Cabinet, or any other body that Congress might set up, would announce to the Senate and the House that the President was unfit to stay in office.

All this has to do with maintaining the 'powers and duties' of the Presidency. But what if the sitting Vice President dies or is unfit? Must the country go without one? Until 1967, the answer would have been, Yes. But then, one other sentence was put into the amendment, almost as an afterthought. The drafters of the amendment thought that while they were at it they might just as well take care of the possibility of a Vice President's dying. The sentence says simply: 'Whenever there is a vacancy in the office of the Vice President, the President shall nominate a Vice President, who shall take office upon confirmation by a majority vote of both Houses.'

That was the only sentence in the Twenty-fifth Amendment

that President Nixon had to act on. He promised to do it 'very soon' but I don't think anybody expected him to do it in two days. The pundits barely had time to draw up long and knowing lists of the men the President was most likely to consider. At the head of the list were three names: Governor Nelson Rockefeller of New York, Governor Ronald Reagan (the ex-B-movie star) of California, and former Governor John Connally of Texas.

The pundits might well have saved their breath on these three. For the Democrats, who have a majority in both Houses, would have a final say on any choice. And the Speaker of the House (who, in the American system, is not a neutral chairman but the leading voice of the majority in the House) made it plain to Mr Nixon in words of one syllable that his party simply would not consider any man who might use the Vice Presidency as a launch pad into the White House in 1976. The Presidential ambitions of Rockefeller, Reagan and Connally are, to put it mildly, raging. Most obnoxious of all was the man who is—like Sean O'Casey's Paycock to Joxer Daly—President Nixon's 'darlin'' man, indeed his first choice: John Connally of Texas. For the simple and repulsive reason that Connally had been a Democrat all his life, weaned on the Democratic bottle by Lyndon Johnson himself. But once he saw the marvel of Richard Nixon's overwhelming victory in 1972, he turned Republican and without a blush started to speak at Republican fund-raising dinners around the country: a blowsy and tedious chore which, nevertheless, is the first sure sign that a man is lusting hard after the Presidency.

After first setting up these three men and then knocking them down, the pundits went on to consider the likeliest alternatives. I won't bore you with their names. They were mostly party regulars of such distinguished lack of distinction as never to be a threat to a real Presidential contender. What the President had to find was a caretaker Vice President who would fill the vacant seat of Spiro Agnew as unassertively as possible till the next campaign throws up a serious ego. If you read enough columnists, you could make your own list of thirty possibilities.

There was one other name whose revived attractiveness must have given the President the collywobbles. He is Senator Barry Goldwater, who has re-emerged through the mess of Watergate, and the government's nineteen pages of appalling charges against Mr Agnew, as the conscience of the Congress. Barry Goldwater will be remembered as the hopeless Republican candidate who was clobbered by Lyndon Johnson in 1964 by what still stands as the largest popular majority in history. Goldwater, it is generally agreed, was beaten because at the time he sounded like a firebrand. He actually wanted to win in Vietnam, and too many voters feared he might bomb North Vietnam and send thousands of American troops into battle. Lyndon Johnson, on the contrary, was the old friendly farmer and Texas schoolmaster (he taught elocution at a junior college), and he preached nothing but piety and restraint. He seemed a more prudent choice, and was elected, and thereupon he bombed North Vietnam and put half a million Americans in Vietnam. Now, Americans tend to recall that Goldwater was always a man of downright character and wiry charm, and in appearance astonishingly like the Jefferson profile on the nickel, with the addition of horn-rimmed glasses.

In the past few months, Goldwater has been the only Senator to speak up with straightforward, tart contempt for the shenanigans of the White House advisers who concocted and dictated Watergate and the collateral spyings and robberies and wire-tappings. He has also not hesitated to say that the charges against Vice President Agnew should be aired and resolved. He did not say, as the President goes on saying through thick and thin (mostly thin), that America is at the dawn of a new era of greatness. He had nothing but scorn for Mr Agnew's farewell address the other night and his saying that 'Our democracy, with its balanced federal system, its separation of powers, and its fundamental principles of individual liberty, is working better than ever.' Senator

Goldwater said, in many no-nonsense phrases, that the government was in a hell of a mess, that the system was being betrayed, and it was time the President released the Watergate tapes, settled the Agnew charges and tried to restore 'some sense and decency' to the Administration. Needless to say, this sort of talk did not endear him to Mr Nixon. But it's an interesting footnote to the seemingly interminable squalor of Watergate that very many Republicans who'd never spoken out on their own should have felt, and said in private, that Goldwater would be just the man to fill the Vice President's seat.

Well, the President turned down Rockefeller and Reagan, Connally (with reluctance), Goldwater (with relief) and all the caretakers who had been mentioned.

Then, on the evening of the 12th of October, he called to the White House a great assembly of Senators and Congressmen and Cabinet officers and justices of the Supreme Court and guests from the diplomatic corps. He would say, we presumed, that the Republic had been shaken as never before by the resignation of a Vice President after the government had drawn up a list of grave criminal charges. He would surely also say that in this grave hour he had chosen a sterling American who had the character, in the always foreseeable emergency, to rise to the Presidency and dignify it.

Mr Nixon said none of these things. He staged the solemn ceremony in the East Room of the White House, in an elegant eighteenth-century setting, under a shimmering crystal chandelier. The Marine band played the President's theme song, 'Hail to the Chief', and he came bouncing in with all the grinning euphoria of a television host about to preside over the finals of the '$64,000 Question'. His family was beaming, everywhere there were gleaming teeth and a festive air and much jollity as the President proclaimed that 'new era of greatness' and announced his choice. He had picked the Republican leader of the House, Mr Gerald Ford, a dependable rubber stamp of any and every Nixon policy, a reliable party hack of amiable small stature. The leaders of Congress, in the flesh and in the spirit, applauded the dazzling choice and no doubt will confirm it. Congress will keep to the letter of the Twenty-fifth Amendment and simply ignore the lessons of the catastrophe, and threats of more catastrophe, that brought it about.

So Congress ducked the issue, and the President made a family party of it. It was like an episode of George Orwell rewritten by Charles Dickens: a time for gravity is a time for jollity, war is peace, and shame is greatness. An unreal, certainly a tasteless, occasion which only time will blur or perhaps sharpen as a memory of the night the betrayal of the Vice Presidency was celebrated with music and dancing and congratulations all round.

# Watergate:
# Act Three

*9 November 1973*

In the past month I have gone from northern New England through the three largest cities of the North-Eastern seaboard, on to Houston and Dallas in the South-West, up to the mile-high city of Denver in the Rockies and out to Los Angeles and San Francisco. And the capsule report on public concern is the same everywhere: 'Nixon's survival, and the oil shortage.' What literally concerns the people's hearths and homes is the Arab embargo on oil to the United States. What concerns their hearts and minds is the question, which is now as incessant as a beating pulse: ought Mr Nixon to be forced out of the Presidency?

A few months ago, only the European papers cried up as an immediate threat the impeachment of the President. They were not by a long shot more prophetic or perceptive than the American press. From my reading, they knew little about the precise required grounds for impeachment or about the impeachment process itself. They were selling papers by playing up an improbable melodrama. The best of the American commentators, and a majority of Congress certainly, foresaw the grave consequences of punishing Nixon by a Senate vote to impeach: they saw ahead, through months and perhaps a year of the House hearings and then the trial, a country left with its government in recess.

But now, the word is on every lip. The notion that the President's resignation is desirable, if not inevitable, is being discussed by even the conservative wing of the Republican Party, which is a very conservative wing indeed. But the latest

Harris poll shows only one American in three in favour of impeachment. It also shows that only one American in four thinks the President is 'doing a good job'. That is not, however, a ground for impeachment. At one time, only one American in five thought Harry Truman was doing a good job.

What counts at this critical point more than the evidence of the polls is the deep anxiety of the Republican Party and the spreading disillusion of Mr Nixon's oldest supporters. Why? Why should they, of all people, believe that his administration is suspect to the point of disablement? Well, consider the catalogue not of rumours but of *acts*, which might come to be interpreted as grounds for impeachment: the 'bribery, high crimes and misdemeanours' that the Constitution lays down. It is a crime for the President to obstruct justice or hamper in any way the execution of the laws of the United States. If his personal aides commit crimes or obstruct justice, the President is held accountable, a hard fact that Mr Nixon has never hinted he will concede. Yet, so far, his Vice President has resigned to avoid a heavy jail sentence for a whole catalogue of 'high crimes'. His old Attorney General and closest adviser is under indictment for fraud. So is his old Secretary of Commerce. No less than thirteen of his one-time top aides have either been convicted of crimes, or pleaded guilty, or been indicted, or fired for misdemeanours.

It is now established that the President himself approved of burglary to keep tabs on radicals. He himself created his own secret service to use wire-tapping and forgery to keep an eye on his political enemies, and members of the press he took to be his enemies. He authorised thousands of secret bombings over Cambodia while telling the people that it was a country whose neutrality must be honoured. He personally approached the presiding judge in a government-prosecuted case and offered him the directorship of the FBI. His own lawyer raised money for the President's re-election campaign to pay off the convicted defendants in the Watergate case.

The last shocker, which may prove to be the last straw, was

the disclosure that two of the nine taped Watergate conversations, which Mr Nixon agreed to yield to the courts, 'did not exist'. As it happened, they were two crucial conversations that would have supported or refuted the charge of Mr Nixon's main accuser that the President was in on the cover-up from the beginning. This is what turned the Republicans' misgivings into anger, for they came to fear, with everybody else, that of course the tapes had existed, that they were too hot to preserve and had been destroyed.

And what do we get from Mr Nixon himself? Almost ceremonial assurances that he has a special knack for handling the Russians and the Arabs, and that his wide, deep knowledge of foreign affairs is too precious to be dispensed with. All we want to know, Mr President, *please*, is when you first knew about Watergate and if and when you started the cover-up.

The clue to his future lies, I believe, in the growing and perhaps irreversible conviction of the right wing of his party that he is probably guilty and that so long as they are saddled with him, they will go down to disastrous defeat in next year's Congressional elections and then in the 1976 Presidential election.

So it could be, after all, that it is not Mr Nixon's announced 'enemies' who will bring him down. Not the liberal press. Not the television reporters he so detests. But his old friends. It is, I suspect, not impeachment by the House he has most to fear just now. It is a deputation of the most true-blue, firm-jawed Republicans who—next week, next month, next year—will wait on him and say: You have to go.

### 3 May 1974

At last, we move on. The House Judiciary Committee—which is the one that must decide whether or not to recommend to the House that the President be impeached—is sitting and this week managed to have him release a transcript of White House tapes that he believes are related to the Watergate inquiry. The transcript runs to 1,200 pages. Not everything that was said, only everything that Mr Nixon believes is relevant. Well, the Committee went into private session on Thursday night and later went into a huff. It voted to reject these edited transcripts. It wants to hear all the tapes, unedited. *It* will decide what is relevant. I believe it will get them.

When we first heard that the President had installed hidden microphones in the White House, we said, well, it's going to be mighty embarrassing to everybody, foreign statesmen and all, whoever had a cosy chat with him. But the suggestion of releasing them, to any good purpose, to a Congressional committee is surely a farce. Because the President knew what he was saying all the time. But did he? To me, simply as somebody who has been a broadcaster for forty years, this is a fascinating line to follow. Because the hardest thing to forget in broadcasting is the microphone. Throughout the last war, and afterwards, I used to sit in the BBC studio in New York and listen to some of the most distinguished men of our time—famous exiles from the Nazis, scholars, clerics, poets, ambassadors—talking into a microphone. Often, what they said was wise and impressive, or learned or whatever. But only very rarely indeed did it sound like one person talking to another. They did not sound like men thinking aloud but like men trying to inform, to be wise, to be impressive, in one way or another, before an audience. They had written fine essays, or speeches, or lectures. And they came out sounding like essays, speeches, lectures. Because, to ninety-nine per cent of them, the microphone was a sword of Damocles over their heads. It made them just slightly, and fatally, self-conscious.

But, with long practice, it is possible to forget the microphone. Charlie Chaplin was in the habit of choosing obscure actors for big parts because he was taken by something in their faces or their movements that seemed to him just right for the part. He even chose non-actresses who gave the appearance of strangeness or innocence or whatever he was after. 'Instead of frightening them with rehearsals,' he explained, 'I would ask the cameraman to keep the cameras grinding for ever—nothing is cheaper in the movies than film—until they forgot it, and in the end I got what I wanted. On a good day, I got the cast to be as unaware of the camera as they were of electric light.'

I believe this is what happened with Mr Nixon, with the microphone on for days and nights, and weeks—and years? Here is an example of a bit of the published transcripts. The President is recalling how he eventually exposed Alger Hiss in the Communist perjury case of the late 1940s: 'I conducted that investigation with two *dot dot* committee investigators ... That *dot dot* Hiss would be free today if he hadn't lied.' The *dot dots* are printed in the transcript between brackets as 'characterisation omitted'. This could only mean that Mr Nixon's words were four-letter words, too crude for us, or the House Judiciary Committee, to see in print. There are scores, perhaps hundreds, of places in this huge transcript where the President's adjectives are listed either as 'characterisation omitted' or 'expletive deleted', and there are many more places where he is being, by the kindest possible interpretation, cagey, snide, foxy, devious.

This is the same man who, when he was running for President in 1960, recalled how 'very proud' he had been that 'President Eisenhower restored dignity and decency and, frankly, good language to the conduct of the Presidency of the United States.' It should be said that Mr Nixon himself was in public—whether rhetorical or informal—impeccable in his language.

Long ago, the English journalist Beverley Nichols put together a collection of interviews with famous people. I remember George Gershwin, Edgar Wallace, Al Capone. He gave the book the cunning title: *Are They the Same at Home?* Evidently, Mr Nixon is not the same at home, even when he has a tape recorder going.

Well, by now, I think that the House Judiciary Committee has more than enough to go on when it comes, say, to the serious and specific charge of 'obstruction of justice'. Here, for example, is Mr Nixon telling an adviser how to evade a perjury rap when he appears before a grand jury: 'You can say, I don't remember. You can say, I can't recall.' And as for the pressing need to bottle up Watergate, at the cost of paying out a bribe: 'Can't you think you have to handle Hunt's financial situation damn soon?... It seems to me we have to keep the cap on the bottle that much, or we don't have any options ... For your immediate things, you have no choice but to come up with the $120,000 or whatever it is.' In the end, it may turn out that Richard Nixon's fatal error was that he forgot the microphone was on.

Do you remember an old Frank Capra movie called *Broadway Bill*? Which was the name of a horse running against great odds in the Kentucky Derby. It had been bred and trained and idolised by two young people who had pooled their meagre savings to enter it in the Derby. They were encouraged along the way by an old, bumbling, affectionate Southerner called 'The Colonel', who was played by the fatuous and delightful Raymond Walburn. He swore again and again that he would back Broadway Bill to his last cent. On the day of the race, he went off sneakily and bet on a dark horse. Broadway Bill won, and as Walburn watched his own clever choice come padding in last, he sighed: 'Duped—by my own chicanery!'

# The Duke

*31 May 1974*

'When it is finished,' says the guidebook, 'it may well be the largest cathedral in the world.' I am always leery of sentences that contain the phrase 'may well be'. But it is certainly a very large cathedral: namely the Episcopal Cathedral Church of St John the Divine on the upper West Side in New York City. Its foundations were laid in 1892. They've been building it ever since, and the end is not yet.

On Monday, the 27th of May, 1974, St John the Divine housed a ceremony that would have flabbergasted its architect and its early worshippers. Every pew was filled, and the aisles were choked, and there were several thousands listening to loudspeakers out on the street. And when the 10,000 people inside were asked to stand and pray, there was a vast rustling sound as awesome, it struck me, as that of the several million bats whooshing out of the Carlsbad Caverns in New Mexico at the first blush of dawn.

It is not the size of the crowd that would have shocked the cathedral's founders (they might have taken it jubilantly as a sign of a great religious revival). It was what the crowd was there for. A crowd that ranged through the whole human colour scale, from the most purple black to the most pallid white, come there to honour the life and mourn the death of a man who had become supreme in an art that began in the brothels of New Orleans. The art is that of jazz, and the practitioner of it they mourned was Edward Kennedy Ellington, identified around the world more immediately than any member of any royal family as—the Duke.

The Duke's career was so much his life that there's very little to say about his private ups and downs, if any. He was born in Washington, DC in 1899, the son of a White House butler, and perhaps the knowledge that Father had a special, protected status inside the white Establishment had much to do with the Duke's seeming to be untouched, or untroubled, by the privations and public humiliations we should expect of a black born in the nation's capital. Certainly, he must have thought of himself as belonging to one of the upper tiers of black society. But his upbringing could be called normal for any of the black boys who were to turn into great jazzmen. I'm thinking of men like Earl Hines and Fats Waller, the sons of coloured parsons or church organists who, almost automatically as little boys, were hoisted onto a piano stool. The Duke took piano lessons but also took to sketching and thought of a career as an artist. This dilemma was solved by his becoming a sign painter by day and running small bands by night.

What got him going was the nightly grind and the daily practice. It is something that nightclub habitués seldom credit, it being assumed that while classical pianists must follow a daily regimen, people like Ellington, Hines, Waller, Tatum simply have a 'natural gift' and just rattle the stuff off on request. Nothing could be more false. I remember ten, fifteen years ago running into an old and engaging jazz man, a white who was employed in a poky little jazz joint in San Francisco. Muggsy Spanier, a sweet and talented man who had had a long experience of the roller-coaster fortunes of a jazzman: one year you are playing before delirious crowds in a movie theatre or grand hotel, three years later blowing your brains out before a few listless drunks in a crummy roadhouse off the main highway in some place called Four Forks, Arkansas, or New Iberia, Louisiana. Just then Muggsy was in a lean year playing in a small band with Earl Hines, who was also at a low ebb (this was before Hines, the father of jazz piano, had been discovered by the State Department and the Soviet government, or been re-discovered by a new generation). Well, Muggsy had left his trumpet in this dreadful night club and found he needed it, on his night off, for some impromptu gig or other. So he had to go into the night club next morning, always a depressing experience, what with the reek of sour air and spilled alcohol and the lights turned down to a maintenance bulb or two. He told me that one of the unforgettable shocks of his stint in San Francisco was coming from the bone-white sunlight into the smelly cave and squinnying through the dark and seeing Hines sitting there, as he did for two or three hours every morning, practising not the blues or *Rosetta* or *Honeysuckle Rose* but the piano concertos of Mozart and Beethoven. To the gaping Muggsy, Hines looked up and said, 'Just keeping the fingers loose.' To be the best, it's a sad truth most of us amateurs shrink from admitting, you have to run, fight, golf, write, play the piano every day. I think it was Paganini—it may have been Rubinstein—who said, 'If I go a week without practice, the audience notices it. If I go a day without practice, I notice it.'

This digression is very relevant to the character and the mastery of Duke Ellington. He was at a piano, but he was there as a composer, day in and night out. For a man of such early and sustained success, it is amazing that he not only tolerated the grind, after one-night stands, of the long bus rides through the day and the pick-up meals, but actually cherished them as the opportunity to sit back and scribble and hum and compose. He did this to the end.

I knew all the records of his first period when I was in college, from 1927 through 1932. And when I first arrived in New York I wasted no time in beating it up to the Cotton Club to see the great man in the flesh. But apart from a nodding acquaintance in night clubs, and becoming known to him no doubt as one of those ever-present nuisances who request this number and that, I didn't meet Ellington alone, by appointment so to speak, until the very end of the Second World War. I went up to his apartment on the swagger side of Harlem. There is such a place, in fact there are as many fine shadings of Negro housing through the hierarchy of Negro social status as there are shadings of pigment from the high-yaller to the coal black. Ellington was at the top of the scale, in a large Victorian building looking out on a patch of greenery.

The date had been for two in the afternoon. In my mind's eye I had the picture complete: the dapper figure of the Duke seated in a Noel Coward bathrobe deep in composition at a concert grand. For those were the days long before band leaders got themselves up in gold lamé and sequins. The big band leaders wore dinner jackets. The Duke wore white tie and tails, and was as sleek as a seal.

Well, I was shown into a large and rambling apartment with a living-room that had evidently seen a little strenuous drinking the night before. Off from the living-room behind curtained French doors was a bedroom. The doors were open and there in full view was a large bed rumpled and unmade. Beyond that was a bathroom, and out of it emerged what I first took to be some swami in the wrong country. It was the Duke, naked except for a pair of under-drawers and a towel woven around his head. He came in groaning slightly and saying to himself, 'Man!' Then *his* man came in, a coloured butler, and they went into the knotty question of what sort of breakfast would be at once tasty and medicinal. It was agreed on, and the Duke turned and said, 'Now.' Meaning, what's your business at this unholy hour of two in the afternoon?

The breakfast arrived and he went at it like a marooned mountaineer. To my attempts to excite him with the proposal I had come to make, he grunted 'Uh-huh' and 'Uh-un' between, or during, mouthfuls.

At last, he pushed the plate away, picked up his coffee cup and sat down and slurped it rapidly and nodded for me to begin again. I had come to suggest that he might like to record a long session with his band for the BBC. This was, remember, the peak period of his big band, and I suggested that we record him not, as we now say, 'in concert', but in rehearsal. He shot a suspicious glare at me, as if I'd suggested recording him doing five-finger exercises. But slowly and warily he began to

153

see my problem and to respect it. Simply, how to convey to a listener (this was before television) the peculiar genius of the Duke, since it was unique in the practice of jazz music. Which was somehow to be, and feel, present at the act of creation when it was happening to the Duke standing in front of the band in rehearsal. Everybody knows that the best jazz is impossible to write down in the usual musical notation. You can no more make a transcription of Hines playing *I Can't Give You Anything but Love*, or, worse, Art Tatum playing any of his cascading variations on *Tea for Two*, than you can write down three rules for the average swimmer to follow in doing the two hundred metres like Mark Spitz. Jazz is always improvisation done best by a group of players who know each other's whimsical ways with such mysteries as harmonics, counterpoint, scooped pitch, jamming in unison. Alone among jazz composers, the Duke's raw material was the tune, scribbled bridge passages, a sketch in his head of the progression of solos and ensembles he wanted to hear, and an instinctive knowledge of the rich and original talents, and strengths and perversities, of his players. They were not just trumpet, trombone, clarinet, E flat alto sax, and so on. They were individual performers who had stayed with him for years, for decades. One of them, Harry Carney, played with the Duke on his first recording date in 1927, and he was with him on the last date, in Kalamazoo, Michigan, last March. In 1927, Ellington had created a weird, compact, entirely personal sound with his band. It was weirder still and richer, but it was just as personal at the end.

Eventually, the Duke appreciated that what we wanted was not just another performance. He agreed, and we had a long and unforgettable session, in a hired studio on Fifth Avenue, where we recorded the whole process of the number dictated, the roughest run-through, with many pauses, trying this fusion of instruments and that, stopping and starting and transferring the obligato from one man to another, the Duke talking and shouting, 'Now, Tricky, four bars!' and 'Barney, in there eight.' And in the last hour, what had been a taste in the Duke's head came out as a harmonious, rich meal.

The Duke was nicknamed as a boy by a friend who kidded him about his sharp dressing. He was an elegant and articulate man and, as I've hinted, strangely apart from the recent turmoil of his race. Not, I think, because he was ever indifferent or afraid. He was a supremely natural man, and in his later years devout, and he seemed to assume that men of all colours are brothers. And most of the immediate problems of prejudice, and condescension, and tension between black and white dissolved in the presence of a man whom even an incurable bigot must have recognised as a man of unassailable natural dignity. He had a childlike side, which—we ought to remember— is recommended in the New Testament for entry into the kingdom of Heaven. He was very sick indeed in the last few months. He knew, but kept it to himself, that he had cancer in both lungs. A week or two before the end he sent out to hundreds of friends and acquaintances what looked at first like a Christmas card. It was a greeting. On a field of blue was a cross, made of four vertical letters and three horizontal. They were joined by the letter 'O'. The vertical word spelled 'Love' and the horizontal 'God'.

He has left us, in the blessed library of recorded sound, a huge anthology of his music from his twenty-eighth birthday to his seventy-fifth. He began as a minority cult, too rude for the collectors of dance music. For much, maybe most, of his time he was never a best-seller. He never stuck in the current groove, or in his own groove. He moved with all the influences of the time from blues to bebop and the moderns and transmuted them into his own, and at the end his difficult antiphonies and plotted discords, the newer harmonic structures he was always reaching for, were no more saleable to the ordinary popular music fan than they had ever been. Most people simply bowed to him as an institution.

In 1931, a college room-mate of mine who was something of a pioneer as a jazz critic, on the university weekly, was graduating, and he wrote a farewell piece. He recorded the rise and fall—during his four-year stint— of the Red Hot Peppers, and the Blue Four, and McKinney's Cotton Pickers, and Bix and Trumbauer. He ended with the phrase: 'Bands may come and bands may go, but the Duke goes on for ever.' Ah, how true! We thought it a marvel that the Duke had ridden out all fashions for four long years. In fact, his good and always developing music lasted for forty-seven years. And we have it all.

So, I am inclined to paraphrase what John O'Hara said on the death of George Gershwin: 'Duke Ellington is dead. I don't have to believe it if I don't want to.'

# Earl Warren

## *12 July 1974*

Some years ago I had the privilege of meeting the world's oldest man. At least he said he was. And he was so dogmatic about it that the promoters of a cartoon strip that specialised in unbelievable oddities brought the old man up to New York from his native Colombia, to have him examined by a team of doctors at the Cornell Medical Center.

He was an Indian, he was four feet four inches high, he had an alligator-hide complexion and a tendency to swing with his right whenever he was passed from one medico to another. He said he was 167, born the same year as the American Constitution. When the name of George Washington was suggested to him, to help him fix his generation, he said he remembered the man well. But he resented coming all the way to New York. He wanted to be left alone to go about his business, which at that time was the business of looking for a sixth wife to comfort him in his approaching old age.

The pathologists and gerontologists who were let loose on him had only to say how old he was. It says something, not very much, for gerontology, which is the science of studying old age, that he fooled them. They put out a report at the end of the day and announced that they had weighed him, tapped him, pumped him, injected him, photographed his arteries and lungs and joints, timed his coagulation rate, chemically analysed all his juices and otherwise subjected him to all the splendid new tests devised by the modern speciality of geriatrics. They confirmed, what the onlooker had already guessed, that he was 'vigorous, alert and observing'. They added that his hands suffered from 'degenerative arthritis' and that his bones were 'in a condition that many a young man might envy'. They also made the profound discovery that he was four feet four and weighed eighty pounds. He was also alive.

Then came the punch-line. 'Non-medical evidence,' they concluded, 'indicates that he is indeed a very old man and possibly might be more than 150 years of age.' The hospital refused to say what 'non-medical evidence' was. Without a blush, the doctors fell back on a consolation known to every female of the species since Eve. 'Medical science,' they pronounced, 'possesses at present no methods of determining the exact age of any adult.'

This conclusion didn't make the subject feel any better about his enormous trek north. When it was over, it was one angry midget who was exposed to a press conference. He began at once to swipe at the photographers. The nervous promoter managed a forced chuckle and said, 'My friend here loves everything and everybody.' At which point, the old man swung at the promoter. A laughing girl went to comfort him and he planted a right on her nose. That was the end of the press conference. On the way out, I remarked, 'If he's gone through life socking everybody in sight, he must have left behind a battlefield of corpses.' No, said one of the doctors, 'He was probably very tame in his youth, old men tend to take on all comers.'

This exchange was very casual at the time, but the doctor's reply ran so counter to the accepted wisdom about old age that I never forgot it. I'd always taken for granted that the ultimate truth about old people had been spoken by Aristotle twenty-three hundred years ago. Which is: 'Unlike the young, the old have lived long'—nobody like Aristotle for getting down to fundamentals—'they have often been deceived, they have made many mistakes of their own, they have seen the pain caused by positive men, and so they are positive about nothing.

158

And when they err, they err in all things by extreme moderation.'

As time went on, and I was able to watch young politicians age and mellow and grow positive about nothing, I noticed that very rarely there was a man who mellowed, like over-ripe fruit, into acidity. They were usually men who'd seemed to be committed all their lives to a bland, comfortable conservatism. And then something happened, something unexplained by the geriatric experts. It wasn't that they grew into the familiar type of the peppery conservative but that they grew at once more mellow and more radical.

Mr Averell Harriman is a handy example. The heir to great wealth, throughout his youth he had two consuming interests: rowing and polo. To be sure, he was converted from his respectable Republicanism by President Franklin Roosevelt and became a New Dealer. But he was never a fire-horse. He became in turn adviser, Secretary of Commerce, Ambassador to the Soviet Union, then to Great Britain. To the astonishment of even his friends, he then ran for Governor of New York. More astonishing still, he won. For he was a dry, poor speaker, a man of few words, the antithesis of a driving politician. Even in private, and when it was well understood that he was talking to a friend and not a reporter, he had nothing very revealing to say. Maybe he was weighed down by the burden of state secrets he carried with him, but the effect of his talk was that of an old bloodhound in a back yard munching on his food with great care in case some of it was mixed in with paper and glass.

Then, in his seventies, he changed. We had been surprised to see that he had remarkable ability as an administrator, especially in choosing obscure first-rate men as subordinates. But now he developed a salty tongue, and a lot of positive ideas. After seventy, he did once say, 'You don't give a damn.' And he was suddenly the ideal man to negotiate toughly with the tough Russians and put through the first nuclear arms agreements. He was absolutely the right man to go to Paris and sit across a table for months and never blink an eye when the North Vietnamese delivered their blazing daily harangues about the wickedness of 'the American ruling imperialist clique'. He told them bluntly what was acceptable and what was not, and when they started their harangues, he simply sat back and turned off his hearing aid.

Well, I hope you'll have gathered from this that the chemistry that turns a conservative temperament into a radical is little understood but remains one of the fascinations of politics. The same thing happened most dramatically to old Alfred Landon, the mild Kansas farmer who, in 1936, was the lost Presidential hope of every rock-bound conservative in the country in the rampaging days of Franklin Roosevelt.

Today we have the opportunity to talk about the most startling example of such a change that we've seen in any American public man this century. For last Tuesday night, in Washington, Earl Warren died at eighty-three: Chief Justice of the United States from 1953 to 1969, the most controversial of American judges perhaps since the first Chief Justice, John Marshall, and the man who more than any other encouraged and presided over the most profound social revolution the United States has known since the Civil War.

He was appointed as Chief Justice, when he was sixty-two, by President Eisenhower, who saw in him (as we all did) a dependable, conservative Republican, an old District Attorney very much for God and mother and very much against sin, crime, national health insurance, the Communists and the Democrats. Just the man to cool the reforming zeal of the majority of Franklin Roosevelt's appointees to the Court. The ideal non-rocker of the boat. Well, Eisenhower came to say that the appointment of Warren was 'The biggest damn-fool mistake I ever made.' Looking back over his life not many months ago, Warren himself said sweetly, 'On the Court, I saw things in a different light.'

Seeing things in a different light is not an unfamiliar experience to Supreme Court justices, though it is rarely mentioned by historians and, odder still, seems never to be anticipated by Presidents. Every President, however much he may grant that the Supreme Court is a third branch of government, independent of the Congress and the Presidency—every President naturally likes to appoint judges who share his general political and social views. But, as I've mentioned before, a President is sometimes deceived into thinking that he has thereby installed a ventriloquist's doll on the Court. Gradually the new man nestles into the realisation that he is going to be paid for life, whatever he decides, that he will never have to seek election, that he can be above the political battle. He can, in short, afford to become himself.

If we look back only briefly at the life and career of Earl Warren up to his sixty-third year, we can easily understand why poor old Eisenhower should have spent the last years of his life exasperated by the character of his choice.

Warren was born in Los Angeles, the son of a father born in Sweden and a mother born in Norway. His father was a train repairman on the Southern Pacific railroad. The son, from boyhood through middle age, appeared to follow the prototype of the all-American Horatio Alger nice boy. He was called, from his sunny disposition and big moon face, Pinky. He went through the public schools. He played the cornet in the school band. He worked as a truck driver and a freight handler on the railroads and managed to put himself through the University of California. Then he went on to study law and practise it, and after time out as an infantry lieutenant in the First World War, he eventually became a District Attorney. He prosecuted malefactors vigorously, joined the Elks, became a reliable true-blue country club conservative, and picked up a reputation as a merciless foe of gambling and pornography (two human weaknesses he never changed his mind about). He was also a fervent spectator of baseball and football.

He had five children, all rosy and handsome, and a California political scout mused, 'How can you beat a man with a family like that?' You couldn't. He became a popular Governor, affable, undistinguished, and a dedicated deplorer of Franklin Roosevelt. In 1948 he seemed geographically just right to balance the appeal of the coming Presidency of Governor Dewey of New York. Consequently, he ran as Vice President on the Republican ticket and was obliterated, as Dewey was, by Harry Truman.

Nobody outside California even then knew much about him. Insiders knew him as a dawn-to-midnight worker and a man so unwaveringly genial to all and sundry that even some liberals forgave him for the dangerously arbitrary act—which since has been thought to be unconstitutional—of putting all the American citizens in California of Japanese ancestry into internment camps during the Second World War. The first shock to his millions of followers came in 1945 when he proposed a compulsory sickness insurance law for all Californians. The legislature defeated it as an invasion of 'galloping Socialism'. (In those days, Socialism in the United States never crept or crawled or sidled. It always galloped.)

From then on, in inconspicuous ways, he began to move slowly away from the Right. But not so that anybody in Washington, President Eisenhower for instance, would notice. In 1953, when the Chief Justice of the United States died, Eisenhower offered the job to John Foster Dulles and then to Governor Dewey. Both of them turned it down. After them, Eisenhower made that 'damn-fool mistake'.

Within eight months of Warren's appointment the Court was faced with the historic case of the little black girl who had to walk two miles to a segregated school (the case of Brown v. The Board of Education of Topeka, Kansas). And the Court ordered the integrating of whites and blacks in American public schools, and so set off the charge for the black revolution of our day. The majority opinion was written by Earl Warren. He went on to champion the rights of accused criminals to have free legal aid, and even the right of convicted criminals to be released if they were not told, at the moment of arrest, of this new privilege. He helped to reshape the old election districts of the country that had manifestly ignored dramatic shifts of population.

In a word, he became the St George of the liberals. And billboards went up throughout the South, and in northern industrial towns: 'Impeach Earl Warren!' He and 'his' Court were accused of pre-empting the sole right of Congress to make the laws. It is true, certainly, that he was inclined to nudge Congress in the direction of what he took to be pressing social reforms. He came to believe, he said, that the Court was more an arbiter between the States and the federal government. 'It is,' he said, 'the people's Court.'

What produced this profound shift of sympathy, this chemical change in his character? We are on the dangerous ground of amateur psychiatry. But I hazard a guess from an episode that I haven't seen mentioned in the long obituaries of him. When he was about twelve or thirteen, there was a workers' strike on the Southern Pacific railroad. His father was one of its ringleaders. The men stayed out for the best part of a year. Warren recalled in private many years later: 'We had a hard time of it in our home getting enough to eat.'

This trauma must have faded, as such things will in healthy boys. But moving into old age, when he went on the Court, he reviewed his life and the secure Establishment to which he had given his energies and his beliefs. And somewhere along the line, not long after his appointment, I imagine, he must have sometimes thought about the time when he was one of the people, the hungry people, in opposition. Anyway, some subdued element of his character rose to the surface and transformed him. And he became, according to taste, either the heroic judge of our time or 'the biggest damn-fool mistake' Eisenhower ever made. Tamed and tailored in his youth, he became in his sixties and seventies—like that ancient midget from Colombia—'ready to take on all comers'.

# Watergate:
# Act Four and Epilogue

*7 August 1974*

Nobody has ever denied America a gift for melodrama, in its history as well as in the great popular literature it more or less invented: the movies. This leads Europeans, more than anybody, to expect melodrama all the time and to report even the gravest American political upheaval as some sort of comic horror film.

Watergate, it's true, started out, two summers ago, as an absurd late-night movie: a raid on the Democratic Party's headquarters by six men (five were caught) claiming that they were saving the country from a take-over by Fidel Castro. Through the summer of the 1972 Presidential campaign, it was known to most people as 'the Watergate caper'. Then the President made a public statement assuring us that nobody in, or ever connected with, the White House had had anything to do with it. Then those two young reporters from the *Washington Post* started digging and found that the real dirt—an enormous pile of hush money—lay, so to speak, in the basement of the White House. Long before the smell was positively identified as coming from the President's Oval Office, some newspapers both at home and abroad began to jump the gun and talk about impeachment. Then impeachment became a serious possibility. And, in the past few months, a probability.

So now, after almost two years, during which the American people floundered, or joked, in a fog of bewilderment and cynicism, they were brought back to a sense of the alertness and toughness of their constitutional system, and the responsibility it gives to the Congress, by the recent—and as it turned out, the decisive—public hearings of the House Judiciary Committee.

I wish these hearings had been televised at length abroad, for I think they would have shown that in a crisis of power, the American federal system has serious and effective weapons that keep the people of the United States, through their elected representatives, sovereign. And only the people.

Not many Americans before the past month or more could have told you off-hand what the Judiciary Committee is about. They may know from the textbooks that it's the body empowered to screen new laws and to look into any legal dispute between the other branches of government that might affect the constitutional power of the Congress. It is also given the job of drafting articles of impeachment: the impeachment of a President, a Vice President, a federal judge or any civil officer of the United States. It is, you might say, the DA—the District Attorney—of the Congress. It prepares the case, or it says there is no case, against the suspected official. Since there has been only one case of Presidential impeachment since the Republic began, naturally none of us on the outside has ever seen the Judiciary Committee at work. I'm always in two minds about the wisdom of televising the proceedings of any national legislature, though I believe it is a good thing to televise the public hearings of Congressional investigating committees. It reminds Americans that they have an incomparable watchdog, which—when it sniffs failure or fraud in any public enterprise, from a rise in unemployment to a rise in the price of baseball tickets, from the President's conduct of foreign policy to Detroit's conduct of the automobile business—can call in the humblest and the most powerful in the land to state their case in public. Everybody but the President.

I'm certain, anyway, that the decision—by the House Rules Committee—to let the Judiciary Committee's hearings be televised in full, gavel to gavel, as we say, was godsent. Here we saw thirty-eight men and women, all of them experienced lawyers, debating with good temper, cogently, often subtly, more thoughtfully than any newspaper editorial had done, the grounds for an impeachment of the President. The first fear that many people had was that the committee would be seen as a simple, deceptive two-way mirror. If you're a Democrat, you look at things one way, and if you're a Republican, another way. The first debates deepened this fear, because the votes to recommend each article of impeachment seemed to follow the party bias. It was possible for last-ditch Republicans to harp on their theme that Watergate was a Democratic plot. But, once the drafting of the articles was done, and the Committee started to argue over them and amend them, it became pretty clear that the opponents of impeachment had a powerful case. From mountains of testimony—from the blowsy and exhaustive evidence of the Presidential tapes—they all agreed that the President had demeaned himself as a man, that the tone of his discussions with his aides was vulgar, tricky and lamentable in the highest officer of the country. But, they held to the necessary point that a man might be all these things, even personally immoral, even dishonest, but unless he was dishonest in the actual performance of his Presidential duties, unless he had failed the oath he takes on the day of his inauguration (the oath 'faithfully to execute the laws of the United States'), he could still not have committed an impeachable offence.

We should not forget that when the authors of the Constitution were deciding on the crimes that would justify impeachment, they were following the impeachment trial in England of Warren Hastings, and they decided that the crimes with which he was charged—'dishonesty and cruelty'—were not enough. There was a powerful move, in the Constitutional Convention, to make 'maladministration' a ground for impeachment. But James Madison, with his usual gift for rooting out a mischief, foresaw that this would leave a President at the mercy of any powerful faction in Congress that didn't like the way he was running things. Hamilton put in the reminder that 'the demon of faction' will always threaten 'all numerous bodies of men'. If 'maladministration' were to be an impeachable offence, said Madison, 'the President would remain in office at the pleasure of the Senate'. The word was dropped. The grounds had to be nothing more or less than 'treason, or bribery, or high crimes and misdemeanours'. (Incidentally, the British took seven years to try Warren Hastings, and they decided that the impeachment process was wasteful, expensive and damaging to good government. They abandoned it once for all just as the United States adopted it.)

In the Watergate case, a bipartisan group began to form on the Judiciary Committee that was opposed to impeachment. It was admitted that there were reams of suspicious testimony, and by inference a mass of charges that could be laid at the President's door. But inference was not enough. There was no clear, direct *evidence* (there was lots of testimony) that the President knew about Watergate or had tried to cover it up before the date he himself had said he first heard about it: March the 22nd, 1973. They stuck with this point.

The seriousness and fairness of the Committee appeared most clearly again when the Democratic legal counsel drew up two extra articles of impeachment. One, that the President had evaded income taxes. The other, that he had lied to the Congress about the secret bombing of Cambodia.

First, it is far more difficult than the ordinary citizen knows for a public man, a President of all people, to keep track of the enormous glut of detail—the expenses, the allowances, the fair deductions—related to his income tax. We are all at the mercy of a tax accountant or a lawyer, or both. The Committee decided, wisely I think, to give the President the benefit of the doubt.

Coming to the secret bombing of Cambodia, which was certainly an unconstitutional exercise in deceit, the Committee reminded itself of President Kennedy's entirely secret plan to invade Cuba. The fact that the invasion failed does not exonerate him from the secret assumption of a power the Constitution denies him. So this, too, looked like very dangerous ground. The Democrats swung over against it, and it was defeated.

On the main charge, that the President had obstructed justice (the nub of the cover-up argument), some Republicans swung over. They reluctantly conceded the point that if you hear of a felony and don't go to a policeman or a judge and report it, you are liable to a criminal conviction. The Committee decided there was enough evidence to warrant recommending that article to the House. When the hearings were over, the first head count of the House showed that the President was certain to have a large majority against him.

Still, right through to the end, there remained for ten members of the Committee (ten out of thirty-eight) a missing link: incontrovertible proof that the President knew about Watergate, and had tried to suppress the knowledge of it, before March 22nd, 1973.

Suddenly, this week, the missing link fell into place as audibly as the lock clanking on a prison door. You remember that the Supreme Court had ordered the President to give more tapes to the courts. His lawyer heard the new batch and was astounded. He had never been told what was in them. He told the President that if he didn't release them, one in particular, he would quit the case and say why. So, with ghastly reluctance, the President released them. And there, as gross as a manacle, was the missing link. It was a tape in which he not only revealed he had heard about Watergate: he ordered Haldeman to get the CIA to stop the FBI's investigating it. The date of that conversation was *June 23rd, 1972* ! Only six days after the break-in, nine months before he claimed he first heard about it. In itself, it was damning in the extreme. But it also cast a new and damning light on many ambiguities of the tapes already out. A single sentence of advice to Haldeman showed that he had known all along, that he had covered up, that he had lied steadily and unblinkingly to the press, to many a public audience, for two years.

Within twenty-four hours the ten holdouts on the Judiciary Committee—Republicans and some Southern Democrats—reversed themselves and announced that they would vote for impeachment. The head count in the House now showed an overwhelming majority against him. His support in the Senate slumped well below the one-third he would need to save him.

In the enormous reverberation of his downfall, we should not forget that what doomed him in the end was the 8 to o verdict of the Supreme Court three weeks ago that he must deliver up what turned out to be the fatally incriminating tape. It was an assurance the country had sadly needed that in any showdown about the supreme power of the land, the Court—representing the people of the United States—is supreme, and not the President, whoever he is.

So now. He could resign and assure himself of $156,000 a year in pension and allowances. Or he could be impeached, convicted and have $18,000 pension as an old Congressman and an old sailor. He could still face criminal prosecution, once he was restored to ordinary citizenship. He might bargain for immunity, as Vice President Agnew had successfully done. He might beg for a pardon from the incoming President. He might go on believing against all the omens that he would somehow salvage one-third of the Senate. These were the alternatives he faced, as three or four of the leading conservatives in the Senate were meeting to decide whether to tell him he had to go. The rest you know.

*Next day, on the 8th of August, he announced his resignation over television, and at noon on the 9th he left the White House.*

# EPILOGUE
## 6 *May 1977*

While the government leaders of Western Europe were
coming face to face with President Carter for the first time, on
what is rather grandly called the London Summit, down on
the lower slopes which you and I inhabit something like
seventy millions of lesser fry in the United States—and
Heaven knows how many more millions around the world—
found themselves riveted to their television sets by the sight
and sound of that old, and we'd assumed long discredited,
performer: Richard M. Nixon.

In the first muddy wake of Watergate, certainly for a year
or more after Mr Nixon's resignation, there wasn't a
broadcasting network that would have tolerated any more
public talk from him. And (which is saying the same thing in
a more pragmatic way) there wasn't a sponsor, not a
manufacturer of soap or potato chips or any other clean, non-
political, product, who wouldn't have run for the hills at a
mere hint from their advertising agency that Nixon was
available. The general atmosphere of revulsion or plain
boredom lay heavy over the San Clemente exile. So much so
that it was a matter of mild surprise when we heard that one
of the most astute of Hollywood agents had taken on the job
of trying to sell Mr Nixon's memoirs.

On the face of it, you might suppose that nothing is more
marketable than the memoirs of an ex-President. But it is
something every new publisher has to learn, that the star-dust
of a President very quickly turns to ashes once he is retired to
private life. Once a President leaves office and starts to recall
the grandeurs and miseries of his term—the meetings, the
memos, the treaties and feuds and setbacks—the prose is
about as warming as a coal grate the morning after. So when
Mr Nixon's agent announced that he was open for offers for
the Nixon view of life, a vast yawn engulfed the publishing
industry. Then, at some point, the agent got in touch with Mr

David Frost, who had the ruinous idea that a large television audience at home and abroad might be interested in seeing and hearing Mr Nixon's television apology for his life. Nobody I talked to at the time with any experience of these things gave Mr Frost or Mr Nixon a prayer of making a penny. And this apathy raged until a month ago, until, in fact, the interviews had been taped. Then somebody leaked to the *New York Times* the text of two or three White House tapes that had been in the hands of the public prosecutor. For some odd and never-explained reason they had not been published. Even Mr Nixon had never heard of them. Yet one of them was damning, if further damnation was called for. This bait dangled in the stream and two national news magazines leaped for it. They saw the videotapes of Mr Frost's interviews. They decided at once to do splashy cover-stories on—nobody but Richard Nixon.

You might think this would have ruined the telecasts and pre-empted the audience for them. Not at all. It did just what Mr Frost had hoped. It whipped up half the American people, and other peoples, to say, 'This we have to see.'

What we saw was surely the most emotionally intimate, sustained look at any politician in modern history. The fact that Mr Nixon and Mr Frost suddenly and surprisingly made a lot of money—and Mr Nixon needs all he can get to pay off a load of back taxes and a fortune in lawyers' fees—seems to me to be no more than a carping, and probably envious, irrelevance. What mattered was the intensity and, better, the quality of the human exchange that came on the screen. Many people, many of my colleagues, I'm sorry to say, felt called upon—by way of boosting their original prejudice or avoiding the discomfort of having to feel new emotions—to rewrite their 1974 judgments a little more tartly than before.

But anyone who gave himself freshly to what was seen and said had a deeper glimpse than we've had before into, simply, one of the most complex and fascinating characters of our time. Hours of unbuttoned self-revelation. I defy anyone, trusting entirely to his reflex instincts at the time, to say that it was not emotionally engaging in the literal sense, the first long view of Nixon to show how deeply intertwined from the start had been his emotions and his judgment. He has plainly done a painful amount of brooding and self-analysis. He has, I believe, a deep and disturbing inability to distinguish tactics from simple honesty. But the pathetic, and I found moving, new element was the admission that by lying he had demeaned his office, and the claim that at the same time he had done nothing criminal. He bristled with a kind of subdued panic only once, when Mr Frost read out to him the text of the statute on what constitutes obstruction of justice. He shook his head. To believe it would have compelled him to face the unfaceable: the word criminal.

It is not to me any longer a question of whether Mr Nixon was hounded by the press or whether he was to the end a victim of his own incorrigible chicanery. In other words, whether he was a dupe or a scoundrel. Such testy questions of right and wrong were transcended, in the face-to-face experience itself, by the substance of a fine novel, by a psychological study of a tragic human being who may not have come to terms with us, or with the law, but who has come to terms, however pathetic, with himself.

In spite of all the crisp editorialising, the defence of positions taken long ago, it seems to me that in the long run Mr Nixon may come out of it better than it seemed he would. Not as a politician, not as a wronged man, not as a President who could possibly have escaped impeachment (he still cannot face the conclusive evidence that the Senate would have given him no more than a handful of votes) but as an engrossing human being, once in high office, trying with astonishing tenacity to prop up the defences of his self-respect: a character of Shakespearian complexity and pathos—pitiable, sympathetic, and gone for good.

# Workers, Arise! Shout 'Fore!'

## 27 December 1974

There is something I ought to talk about and something I must talk about. What I ought to talk about is the end of the annual General Assembly of the United Nations, a leaden piece of Christmas cake I have obediently chewed on for the past thirty-odd years. What I must tell you about is an encounter I recently had with the Russians that is altogether cockeyed and hilarious, but it is not without deep significance of a ritual kind. Let us skip the cake and come to the icing.

A few weeks ago, I was staying in San Francisco, and I had a call one morning asking me to lunch with the Russian Consul General and his deputy. The invitation came from an unlikely host, a friend, a lawyer, an affable and fastidious gent, a Republican and a first-rate golfer, to whom the great game is not only a major exercise in military strategy and tactics but also a minor rehearsal of the Ten Commandments. He is, indeed, the chairman of the championship committee—and will without doubt soon become the President—of the United States Golf Association. His pairing with the Russian Consul General seemed improbable in the extreme. Where, I asked, shall we meet? 'At the golf club, of course,' was his mad reply. But why, why? 'It is very important,' he said. 'I should surmise that the Consul General is coming under orders, and the whole point of the lunch is to talk golf.' This was like being invited by a rabbi to lunch with the Pope to discuss stud poker. I accepted instantly.

The co-host was a young American, a boyish type who is associated with his famous father in the most successful golf

173

architecture firm on earth. Golf architecture is the art and science of designing and building golf courses, and it involves much knowledge of landscape, soils, grasses, water drainage, engineering, meteorology and sometimes—I feel—black magic. Let us call the young man Mr Jones, for that happily is his name.

It seems he had recently got back from Moscow, where he and his father had responded to what must have sounded like a joke more unlikely than the reason for our lunch: a call from the Mayor of Moscow to consider building the first Russian golf course. The impulse, apparently, had come from a Soviet diplomat who had been exposed to the decadent West and had become one maniacal golfer. This in itself should give us a pause. I should have guessed that any Russian who had yielded to such a capitalist diversionary activity as golf would have been, on his first homecoming, bundled off to Siberia, where he'd have been condemned to play golf with a red ball and a snow sledge. But he was a close friend of the Mayor of Moscow. When he returned from a foreign, Western, post, he came into the airport carrying a golf bag. The customs men—as also, I imagine, the military and the narcotics squad—examined the weaponry but reluctantly gave him the benefit of his diplomatic passport. Somehow, the man sold the Mayor of Moscow on the idea of a city—public, of course—golf course. I don't suppose things rested there. The matter went up to the Kremlin. And, from all I could gather, Mr Brezhnev gave the nod.

Well, we sat down to lunch, and the Consul General—a stocky man in the regulation Sears Roebuck suit—turned out to have a puckish humour. When we asked him if the Russians would take to golf, he said, 'I think, because, you see, the Russian people like quick games.' Somebody said, 'Like chess.' He came back on the hop: 'Yes, we like a quick win.' He plainly and admittedly knew nothing. But he asked everything. And to help him with the rudiments—of building rather than playing—young Mr Jones put on a lantern lecture, with colour slides showing rice paddies in Bangkok being transformed—

slide by slide—into a bulldozed mess, then into terraced ground, then into ground being planted with gravel and soil and seed, and eventually emerging as a pastoral golf hole. Through a series of other slides, we went to Hawaii and Florida and Scandinavia and, in the end, to the five sites around Moscow from which they will choose the one on which to build the course.

After that, the Consul General was given a lesson in weaponry. ('Golf,' said Winston Churchill, 'is a game whose aim is to hit a very small ball into an even smaller hole, with weapons singularly ill-designed for the purpose.') We went off in electric carts, like a little motorised battalion, to the eleventh tee on the noble San Francisco Golf Club course, a swaying landscape of lush green meadows flanked with towering cypresses and pine and occasional stands of eucalyptus.

The eleventh hole is a par three: that is to say, you are required to hit the green with your first shot and then sink the ball with two putts.

Our lawyer host, Mr Frank (Sandy) Tatum, straightened his waistcoat (all *ex officio* members of the United States Golf Association board are very sensitive to the ancient amenities and insist on playing in ties and waistcoats, like the respectable Scots in the old prints). Offhand, I would bet that this Tatum, on that hole, would hit the green ninety-nine times in every hundred. He hit about six inches behind the ball, which rose in an unsteady arc and landed about 150 yards away, well short of a cavernous bunker. 'Dear me,' he said with splendid restraint.

'So,' said the Deputy Consul (a pretty fresh type, I thought), 'the first pancake is never any good.' Ignoring this gem of Russian folk wisdom, Mr Tatum set up another ball, and this time was comfortably on the green. Now, with many open-handed gestures and facetious bows, the Consul General was motioned to 'have a go'. He took off his jacket, looked down at the ball, gripped the club with all ten fingers (the so-called baseball grip, which about one professional in a thousand uses). His two hands were far apart. He missed the ball at the first swipe, but at the second it fell just a little short of Tatum's first effort. There was general applause. 'A natural talent,' purred the gallant Mr Tatum. 'Please!' said the Consul General.

Then the Deputy had a go, and he slithered the ball about thirty yards along the ground. 'That Deputy,' one of our group whispered, 'he sure knows what he's doing.' Well, then we all departed for the clubhouse, had our pictures taken, and the Consul General was presented, by young Mr Jones, with a copy of an article I had once written on the origins of golf. Mysterious, this. 'Why?' I asked young Jones. He looked for a second over his shoulder. 'Don't you see,' he hissed, 'it supports the main argument?' And what would that be? 'What we kicked around at lunch.'

I realised then why I had been seated at lunch next to the Consul General. He had dropped several uncomfortable hints that he knew golf was a rich man's hobby, and I sensed that Moscow had asked him to check on this repulsive legend. I hastened to disabuse him with—young Jones later assured me—deeply moving eloquence. 'No, no,' I said, 'that used to be so long ago, even then only in England and America, never in Scotland.' I painted a picture, all the more poignant for being true, of poor little boys going off with their sticks and paying a few pennies to play some of the most hallowed courses on earth. 'In Scotland,' I said, 'the people learn to play golf as simply as they learn to drink tea. And St Andrews, which is the Vatican—pardon me, the Kremlin—of golf is a public course. On Sundays they close it so that little old ladies and dogs and babies can frolic—can walk around—for it is a public park *absolutely for the people.*' 'No?' said the Consul General. 'Yes,' I said.

'What,' he asked, 'will our people do, will they succeed at this sport?' 'No question,' I said, 'ten years from now'—we were well along with the vodka martinis—'I swear to you the British or American Open Champion'—('Open? What means this open?')—'the golf champion of Britain or America will be a Russian. After all, not so many years ago, you sent over a Russian basketball team, and Americans shook with laughter. Until you wiped the floor with both the Americans and the Canadians.'

'Wiped?'

'Beat, trounced, massacred, defeated!'

'It is so,' said the Consul looking gloomily into his glass of vodka.

'Very well, then,' I went on, 'maybe the big switcharoo will come sooner than ten years. Maybe four, five years from now, there will be a match between the best player in the world, Jack Nicklaus and Nicholas III.'

'There was never any Nicholas III,' said the knowing Deputy.

'But there will be!' I cried. 'And he will win!'

'Is possible?'

'Is certain.'

I went back to town feeling I had done creditably on my first assignment as ambassador without portfolio. There were, of course, certain little nuisances: of having to learn to play the game (from whom?), to find courses to learn it on, pros willing to spend a couple of years teaching the first Russian golfer how, for God's sake, to hit a golf ball straight. I thought of Nicklaus, at the age of eight, going on the practice tee every day for a year to have his head gripped for an hour on end by the hand of an assistant pro so he could learn to keep his head still. Perhaps I should have stretched the apprenticeship period to ten or twenty years.

Still, if they get around to building the Jones course, I like to imagine Mr Brezhnev or his successor, or *his* successor, standing on the first tee and approaching a ribbon with a mighty pair of shears. He will carry in his hand a note or two from our San Francisco Summit, and he will proclaim to a vast assembly of the peoples of all the Russias: 'So! I have the extremely great honour to say to the citizens of our Soviet

Socialist Republics—let us begin to play Goalf! The pipple's sport!'

# The Benefits of Clergy

## 4 April 1975

Over the Easter weekend in the Delaware Valley of Pennsylvania, more than four hundred married couples, young and old, held hands in an auditorium lit by candles and chanted in unison, 'I have made a decision in love.' For most of them the decision had been made years ago, for some— decades ago. Mostly, though, they were young people brazenly defying the current maxim of the liberated that there is no such thing as a happy marriage.

Eight hundred people don't, of course, come together spontaneously, except to watch a big fire or—as I shiver to recall my first American news assignment—a young man taking thirteen hours to decide whether or not to jump from the top of a Fifth Avenue hotel. These hand-holders were organised by something called Marriage Encounter. And never mind that these long-delayed second honeymoons were called Encounter Weekends. The ceremony was performed at the same time in nineteen other countries.

It sounds like a typically American notion but it was, in fact, started nearly twenty years ago in Spain and has since spread to several countries of South America and then to the United States. The idea came—as you may have guessed by now— from Roman Catholics.

This year's ceremony coincided with a national survey which reports that in this country Roman Catholic families have by far fewer broken homes, more good students— especially in the sciences—much less juvenile delinquency, and a close family life. To get a true picture of how stable or how anxious those families could be, you might have to make many more exhaustive surveys, asking what is meant by a broken home, and what constitutes delinquency, and what is the emotional price paid by children whose instincts to rebel are curbed by their religious taboos.

Anyway, both the American ceremony and the survey are not to be sniffed at in a country where—out of a population of 212 million—there are forty-eight million Catholics. This is almost twice the number of the next largest sect: the twenty-one separate denominations that make up the body known as the Baptists. There are, by the way, only three million Episcopalians (the closest thing to the Church of England) and fewer than a hundred thousand Methodists.

It almost goes to suggest that the bulwark of the institution of marriage in America is the Roman Catholic Church, a conclusion that no Congressman—unless he came from Boston, Philadelphia or Chicago—would dare to draw. It should, at any rate, jolt the popular picture abroad of the United States as the headlong, swinging capital of the world in which the loophole of divorce is woven into the marriage contract, wife-swapping is rampant, and more young couples live together without than with benefit of clergy. These practices, it is safe to say, are aberrations in American society. As such, they naturally get most of the publicity and all the tendentious magazine articles on the imminent collapse of marriage itself. Heaven knows, and no doubt shudders, that there are in Britain and most other Protestant countries thousands and thousands of young people from what used to be called respectable homes who not only live together without a marriage certificate but have children without a hint of legitimacy. Indeed, many famous actresses have become the Vestal Virgins of this cult, on principle, to show that God, at least, does not need written permission to inseminate the female.

It's anybody's guess how long this has been going on, but I think most of us would agree that the unwed couple is a product of the 1960s. And, I must say, most of the couples who have made a go of it seem to think it's the wave of the future.

Well, it's just beginning to occur to a lot of them that marriage, being a legal contract, does help to straighten out the tangles when the relationship breaks up or down. In San Francisco, there is an attractive young couple that does not live together. The girl is married, the man has been married, but they have become partners on a project. The only baleful thing to note about this sunny couple is that they are both lawyers. They have written a book to explore the jungle of legal problems that is invisible to most young people who set up house out of wedlock. 'It can get very sticky,' says the woman lawyer, 'I once had a case involving a fight over the custody of a rubber raft.' Her legal partner opens up the murky prospect ahead of parting couples by saying, 'Hardly anyone gives a thought to the practical aspects of living together at the beginning. Usually, everything is very informal until the end, and then each person has a different view of property, debts and obligations.'

The book is called *Living Together and the Law*. It is intended as a handbook, for frequent and maybe desperate consultation, by couples who are astonished to discover that even without a wedding ring they are—like the rest of us—subject to the law. To the laws of property, indebtedness, bankruptcy, insurance, inheritance, and—I shouldn't wonder—of piracy and barratry. The authors sweetly declare that they are not out to judge people, but simply want to help 'people who are in over their heads'. When you consider the prolonged bouts of recrimination that legally married couples can get into once the marriage crumbles, you don't need to be a Ph.D. in human nature (such courses are offered in some colleges) to guess at the pandemonium that ensues when either or both of the non-legal, ever-loving partners discover that there appears to be no law to compel the now detested mate to do anything.

The handbook, though gamely trying to avoid all moralising, does in fact produce its own set of rules, and some of them are more rigid than the ones that married people swear to live by or, at worst, come to recognise as being in effect the law.

Debts, for instance. Apparently, there is no legal obligation for an unmarried couple to be responsible for each other's debts. Property: the house you buy, the rooms you rent, are other nasty hurdles to the love life everlasting. If one of the partners has been in the habit of paying the rent and skips town, is the other partner responsible? In some States, yes. In most States, it will have to go to court. Then, it is a common thing for a couple to swear enthusiastically—in spite of their refusal to swear anything on a Bible—that they trust each other implicitly and, of course, will share the bank account and the charge account. In an unusual burst of spleen, the tolerant authors describe such couples as idiots. The banks may be wary of allowing this practice but when they do, they too can discover that the surviving partner of a wrecked alliance is not responsible for the bank loan taken out by the departed lover.

There are smart couples who think to get the jump on the law by pretending to be married whenever marriage seems to offer a social or financial advantage. They learn, for instance, that they will pay more taxes as single people than if they claim to be married. So they file a joint return. Once the Internal Revenue Service spots this trick (and nowadays all returns go through computers, which take a dimmer view of human beings than humans do) then the couple is liable to arrest and, quite likely, a prison sentence.

The worst nightmares for a broken partnership have to do with the rights of shared property, and—worst of all—the rights of previous husbands and wives and children by a previous marriage, not to mention children by the non-marriage. I have been told by young people who coupled in haste and are repenting in panic what an awful shock it is to learn that the laws which sanction marriage were also designed to protect men and women from the very pitfalls that confront couples who are not married. To put it most heartlessly, they become aware for the first time that the marriage licence, which square couples insist on, is not so much a bond or shackle as a shield against adversity, adultery, a change of heart, which was given to each partner, not least to the woman, certainly as long ago as the Romans. From whom, it is the ultimate humiliation to learn, our marriage laws derive.

I'm telling you all this with the blank air of a reporter, intending no I-told-you-so sarcasm of an older generation. These legal horrors had frankly never struck me until I read *Living Together and the Law*. Among the friends of my generation, I must know a score with sons or daughters, or both, who have set up house with somebody else's unmarried son or daughter. Among the parents, there are the rich and the poor, business people and bohemians, lawyers, artists, social workers, ambassadors, advertising executives, cooks, religious couples, agnostics, atheists, Jews, and lackadaisical nothings. But—it strikes me now—no Roman Catholics.

There are no doubt some listeners in the class who claim to belong to that most alarming of liberated groups: the unshockable. They most likely have children of their own practising the trend of bed and board with no strings attached. They too—according to *Living Together and the Law*—are more surprised than anybody to learn that while the strings which attach to unmarried couples may be invisible at the start, they are in the end as irresistible as the wires on a puppet. And that when they get ravelled—by the irritable hand of either partner or perhaps by the usual hand of mischance or fate—then the question is: Who can be called in to liberate the liberated couple? Usually, I fear, the unliberated parents. It takes money to do the disentangling, and usually, it seems, it is the now outraged in-laws who are going to have to do it.

As, for instance: Who takes the baby? Who pays for its education? Whose name does it assume? Who redeems the joint charge account? Who has title to the half an acre? Who may sell the pooled property—the four chairs, the cooking pots, the tape deck, the skis, the slope-front desk that was contributed by the girl's indulgent father but was used as a working tool by the male partner? The green stamps? The works of Germaine Greer and Betty Friedan? Who takes the car on which the committed couple committed themselves for a while to make alternate payments? Who keeps up the mortgage? Which child of which marriage, legal or otherwise, has access to whose home? Who takes the telly? Who gets custody of the rubber raft?

It's enough to make a heathen rush to Rome. It makes marriage seem like the greatest new swinging thing, a really cool institution. Or, as the very latest swingers say about something really splendid: 'Bad, man, real bad.'

# The End of the Affair

## *11 April 1975*

Throughout the nineteenth century and on into our own time, military disasters were reported to the home front as, at worst, military setbacks. Thanks, I suppose, to strict censorship at the front and the unquestioned existence of official secrets acts and such, which concealed the unvarnished truth for so many years that by the time it was open for inspection, the people at home had other things on their minds. It was left to the historians to analyse and thrash over the ashes of once burning issues.

I think of the ill-fated expedition to Dakar in the Second World War, and the ill-conceived British landings in Norway. True, they caused a rumpus in the House of Commons, since the brave invaders quickly came home again. But there were no nightly pictures on the telly to show, for instance, our men landing in Norway without skis, on the assumption of generals bred in a temperate climate that the men were going off to fight a rifle-to-rifle battle in Surrey or on the fields of northern France.

The enormous catastrophe of the Dardanelles campaign in the First World War was, I well remember, reported to us as a difficult but heroic undertaking. And when it failed, the tip-toe evacuation of all our forces was glowingly represented as a triumphant success. In those days, they did not publish the human cost. Only the schoolboys of a later generation learned to be dazed by the news that Gallipoli cost each side a quarter of a million casualties. And those of you old enough to remember Dunkirk will recall how the relief at the evacuation of so many men from beaches under aerial bombing was turned by the government of the day, by the newsreels, and then by Hollywood, into a glorious thing. Until Mr Churchill brought us to our senses with a speech in the House of Commons in which he bluntly declared, 'It is a colossal military disaster ... wars are not won by evacuations.' But there can never have been a time like that of the mid-nineteenth century, not in Britain anyway, when the romantic legend of our brave chaps out there was so deliberately separated from the reality. The dreadful idiocy of the Battle of Balaclava was celebrated—by the Poet Laureate no less—as an act of epic valour: 'Theirs not to reason why, theirs but to do and die.'

Well, the United States has just suffered the most unmitigated defeat in its history, and we know it. The cost, in casualties, and money, and pride is being counted *now*. And everybody is arguing 'the reason why'. What Kennedy started with the quiet infiltration of 'military technicians' is about to end, fourteen years later. It would no doubt have ended much sooner if the United States hadn't believed in the beginning that it had a duty to stem the advance of Communism in Asia and, what turned out to be more fateful, believed it had the capacity to do it. The most unrepentant hawks will maintain on their deathbeds that the United States did have the capacity, by a general invasion of North Vietnam or by the use of tactical atomic weapons. But none of the four Presidents who bore the burden, and the curse, of the Vietnamese war was ready to do that. All of them knew that if America could keep its treaty commitments only by means of even a limited nuclear bombardment, America would be a monster's name everywhere on earth.

So the country is just now in a stew of recrimination. No doubt in time the arguments will straighten themselves out and people will come to take up one of two positions, which won't necessarily be closer to the truth because they've been over-simplified.

The most striking thing to me about this turmoil of public opinion is the way, while the Right is holding its ground, the Left is shifting its ground. The leftist and liberal commentators who have been against the American presence in Indochina more or less since the beginning have always tended to stress the corruption of the South Vietnamese government and the brutality of its treatment of prisoners and political dissidents, but has always turned a blind eye towards—or refused to credit—the Hanoi government's brutal treatment of prisoners and political dissidents (if any were ever known to speak up). The Left has always said that if the United States got out, and if South Vietnam capitulated, then the people of South Vietnam would receive their conquerors with relief and, after thirty years of nothing but war, would settle down peaceably to be ruled by them.

But now that we've seen thousands of bedraggled and wounded civilians fleeing from their homes and jamming every escape route to the south, the Left is saying how shocking that we didn't evacuate these people sooner instead of leaving them to the mercies of the oncoming armies. This shock implies a belief in something that the leftists and the liberals have never been willing to concede: that vast numbers of the population of South Vietnam have been and still are terrified of the Communists and want to get out.

In other words, since the United States is no longer there as a military force, it has got to be blamed for something. And it is now being blamed for deserting the South Vietnamese in their hour of need. Some reporters, especially foreign correspondents who throughout the war have been privileged to enjoy the luxury of neutral high-mindedness, have written dispatches burning with indignation at the thought of President Ford playing golf while babies were being bundled into planes and flown to camps in the United States (and—something I've not seen in an American paper—to homes in Britain and Australia).

Well, it was maybe a tactless time for the President to be

practising his backswing, but the inference of these angry men is that President Ford and his advisers callously refused to send in planes, and the old Marines, to arrange a mass evacuation when the Central Highlands were about to be overrun. But neither the President nor the Pentagon, nor an American military mission on the spot, seems to have been given much notice of President Thieu's independent decision to abandon the Central Highlands. The White House and the Pentagon seethed with their own sort of indignation when it happened, and had to improvise a makeshift Dunkirk operation. Naturally, they said hard words about President Thieu. And their anger gave him a godsent excuse to declare that the United States had betrayed its ally.

In turn, the conservatives here who have gone on thinking of President Thieu as the poor man's Chiang Kai-shek were only too eager to pick up his accusation and turn it, not so much against President Ford, whom they've come to consider a well-meaning drifter, as against the Democrats' majority in Congress. Certainly, if the retreat of the South Vietnamese could have been held up by more millions of dollars from Congress, then those Democrats in power are to blame. At this point, the country is heard from. Over seventy per cent of the American people are convinced that South Vietnam and Cambodia would be lost, sooner than later, no matter how much money the Congress voted.

Meanwhile, less positive people—middle of the roaders, weary newspaper students of the long war—are going back to see where the rot set in. Who was to blame? President Johnson blamed the doubters for having little faith. President Nixon called his opponents traitors. President Ford is going back to Kennedy's line—a rather forlorn battle-cry so late in the day: that the United States has 'solemn commitments' and must honour them. He blames Congress. And he's helped by Henry Kissinger who sees, in the Congressional echo of public sentiment, a dreadful determination 'to destroy our allies'. Others again, looking pluckily on the bright side, say that the

Administration is making a fundamental error in confusing the collapse of Indochina with America's real interests. They say that to let Vietnam go is no proof that the United States would let Japan go, or Israel, or Europe.

However, it is possible to recognise a pall forming over all this dissension in the reports that are coming in from Thailand, and Malaysia and Israel and other places whose governments—rightly or wrongly—are beginning to wonder whether the United States is an ally you can depend on. Hardly reported at all are the fears of the Australians, to whom what we call the Far East is the Near North, against which they had better prepare their own defences.

And through this bedlam of charge and counter-charge, a still small voice rises, from people who were once dogmatic, and from people who are merely puzzled: what if, after all, the domino theory is correct?

# The President
# Goes Up to the Mountain

## *13 August 1975*

One of my favourite journalists calls August 'the moronic month', a time when it's all right to put our intelligence back on the bookshelf as if it were an encyclopedia we had just consulted. Certainly August is about the only month in which this happy prejudice is extended to Presidents. And President Ford has gone up into the Rockies, there to take deep breaths and think deep thoughts and maybe get in a little mountain golf, with no complaining mutters from the citizens wrenching away at the crabgrass, or catching trout, or lying in hammocks with a beer or an unread tome.

Last August, I myself felt almost as drained as a White House aide by the intolerable tensions of the coming abdication. And on the pretence of looking into the work of the government's atomic energy research centre, I took off for Los Alamos, New Mexico, the once very secret place where the first atom bomb was manufactured by famous men with bogus names. The idea was to get in a little mountain golf myself, after a morning of polite attention to people who spend their lives feeding a two–hundred-yard beam through invisible targets and measuring which protons deflect and which are absorbed.

The first evening, there was a cocktail party with the Los Alamos staff. I felt at home at once, as I sidled up to a large, rangy man with a roguish expression, a Western accent, and the hands of a blacksmith. I put him down as a five handicap and attended promptly to a conversation he was about to initiate with a very pretty dark girl. 'Excuse me, Miss

Hayward,' he said, 'what are you in?' With absolutely off-hand aplomb, she said, 'Well, it used to be shattering protons but now, I guess, I'm into pion bombardment.' Is that so, asked the rangy stranger, also not put off. 'Well,' he said, after a swig of martini, 'it's like a two dollar bet on a hundred-to-one shot, but *if* the horse comes in, just think!' 'That's right,' she said, 'you'd leave the healthy tissue untouched.' 'My, my,' said the stranger, 'not exactly the end of the X-ray but what a mighty jump forward.' 'That's right,' she said.

I drifted off in search of some other pretty woman who was 'into' something more my style: organic vegetables, say, or bathing suit design. I just nodded and said sure, when practically everybody who came up to me said something like, 'How d'you feel about the interlinear scanning with the portis friggis?' In the end, just before dinner, I snuck off to the library to look up 'pion'. It is a word you won't find in the *Oxford Dictionary*. But, as usual with anything having a scientific connotation, it was in the *New Webster*. A pion, then, is 'Any of three mesons that are positive, negative or neutral, have a mass approximately 270 times that of an electron, and play an important role in the binding forces within the nucleus of an atom.' Right?

Next day, I left them to it and took a camera and photographed some of the flora—and flashes of fauna—of six life zones. There are not many places where you can start in pretty nearly true desert, at a hundred degrees, with mesquite and cactus around, and half an hour later be up in grazing lands with deer watching you go by. And fifteen minutes after that be in timber country, where bobcats hop out for the view. And then wind on and up cold slopes at 8,000 feet stiff with Douglas fir and spruce; and up again, above the timber line, where only sheep and the Siberian juniper flourish; and at last to the so-called Arctic-Alpine zone, where—at 12,000 feet—there are no discoverable mammals and only rushes and a little larkspur, and the Colorado poppy fluttering in the wind.

President Ford didn't go quite that far up, in his section of the Rockies to the north. But he was a mile high and the papers reported that he had enjoyed the agreeable sensation, which has to be felt to be believed, of seeing his drives go twenty or thirty yards longer than usual. Whenever I'm on a vacation, I scan the papers for all Presidential news with guilty thoroughness. This may be due to the scar tissue left by the wound of a piercing cable I once had from my editor while I was roaming the Big Bend of Texas looking for white-tailed deer and learning to recognise the oddity of a weeping juniper. Our friendly forest ranger came down one morning from his shack on stilts and said, 'Ol' Harry done it! He fired MacArthur.' The man was a simple soul and plainly demented. We thought no more about it till we got back to Alpine, Texas, where the editorial cable from Manchester, England, was waiting for me. It said: 'WHERE ARE YOU STOP GET TO SAN FRANCISCO AT ONCE AND WATCH HIM WADE IN.'

I was suitably soothed to hear that President Ford was relaxed enough to be banging a ball, even though Portugal was in ferment, the biggest, or perhaps the most notorious, American labour leader had mysteriously disappeared, and much villainous stuff was coming out about the sneaky intervention of the CIA in various South American republics. President Ford was right. If there's one human species that ought to be put out to pasture at regular intervals and allowed to snooze or bang a ball, it's Presidents and Prime Ministers. Their working day, every day, goes through twenty-four hours most of the time. And they're expected to know everything and do something, and be clever or deep or concerned or compassionate every hour of the day.

President Ford, another little item revealed, gets up in his mountain retreat and cooks his own breakfast. After that, any similarity with your routine and mine is at an end. Dr Kissinger or some whiz-kid from the Treasury is along feeding him the terms that Cairo is feeding to Jerusalem. The Department of Commerce is on the phone telling him he's going to have to shell out another three hundred million dollars for public transportation for some cities whose railroad link has gone bust. A special switchboard is installed in his mountain cabin, with lines out to Washington and Europe, and the hot line is always there to Moscow. Closed circuit teleprinters chatter away, pouring out the contents of the diplomatic bag, with messages marked 'Urgent' or 'Top Secret' or 'For President Only' about a civil war in Angola, how Tokyo felt about Prime Minister Miki's visit to the White House, how serious are the recent clashes between the Afghans and the Pakistanis, and what the FBI is doing to track down Jimmy Hoffa and Patty Hearst. A delegation of local ladies has made the climb with a posy of columbines and an invitation to address the local Republican club. He has to send three cables to applaud the birthdays of a valued Senator, a Scandinavian prince, and a big Buddhist priest in exile. A secretary (he has a pack of travelling secretaries) tears in to announce that he'd forgotten to telegraph condolences to the widow of a famous football coach. He goes through a raft of mail inviting him to address the annual convention of the Plumbers of America, the annual dinner of the Camelia Society of Mobile, Alabama, and an impromptu dance got up in his honour by the girl guides of Sheridan, Wyoming.

And when, finally, he gets away to the golf course, just to play a round with the local pro, trailing behind his caddie is a motorcade of other golf carts carrying the Secret Service men. And close at hand, you may be sure, is that lonely, eerie and ever-present creature who stays never more than ten seconds from the President: the man who carries in his pocket the day's scrambler code that can flash the proper combination to the Red Box nuclear alert system of the Strategic Air Command in the bowels of the earth below Omaha, Nebraska.

At the end of the day, he is at last able to stretch out and take a drink and remark to a couple of old newspaper friends that he likes to fill his days and keep on the hop. 'Eating and drinking,' he said, 'are a waste of time.' Oops! The guileless sentence was no sooner in the papers next morning than the chefs and proprietors of a score of restaurants were on the phone to the White House (and the phones of whichever place the President is in are re-labelled 'White House'), and the presidents of the *Good Food Guide* and some *haute cuisine* society shot off interminable letters lamenting the wounding blow the President had just struck at the food 'industry' of the United States.

Mrs Ford, whose health had been worrisome for a time, was now feeling well enough to agree to have an informal interview on a national television network. So the interviewer said, 'How would you feel if your daughter Susan came to you and said, "Mother, I'm having an affair"?' 'Well,' said Mrs Ford, very easy and free-wheeling, 'I wouldn't be surprised. I think she's perfectly normal.' A thoughtful pause. 'Susan, after all, is eighteen, she's a human being, like all young girls . . . She's a big girl.'

The fat exploded in the campfire. Campaign managers for Mr Ford's next Presidential try moaned from coast to coast. A Catholic bishop was stunned. The President of a Protestant denomination cried, 'I was aghast, aghast, to imagine the First Lady sanctioning promiscuity for her daughter . . . the First Lady!' Of course, she hadn't sanctioned any such thing. She said she'd like to look the young man over, and hope he was good news. This provoked in yet another group of conscientious citizens the accusation that she is a busybody supervising her daughter's affections. An old politician in Boston, the heart and capital of the Irish Catholics, said, 'Bang goes the Massachusetts vote.'

One of the Elders of the Mormon Church called a news conference. 'We feel very strongly about this,' he said, 'we deplore the deterioration of morality around the world.' The unkindest cut came not from any public character but from Mrs Ford's own son, Michael, who is a theology student. He could not agree with his mother's views on pre-marital sex. 'I guess,' he said, 'I'm more old-fashioned.'

I see President Ford, finally alone with his wife at the end of that rocky day, and hear her saying, 'Never mind, dear, you can't win 'em all.' And he says, 'It's not true. You can't win any of 'em.'

# Pacific Overtures

*16 January 1976*

I saw something the other night that reminded me of the Spanish, nearly five hundred years ago, going into Central America and coming over the mountains and petrifying the natives with two horrors nobody in the New World had ever seen: a cannon, and a horse.

What we saw this week was a brilliant theatrical representation of a flock of similar horrors that terrified the Japanese on a famous—or infamous—day in July 1853. The people who were looking out across the bay of what we know as Tokyo saw on the horizon what they took to be enormous sea dragons snorting fire and smoke, precursors of the great Godzilla who, in the Japanese movies, rises sometimes from a lake, sometimes from the ocean, and gobbles up the condescending American scientists who have dared to titter at the local warnings of just such Loch Ness monsters. The monsters gliding toward Tokyo on that summer day of 1853 were an American armed squadron, including a new steam frigate. And it anchored in the bay.

This is the famous incident that is known in American school history books as the *opening* of Japan—to the Western world. But, as a celebrated Irish-American commented, 'We didn't go in, they kim out.' I could cut short the history lesson right there, for fear you are already reaching for the knob. I could say quite flatly that I am talking about, or am going to, American musical comedy. But what I have to say will make more sense later on if, for a minute or two, we go on with the story of the Americans crashing into Tokyo Bay.

The Americans were not by any means the first who had tried to coax the Japanese out of their obstinate isolation from the rest of the world. You have to go back to the early 1600s, when Europeans were busy exploring, exploiting or colonising old lands and new. The Japanese would have none of them. They knew what the Spaniards had done to the natives and the native cultures of America. They expelled the first Spanish and Portuguese intruders. They made the British give up their only trading post. They told their own shipbuilders not to construct anything big enough for overseas trade. And they locked themselves in their islands. When they made this decision, there were about a hundred thousand Christians, native and foreign, still left, and the Japanese rulers massacred more than half of them. Thirty-odd thousand escaped to a castle fortress and dug in for three months. When they could take no more of the siege they surrendered and were systematically slaughtered. After that, the ruling clan forbade all foreign travel and for two hundred years maintained the habit of executing foreigners who sailed in or had the ill-luck to drift in from a shipwreck. As a sustained, two-hundred-year effort at racial purity, it is a record that Hitler might have greatly envied.

But, by the middle of the last century, the British, the Russians and the Americans kept begging the clan to open up to foreign trade. They said no. It was the United States that decided to force the issue and steamed into Tokyo Bay with that frightening fleet. Plainly, it took remarkable courage or gall on the part of the American commander, one Commodore Matthew Perry. However, he was a tactful invader. He made it clear while he was off-shore that he had not come to stay. He left a series of trading proposals and then sailed away to China to give them time to think it over. He came back eight months later, by which time the Japanese had decided to say yes. There was an elaborate exchange of gifts: the Japanese offering brocade and rare lacquers, the Americans presenting such home-made marvels as telegraph instruments, farming gadgets, a miniature locomotive and several barrels of rye whisky. This was Japan's first taste of Western progress, or corruption, or whatever we now care to call it. It seems that even then the Japanese were developing their great gift for catching their breath with admiration for some ingenious foreign invention, and then in no time improving on it. Fifty years after they had been struck dumb by the terror of the American armed squadron, they had challenged and thrashed the Russian navy. Within a hundred years, they had surpassed the Germans in the manufacture of exquisite optical instruments. I won't make you wince any longer by listing all the technological wizardries in which today they equal or excel us.

What has all this to do with American musical comedy? My friends, you have just been privileged to hear the plot of a new American musical comedy that in a modest way is as startling a breakthrough in its own line as Commodore Perry's breakthrough in international trade.

The musical is called *Pacific Overtures*, and in many more things than its plot strikes me as a landmark in the history of American musical comedy. Landmark is a bold word. Show business is populated with people who live in a frenzy of tiny shocks and fashions. Half a dozen times a year they make discoveries—of a new actress, a new restaurant—that are immediately described as 'fabulous' or 'fantastic'. The question always is, yes, but are they good? A 'landmark' is so much part of the working vocabulary of the theatre that I once heard a director so describe the day they took the floppy bows off the shoes of the little girls who danced in the chorus. Another landmark was the replacement of these little dancing girls, who were known as 'ponies', with very tall, non-dancing girls who strutted with a kind of kangaroo hesitation step and were known alternatively as showgirls and 'long-stemmed American beauties'. So I am nervous in this context of using a formidable word that I would normally use to describe something like the arrival on the European scene of Adolf Hitler or the arrival on the moon of the first human being.

Well, it seems to me that *Pacific Overtures* is the most ambitious, the bravest and the most enchanting breakthrough in American musical comedy since *Oklahoma!* in the early 1940s. *Oklahoma!* banished once for all the floppy little ponies and the long-stemmed beauties and made the revolutionary demand on all subsequent chorus boys and girls that they should learn to dance, as stage dancing was defined and taught by Agnes de Mille, who—if anybody is—was the inventor of modern ballet. To see this done, not in a concert with pretentious programme notes but in an otherwise rollicking and professional musical comedy, was enough to send people out of the theatre saying, and knowing, that musical comedy would never be the same.

I don't quite know where to begin in enumerating the innovations in *Pacific Overtures*. To appreciate it you have to go back and recall a procession of other changes in American musical comedy over, let's say, the past sixty years. Let's briefly do that.

The first shocking novelty in *my* time—and what a blessing it was to a boy brought up on genuine romantic literature like Dumas and Scott—was the banishment of roistering musicals about Ruritania and big-bellied dukes of Burgundy in favour of musicals about young Americans of independent means who were pursued, from the Riviera to Atlantic City, by platoons of comely girls in one-piece white bathing suits. This sounds like trading one sort of silly plot for another. So it was. But Ruritania had to go because it couldn't cope with the new musical idiom that came dancing in after the First World War: with, that is, the fountain of racy and tender melody that sprayed us all in the 1920s: the music of Irving Berlin, and Jerome Kern, and Vincent Youmans, and Richard Rodgers, and the incomparable Schubert of the American musical—George Gershwin.

So, in the 1920s, the revolution was a musical one. Then

came *Oklahoma!* and the ballet chorus, and more sensible, at least more plausible plots. And a small but admirable breakthrough with Leonard Bernstein's *On The Town*. You could say that in the past ten years, musical comedy has enjoyed, or suffered, a crashing breakthrough with the raging rock musical. I am deeply prejudiced in this matter, and I'd better say that so far as I'm concerned—and not too long after *Kiss Me, Kate* and *South Pacific*—musical comedy either vamped till ready on well-worn themes or suffered, through the aforementioned rock orgy, not a breakthrough but a breakdown, of the sort that Gibbon chronicled in the Roman decadence as 'freakishness masquerading as originality . . . and enthusiasm as vitality'.

You will already have gathered that the plot of *Pacific Overtures* is refreshingly intelligent and original. When I went to it, I had no notion what sort of entertainment was in store. Somewhere at the back of my mind, I imagined a poor man's *South Pacific*. Imagine the shock of entering the theatre and hearing a plaintive flute, and seeing planted downstage left two Japanese men and a Japanese woman plucking or piping on Japanese instruments. To find that the whole play is performed in the formal style of *Kabuki*. To discover that all the cast is Japanese, including the jokers who represent the Americans, the British and the Russians. To watch them move in their grave and decorative way against a shifting dream-world of sliding screens and friezes that compose a ravishing stage picture. Then to sit back and listen to the music of the most gifted, the most artful and serious of all living composers for the American musical theatre: Stephen Sondheim.

Mr Sondheim, who wrote *Company* and *A Little Night Music*, will not stay put in a profitable commercial groove. And he is to be honoured for it. He has absorbed the moods of Japanese music and adapted them to his own wistful idiom. I'm afraid this is where he may have come a cropper, on the assumption (which is well grounded in the box-office receipts of many a Broadway winner) that a Broadway musical is written to invite and delight people, from New York and from Keokuk, Iowa, who are musical slobs. Mr Sondheim, on the contrary, dares to assume that you have taken in through your eardrums the harmonies of Ravel and Debussy and on to Stravinsky and maybe some Schönberg and then some.

This is asking a lot of high-paying customers. Mozart would not last a week at the box office. He runs for a night or two at the Metropolitan Opera on a subsidy granted in the first place by, so to speak, Mrs Astor: a subsidy never large enough to cushion the monstrous fact that every time the curtain goes up, the Met loses $48,000.

I hope I misjudge and belittle the chronic Broadway theatre-goer. The first night of *Pacific Overtures* was one of those very rare nights in the theatre when you feel that a whole generation of pleasant but clotted clichés has been shed like a skin, when—as Handel put it—the people that walked in darkness have seen a great light. I should like to think that it will shine for legions of foreign visitors to New York, and that they will have their faith renewed in the vitality of that remarkable twentieth-century invention: the American musical comedy.

# Haight-Ashbury
# Drying Out

## 16 April 1976

Even the guide books say that San Fancisco is a tolerant city.
Well, in the beginning it had to be. The gold stampede that
turned it from a shanty town on windblown sandhills into a
city was made up of every sort of adventurer and honest toiler
from Ireland, Germany, France, Italy, New England and
Cornwall—not to mention the labouring poor from China,
and the resident Mexicans who waited, not for long, for their
town and province to be taken over by the gringos.

Since then, in the hundred and thirty years of its
phenomenal growth, San Francisco has suffered from—I was
going to say enjoyed—a reputation as a haven for eccentrics,
since it has had to put up with nuts and layabouts and felons
and debtors and professional bohemians and chronic drunks
who have come toddling in on the assumption that their
particular frailty qualified them as welcome eccentrics. Today,
San Francisco has more drunks than any other American city,
a high suicide rate, and such a large population of declared
homosexuals that the city council practically has to have one
member who is there to look out for their civic needs.

It also has, or had, Haight-Ashbury. And only a year or two
ago, a stealthy evening trip to Haight-Ashbury was almost a
tourist compulsion. Indeed, it has pained me on recent visits
to London to discover that the picture of San Francisco in the
heads of Cockney taxi drivers is no longer that of an exotic,
toppling city on a beautiful bay but a seedy and violent
composite of the TV show, *The Streets of San Francisco*,

and the 'Wot d'ye call it where the 'ippies live: that there Eight Asperry.'

What gained the city this world-wide shabby reputation is a poor section of the city where young people, most of them from middle- and upper-middle-class families, achieved a squatters' exile from the society they despised and the families they mocked. They had not much in common with the earnest ones who pooled their allowances or their trust funds, bought a few acres in some empty landscape, grew organic crops and more or less followed the style of the nineteenth-century American communes. Some of them were admirable in their determination to renounce the materialism of the society they had been brought up in. Some of them merely sought a pretext for drifting into lassitude and calling it meditation. I suppose the nightmare caricature of the remote and self-ruling commune was the little company of half-demented youngsters, girls mostly, who lived with their king and idol, Charles Manson, and who still parade near his prison and stay loyal to the hideous gospel of his own apocalyptic version of Murder, Incorporated.

Haight-Ashbury was neither rural nor organic, nor dedicated to anything but a vagabond exile. It is bang in a dreary section of the city, and the new arrivals fell not into a religion but into a routine of squatting in some garret or basement, roaming their own night spots, getting high on speed or amphetamines or heroin, or all three, and sleeping it off by day. They bolstered their egos by spouting to each other a group jargon about the detestable life of the Establishment and sharing absurd reminiscences of Squaresville, the town in which they were raised. And through the big protest years of the late Sixties they could bolster their ideology by reading Eldridge Cleaver's *Soul on Ice*, pondering the social necessity of rape and recounting with enthusiasm what Jerry Rubin had said at the trial of the Chicago Seven.

Well, as Duke Ellington said, there've been some changes made. And the change was evidently so gradual that it escaped the tourists and, until just now, the watchdogs of the press. Haight-Ashbury is still there. It is still rundown. It still has its quota of the tired and listless, but by now the hippies and the flower people are outnumbered by the regulation San Francisco winos. There has been a slow but steady exodus of the original colony of the social dropouts, and at last one reporter has had the wit to follow up a general survey by tracking a lot of them down and finding out what happened to them.

Only one in ten of the residents, it appears, is a hippie or a yippie. After the innumerable explosions of hot air on the youthful Left, something was bound to give. The gurus themselves have gone through a drastic change of life. Eldridge Cleaver fled the country, lived in Paris and Africa, and now has come back of his own free will to stand trial on a murder charge. He says it took a couple of years or so of exile in other countries for him to feel a strange, and wholly unexpected, respect for his native land and, what is more, for its government! That must have been a wounding blow to his disciples who, as a point of honour, spelled America with a K. Worse followed. Jerry Rubin, the liveliest and most impenitent of the rebels, is rebelling no more. He has written his autobiography. He winces at the memory of his old self, and in his more recent reincarnations has tried everything from yoga to yogurt and psychoanalysis to Est. And now he has proclaimed, not simply said, that he and every one of the Chicago Seven were as guilty as could be.

These confessions and reformations have bruised the ideology of the Haight-Ashbury yippies by depriving them of the idealists who wrote it. But the spirit of penitence, or perhaps of boredom, was in the air. Also, the spirit of alarm. Professional dope pushers moved in and organised the trade, and roughed up the dreamy young junkies, including simple-minded flower people, till many of them realised they were now the victims of an underground Establishment a good deal less laughable than the Establishment of Mom and Dad.

Well, now, nine-tenths of them have gone. Some have vanished without trace. Some have seen the ecological light and gone into rural communes. Some have begged forgiveness and actually taken up college courses where they left off six or seven years ago. But, the survey discovered, more than half of them have gone back to their home towns and been reconciled with their families. That is a tremendous figure and one that the most cynical would not have guessed at as a wild possibility in the rampant days and nights of independence.

I don't know what the moral to draw from all this is. It must be a matter of joy, of relief at the very least, to thousands of parents who in the worst days dared to muse that their child might be better off dead than alive and numb in Haight-Ashbury. Sooner or later, we may hope, these sincere sheep will come out in some other uniform than torn jeans, jangling beads and leather windbreakers. Some of them, if they can yet assert any individuality after years of nonconformist conformity, may even put down the guitar and take up some other instrument of their very own choice. There is even revolutionary talk that the day of long hair is over. A group of younger liberationists on the campuses is trying to bring back the crew cut. Which is where the hippies came in.

All in all, it looks like the end of a—you know what. It was poetic, and fitting in a sad way, that San Francisco was where Patty Hearst finally holed up, and was caught, and was taken off to prison, after which she will no doubt revert to her original type. I say this in hope as well as in all seriousness. For I have had personal experience of the gruesome and unbelievable process of brain-washing: of seeing a healthy and humorous child re-cast in the mould of a morbid automaton. Once it is over, it is a time, believe me, for great rejoicing.

If you look in the San Francisco phone book today, you will finger down a list of unemotional addresses and numbers, which represent the emotional deposit of the Haight-Ashbury of the 1960s. The Haight-Ashbury Center for Alcohol Problems is the first. It is followed by the Haight-Ashbury

Community Radio, then by the Ecumenical Ministry, the Free Clinic, the Heroin Detoxification Section, and the Rock Medicine Section, the Physical Therapy Center, the Research Institute, the Senior Services, the Haight-Ashbury Training and Education Project. They are the price—the morning-after price—that always has to be paid for the long, lost weekend.

# I'm All Right, Jack

## 21 May 1976

Somewhere, in Shakespeare certainly, but maybe also in some simple nursery rhyme, there must be a wincing reminder that when a small painful thing happens to you and me, it blots out a catastrophe that staggers the headlines. Nobody has made a keener comment on it than James Agate in a passage of his 'Ego' diaries. He had been to watch a day in the trial of an architect's wife and her lover. She was thirty-eight. The chauffeur-lover was eighteen. Came the day when the husband was hit over the head with a mallet. The couple was on trial for his murder.

It sounds like a humdrum, squalid business—except, of course, for the accused couple. Anyway, Agate was in court when the woman was asked what was her first thought when her lover came to her and told her what he'd done. She replied, 'My first thought was to protect him.' It's the sort of surprising line that a dramatist would give his right arm—a dollop of his royalties, anyway—to have thought of. Agate remarked it was the kind of thing that Balzac would have called 'sublime'.

In the following days, Agate couldn't get the woman's reply out of his mind. And just then, there was an immense earthquake in Quetta, in India. Agate wrote in his diary: 'This trial has moved me immensely, probably because I saw part of it, while the dreadful affair at Quetta makes no impression. The 20,000 said to have perished might be flies. I see no remedy for this; one can't order one's feelings, and to pretend different is merely hypocrisy.'

I imagine that we all have secret ways of compensating for

this awkward truth. I make it up to myself by admiring immoderately those people—hospital volunteers, the Salvation Army, most of all people who work every day with the disabled: the people *who do something about it*, even though they obviously have lives and troubles of their own. I think I was saved from living the life of a secret slob by my father-in-law, an austere old New England puritan. When I came back to the United States for keeps, he explained to me—as you might to a child about to receive its first weekly allowance—how 'we Americans' divide the breadwinner's salary: 'You try to pay between a fifth and a quarter of your income for rent, never more than a quarter, and you set aside ten per cent of your income for charity. The rest goes for food and savings.' For a time, I followed this punctiliously, for I had applied for citizenship and took it to be a requirement of the Constitution. Later, I regret to say, rents went up, and so, but not for a long time, did the income.

Well, the past two weeks have reflected once again the embarrassing truth that the downfall of a dictator is significant, but a toothache is an emergency. I ought to be talking about Dr Kissinger's decision to resign as Secretary of State after the next election. I ought to go on about the recent earthquake in the Soviet Union, which had a force one-third as great again as the 1906 San Francisco earthquake. There is a lot of room for comment in the fact that the Russians have been very tight-lipped about it. But Dr Kissinger and the Russian earthquake fade away like ghosts at dawn before the sentence shouted at me during the past fortnight by my wife whenever I am on my way out. 'Don't go out,' she'd scream from some distant room, 'without taking down the garbage.'

What is this? Am I moonlighting as a spare-time dustman—or, as we slangily say in the United States—a sanitation department employee? Of course not, though there must be scholars and clerks and other members of the sedentary professions who are greatly tempted by the report from San

Francisco that the dustmen of that city successfully struck for a guaranteed high wage of $27,000 a year.

No, what has been happening here is a strike of handy men and the other 'maintenance personnel' of our apartment houses, or blocks of flats. (By the way, although I'm always maintaining, in the presence of Americans, that the British still hold to Anglo-Saxon English in contexts which Americans fog up with pompous Latinisms, I am bound to say that it is the British who have succumbed to the euphemism of 'industrial action'. In America, they still strike.)

Well, the men who keep things humming in the big apartment houses walked out two weeks ago. So it was left to the tenants to run the lifts, stoke the furnace, stack the garbage, sort the mail, guard the front door and work in shifts round the clock keeping tabs on all visitors and demanding to see their identity cards, if any. If not, the house phone rings and a voice—plainly not that of the regular doorman—says, 'There's a gentleman down here who claims to be Mr Tim Slessor and says he has a date with you.' And you answer, according to mood, 'Send him up,' or 'Throw the bum out.'

It was a trying time for us tenants. But we learned some useful things. A friend of mine phoned me one morning. He'd been running his elevator for four hours that day. He said, 'D'you know something? It's not true that being an elevator man is an unskilled job—you have to know all about the weather.'

Well, it's over now. The strike ended at four p.m. and at five the men were back in uniform helping old ladies out of cabs, carrying bags, handing out mail and recognising friends and tenants without peremptory challenge. They struck—as almost everybody does these days—for more pay and a shorter working week. They didn't get what they asked for, since it's well understood that the first increase they demand (it's always 'demand') is like the first price a Persian quotes to you when you admire a rug. You simply walk round the block, get a second price, go out to lunch, come back and settle for the third price.

In most strikes today, the non-striking people on the outside, commonly known as the public, make an assumption, I think, which a friend of mine in California tells me is very naive. I find it hard to label his profession, since it is a comparatively new one. Not quite a labour lawyer but a contract adviser or, as he puts it, a hassle soother. Sometimes he's hired by a company, sometimes by the union, either to draft the next contract or, if things are already out of hand, to help settle a strike. Most of his adult life has been spent in bargaining between the two contending parties about such things as time and a half, pension payments, re-defining overtime, pregnancy benefits, a new recreation ground, redundancies (another British euphemism, by the way, for men you no longer need).

According to this cunning negotiator, the naive assumption we all make is that in every strike the dispute is between the employer and the employee, a conflict which is dramatised in the newspapers either as a fight between the ruthless union and the company going broke, or between the ruthless boss and the ground-down faces of the workers. He says this is 'a bunch of—er—nineteenth-century ideology'. He says that almost invariably both sides *want* the strike. Generally, to prove their need of recompense—more wages or a fairer profit margin—to some third party: the government, the city council, or even the consumer himself. Well, it was strongly hinted in our apartment strike that both the union members and the landlords were eager to prove to the State government in Albany and the city fathers of New York City that rent control has to go.

I think I'm right in saying that no other city in America still retains the rent control laws that were imposed nationally during the Second World War. There are many thousands of apartment houses in this city—rundown buildings, modest blocks of flats, handsome big apartment buildings—which must conform to the rents set by a city control board. This board yields, about once a year, to the landlords' plea that their costs—of fuel, insurance, staff, maintenance in general—far outrun the biggest rents they are allowed to charge. The rent control board yields them an extra seven and a half per cent a year. And though I ought to keep my mouth shut, I must say I feel a little sheepish when I run into a young couple in an uncontrolled building who pay for two rooms what I pay for eight. When a baby comes, they do not tie pink ribbons, they wring their hands.

If they are in 'the professions', they go to their boss and say, in some dudgeon, 'An electrician earns more than I do.' They become—what miners become, and nurses, and truck drivers, and all of us when we feel the pinch—'a special case'. In fact, it sometimes seems to me that an ever-soaring inflation rate was guaranteed the day that the ordinary citizen, who is against both inflation and strikes on principle, started to say that his case was different.

Until ten or twenty years ago, I think it was as true in America as in less affluent countries, the socially sanctioned scale of wages has held since the nineteenth century. I say *scale*, not wage rates. It was an unwritten law that working people, so called, could earn only a certain maximum, which stopped short of the general level of wages paid to the professions. This is so obvious that it's either not worth saying or it's one of those simple discoveries that nobody thought of before Aristotle. It's so obvious, anyway, that nobody seems to have said it. We have gone on, down all the years during which labour–management relations have grown more complex and more acrid, talking about the labourer being worthy of his hire, while the industrial and craft unions have been developing a wholly new view of their monetary worth to society. While the professions—the learned professions especially—have gone on living on the old assumption that being upper- and not lower-middle class, they must be living better than the average skilled factory worker. They slowly and sadly learned that it is not so, that they—along with the old and the pensioned professionals—are the worst victims of inflation. It is odd that the more educated should have done nothing to define or justify their relative worth, while the less educated— with the help of such as my labour negotiator in this country, and the shrewd shop steward in other countries—have done everything.

# No Cabinet
# Officers Need Apply

*24 December 1976*

One of the most curious but absolutely dependable chores of political journalism in the United States is undertaken around Christmas time once every four years. Whenever we are only a month away from the inauguration of a new President, the papers are full of speculation about who is likely to be a Cabinet officer, and of profiles of people who've already been picked. I say it's a curious custom because the American Presidential system is not a Cabinet system. This is something that Cabinet officers usually discover, to their chagrin, rather late in the day. The system puts all the responsibility for a riot, say, not on the Secretary of the Interior (the British Home Secretary) but on the President. A cruel budget is not attributed to the Secretary of the Treasury but to the President. If there's a public outcry about selling wheat to Russia at bargain prices, the howls are piped into the White House, not into the Department of Agriculture. And so on.

But there is one Cabinet appointment just made that has set off a tremendous uproar, especially among the blacks. The concern is not particularly ideological, though while Mr Carter says that the new man has a 'superb' record on civil rights, the black leaders says he has a very dubious record indeed. What has aroused the blacks is a provocation which I don't think would come up in other white democracies. The appointee is Mr Griffin Bell to be Attorney General, who—as the head of the Department of Justice—is therefore the chief law enforcement officer of the United States. Mr Bell is an Atlanta lawyer and a close friend of Mr Carter. The sin with which he is charged stresses once again the vigilante role of the American press that makes the life—the private life and public life—of any man or woman an open book. To sharpen the contrast with Britain, say, let me put it this way. When you hear that John Wallaby has been made Foreign Secretary, or Richard Stretchford Chancellor of the Exchequer, do you instantly wonder how many companies he has shares in? Are you impatient for the newspapers to list the clubs he belongs to? Do you, every now and then, expect questions to be asked in the House, and have them followed by a regretful little speech from the Prime Minister withdrawing the appointment? I think not.

Well, Mr Bell had been Attorney General designate for no more than twenty-four hours when the diggers of the press dug up the hair-raising fact that he was a member of two private clubs in Atlanta that have no blacks or Jews as members. What amazes the politicians is that Mr Carter should not have routinely questioned his appointees about such affiliations. Because when it comes out, it always triggers a shock wave, which always subsides when the appointee regrets the insensitivity of his past life and resigns from the club or clubs. Which Mr Bell, after a little self-defensive hectoring, will undoubtedly do.

When Mr Carter heard about the sin of Mr Bell he said rather wanly that he 'hoped' all his Cabinet officers would give up their membership in any society that discriminated against minorities. (In California, it may soon become a scandal if you belong to a club that does not admit Chicanos, that is to say, Mexican-Americans, whose vote is large.)

This has brought up in the minds of many people the question of whether it is legal today to form a club with any sort of exclusive membership. Well, yes, it is, no question. You can form an Irish-American club, or a rifle club, or a tennis club, or a drinking club *provided* you don't meet in a building, or on land, or employ services, owned by your city, your state, or by the federal government. All the test cases that have come up before the Supreme Court since its integration decision of 1954 have challenged the right of exclusivity of any organisation that is supported in any way by public funds: schools, restaurants, buses, toilets, housing projects, recreation grounds, clubs and so on. The grounds here are always the same, and the Supreme Court has reiterated them again and again: that such discrimination violates the Fourteenth Amendment to the Constitution, which says, 'No state shall make or enforce any law which shall abridge the privileges or immunities of citizens of the United States . . . nor deny to any person within its jurisdiction the equal protection of the laws.'

No one, I think, has yet tested the right of private clubs to exclude people on the grounds of race, religion or whatever. And I doubt they're likely to. Mr Bell's clubs were privately owned. Like most such clubs everywhere, they were organisations of congenial people who shared a certain interest, people who are like-minded, like-coloured, alike in their enthusiasms or even their prejudices. Senator John F. Kennedy belonged for years to a private and very exclusive club in Washington which, in the most gentlemanly way in the world, quietly excluded Negroes. When he became President, he resigned at once. Similarly, Mr Bell is not up against the law. He's up against the strong public feeling that anyone who chooses to become a government official, dedicated to the service of the whole country, should not be associated with any group that bars any sort of American.

We had, a few years ago, a prime example of the power of the press to embarrass any public man with ambitions to govern into shedding a lifetime's fellowship with his own kind. When Mr Nelson Rockefeller came out for the Presidency, the press discovered overnight that he was a member of an exclusive New York City club that had never had a Jewish member and never seen a Negro, except one bearing a tray. 'What?' cried Mr Rockefeller, 'no Jews or Negroes?' He was shocked to his marrow and he got out at once. It then came out that one of his sons—I believe it was the littlest and the last, a toddler—had a sizable block of shares in the club. Well, I never—said Mr Rockefeller, and scrupulously and immediately sold it.

Within a matter of days, Mr Richard M. Nixon let it be known that he too was thinking of the Presidency. So the press obliged by discovering that he was a member of a famous golf club in New Jersey that might have heard of Jews or blacks but had never seen one out on the course or on the receiving end in the clubhouse. Mr Nixon's approach was, as you might expect, less hasty, more thoughtful, more humane. Mr Nixon said, 'Ah, yes,' he was well aware of the discrimination but he was 'working from within' to end it. This admirable crusade, which he had naturally not publicised, was brought to an abrupt end when—within a day or two at most—Mr Nixon resigned.

This, by the way, was the club that was chosen, in 1967, as the site of the US Open, the American national golf championship. I remember it well, because I was called on by my paper to cover the championship at the last minute. It seemed that our golf expert, the eminent Pat Ward-Thomas, was detained in Britain on other business. This put me in a bind. The Security Council of the United Nations had been meeting night and day over the Arab-Israeli war. Its last session finished considerably at three in the morning of the day the United States Open was to start. And I recall the puzzlement on the face of the most artful of American sports writers, a prose demon named Red Smith, when he saw me on that first morning, before the play had begun, bent over my typewriter in the press tent banging out a couple of thousand words. What could I possibly find to write? Then he looked over my shoulder, saw that the dateline was 'United Nations, NY' and he relaxed with an 'Oh, that. I thought you knew something the rest of us didn't.' This was my last dispatch on the Middle East.

The tournament was played in one of the most drenching heat waves even of an American summer on the infernal

Eastern seaboard. On the last, the fourth, morning of the championship, it was 112 degrees inside the press tent. At some sweating pause, in mid-morning, two or three of us were standing around looking up at the scoreboard that blanketed one wall of the tent. The scores are recorded cumulatively, so you can see at a glance who is leading. You look first for the players whose scores are up there in red: the ones who are playing the course under par. At the start of the last round, there was only one name in red. It was that of an unknown, a fellow named Marty Fleckman. As we were goggling over this, and hoping for some official to come through with a quick, potted biography of this redoubtable Fleckman, an old stockbroker who cuts a considerable figure in the administration of American golf, an old gaffer not famous for his tact, followed our gaze and barked out, 'Who is that Fleckman in the lead? Is that that Jewish boy from New Orleans?' 'The same,' somebody said. Somebody else said, 'Boy, wait till the Arabs hear about this!' Red Smith said wistfully, 'Forget the Arabs, wait till the club hears about it!' This funny remark is something which, in the United States today, you'd have to be careful to pick your audience for.

The ironical thing about discrimination, against Jews in particular, is that it is practised with the quietest tenacity by white professing Christians of the genteelest kind. It's a rueful thought, at this time of the year, that they would have been the first to black-ball the Founder of Christianity himself.

# Christmas in Vermont

*31 December 1976*

I spent a four-day Christmas with my daughter in northern Vermont after flying out of New York City on one of those brilliant blue winter days that ring like a bell. There was not a smidgeon of snow anywhere. But very soon after we flew over Long Island Sound and into Connecticut, the smears were lining the roads, and by the time we were over Boston every lake and pond was a white rectangle and the forests were as leafless as a storehouse of telegraph poles, the towns collections of little wooden boxes strewn around bare ground. Then the real snow came in, first fringing the mountains then blanketing them, and as we veered and banked over the white-peppered evergreens the only bare land you could see was the long curving ribbons of cement, of the federal highways snaking through a planet of snow.

When you're not used to it, it's always a shock to get out of a plane and feel that somebody's slapped you in the eyes with a towel. This is simply the first adjustment to the blinding northern light. I went padding towards the tiny airport taking deep breaths of oxygen as sharp as ammonia. I was met by my daughter and son-in-law and grandson, a grinning Brueghel trio if ever I saw one. It had been fourteen below zero when they woke up, and though it had gone up to a suffocating twenty above, their outlines were thickened by the snow boots and the billowing pants and those parkas that look like balloons but weigh about an ounce and are warmer than all the wool and sweaters in the world. My family, in short, looked like the first family of spacemen out there to greet a wan man-creature from remote New York.

With suspicious casualness, my daughter told me to put my bag in the back of the station wagon. I found it was impossible, because rearing up there and making a frightful honking sound were two of the fattest geese outside the *Christmas Carol*. About twenty minutes later, when we'd arrived at the graceful little white wooden eighteenth-century box they call home, I should say not more than ten minutes after we'd arrived, the two fat geese honked no more. They had departed this life, having had their necks wrung by my son-in-law and my son—a flown-in refugee from another distant planet, California. I didn't see these two for the next hour or two, which is just as well for a squeamish city type, since they'd been busy cleaning and plucking the birds against the Christmas feast.

The kitchen, which on any working farm is the centre of things, was dense with odours and tottering with platters and bowls, and my wife and daughter up to their elbows in parsley and onions and forcemeat and chanterelles, and pans bubbling with morelles (plucked, according to a sacred tradition of my children, from dark corners in the woods by the light of a waning moon). The only time I ever saw anything like it was in rural France when I was invited to see what was brewing in the recesses of one of those country restaurants that manage to snag three stars from the Parisian dictators of such things.

My daughter and son-in-law lead a hard—but on these occasions and strictly to an outsider what looks like an idyllic—life. The food is not everything in some families but it happens to be my daughter's passion. And why not? After all, she has a lot of time hanging on her hands. She gets up before six, feeds, dresses and civilises two small children, then goes out to see to the chickens and—in summer and fall—the raising of the fruits and vegetables. All that's left is to clean the house, stack the wood for the stoves, clean the barns, shovel the knee-high, fresh snow into parapets so as to be able to get to the big sleeping polar bear which tomorrow, the next day maybe, will turn into an automobile. Ferry the four-year-old over the ice and snow to school, and put in an hour or so campaigning for the public (non-commercial) television station. So this leaves her ample time to prepare three meals a day, which are never snacks, at any time of the year. The first night, we started—started, mind—with a platter of smoked bluefish, one of a dozen thirteen-pounders her husband had caught in the summer off the end of Long Island. We smoked them within hours of the catch and they froze beautifully. After that came the irresistible piece of resistance: venison. Ten days before, my son-in-law had shot a doe and I'm happy to say I was not on hand to watch him and my daughter spend the next six hours skinning, de-gutting and butchering it before leaving it for the statutory week or so to hang.

I ought to say that I've had venison in farmhouses in Scotland and in lush restaurants in London and Paris. And, with an immense to-do and gaudy promises of food for the gods, in Texas. Texas does not, like any other region, simply have indigenous dishes. It proclaims them. It congratulates you, on your arrival, at having escaped from the slop-pails of the other forty-nine States. Welcome to Texas, and the incomparable three dishes of the Lone Star State: venison, *chili con carne*, and rattlesnake. (To the goggling unbeliever, they say—as people always say about their mangier dishes—'But it's just like chicken, only tenderer.' Rattlesnake is, in fact, just like chicken, only tougher.)

Well, about venison and its hunters and preparers, I can only say that they all wag their fingers against their noses and confide to you, as a privileged guest, their dark and secret recipes for hanging and cooking and having it 'come out just right'. And it's always smelly and gamey and a little tough. In a restaurant, you can let the whole thing go with a sickly nod at the waiter. But the Texans are nothing if not considerate and eager hosts. They always beg you to tell them truthfully if you've ever eaten venison like that. The true answer is yes, unfortunately, always. But they are kindly people and you have to think up some variation on old Sam Goldwyn's line when he was pressed for an opinion by a brother film producer who'd just shown him his latest masterpiece in a sneak preview. 'Louis,' Goldwyn used to say, looking the man square in the eye, 'only you could 'eff made a movie like thet.'

Well, I want to tell you that that first evening I had naturally assigned the venison to Christmas day and the big feast. I started to slice into a very fine tenderloin steak. It was so tender you could have eaten it with a spoon. But a round of uh-ums alerted me, rather late, to the fact that this was the venison. With delicate chanterelle sauce. A salad with raw mushrooms. Then Susie's fat and creamy cheesecake, with some of the fruit of the 270 strawberry plants I'd seen her putting in earlier in the year, up to her knees in mud on some idle day. Just to keep things in the family, the wine was a remarkable claret from the vineyard my stepson farms in the beautiful Alexander Valley eighty miles north of San Francisco.

Well, it went on like that. And on Christmas day, we had the geese, succulent and very serene in death. And a billowing cheese soufflé. And from time to time, there wafted in from the kitchen the scent of the four sorts of bread my daughter had baked. I once said to her, 'Any day now, Susie, you'll be making your own soap.' It was too late. She'd done it.

At the Christmas feast, with old Thomas Beecham whipping his orchestra and principals into proving once again that he is the Handel master of all time, I was asked to turn it down a shade while my son-in-law—a New England version of Gary Cooper—proposed a toast. He is not a gabby type, and this extraordinary initiative must have been inspired by the Alexander Valley grapes. Anyway, he said he didn't know what a proper toast should be but all he could think of with— 'well, pride I guess you can call it'—was the fact that everything we'd eaten in three days had lived or roamed or been grown right there, or in the woods that rise from the long meadow that goes up to the hills. Nothing, as they say in New

England, had been 'store boughten'. And, he ended, 'If it doesn't sound pretentious'—wriggling at the fear that it might be—'I think we should drink to the bounty of nature.' A very weird thing to toast in the last quarter of the twentieth century, when you can hardly buy a tomato that hasn't been squirted a chemical red, and chickens are raised in little gravel cages, and since they are immobile from birth and failing fast, must for our protection be injected with antibiotics and God knows what. (I know a very knowledgeable food writer in France who says he now recalls that the last time he tasted a chicken—a real free-range chicken—in a restaurant was in 1952.)

That evening we sang carols, in close if creaky harmony, with the four-year-old Adam piping *God Rest Ye Merry, Gentlemen* right on pitch. Next morning, I woke up and he was out on his skis. They are small skis and he got them a year ago. He was plumping up the hills and skimming down them with the poles helping him on the turns. And I thought, what an extraordinary childhood. He was born in twenty below zero (outside; of course he was born inside). Winter brings about 100–120 inches of snow. May is the squishy month, when the thaw sets in. Summer bangs in with ninety degrees. Fall is a fountain of scarlet and gold, and inky forests of evergreens on the mountains. And here, at four, he's skiing over the deep and crisp and even like a Disney doll. And this is all the life Adam knows.

One day he will grow up and, I'm afraid, taste of the forbidden fruit. One day, he will read the *New York Times*. And Adam will be out of the Garden of Eden, out of Vermont, for ever.

# The Obscenity Business

*18 February 1977*

The other evening we were talking—some grizzled veterans of the Depression—about New York in the early Thirties. I beg no youngster to groan and say—yes, we've heard it all before: the breadlines, how a four-course dinner cost seventy-five cents, how twenty-five dollars a week was a godsend, how the ambitious young, in or out of college, were content with a one-room pad where they could drink cheap wine, reform the world and toss bananas and cookies at each other.

That wasn't our theme. We were talking mainly about something that happens to the eyesight, as you get older, which the eye doctors may know about but never mention. How your visual view of age changes and never goes back. It came up because I mentioned how I am constantly surprised these days—mostly at airports—seeing girls of about twelve with a couple of children on their kaps. The age of consent in my day, I felt, was very much higher. This led on to a corollary: how one's view of old age lengthens into tolerance.

Some years ago, the novelist and playwright, Somerset Maugham, decided that the time had come to sum up his life. And he wrote a book with the title *The Summing Up*. Fair enough. He was, after all, sixty. And I remember at the time thinking that he'd made his decision none too soon. The fact that the old rogue lived for another thirty years could not be anticipated. Which reminds me how moved I was, as a young man, to read Walter Savage Landor's brief epitaph on himself as he tottered off into the grave: 'Nature I loved, and next to Nature art;/I warmed both hands before the fire of life,/It sinks and I am ready to depart.' Very touching, and nobly said. (It took many more years for me to discover that *this* rogue was only in his forties when he wrote that, and wasn't ready to depart for another forty years.)

One thing that Maugham wrote, in the preface to his memoir, was that he had got into the habit, as soon as he picked up his morning newspaper, of turning at once to the obituary page, to see who 'had had it'. This struck me as cruel and morbid, though I'm sorry to tell you that I now do the same thing myself and find it one of the irresistible amenities of breakfast time.

I did this yesterday, but the effect of what I saw was to make me feel older than Noah. It said: 'Joseph March Dies.' The headline alone made me know that the writer or typesetter or whoever was very, very young. The man was never known as Joseph March. He was always, and only, Joseph Moncure March. It was as if you'd seen a headline: 'George Shaw Dead'—and then discovered from the accompanying fine print that they were talking about George Bernard Shaw.

Well, it was that headline which threw our little group back on memories of the Thirties. We were not shocked that Joseph Moncure March was dead but that until yesterday he had been alive, at the age of—I should have guessed—120. He wasn't 120, he was only seventy-eight, and that's what slew me. I met him in my first winter in America, with a little fright on my part, because he was then considered the most daring of contemporary writers of fiction. He was, to be truthful, not a good writer. But he had written a book—in a florid, telegraphese sort of doggerel—called *The Wild Party*. It was certainly the most shocking book of its time. It fulfilled all the worst fears—or, perhaps, the secret hopes—of the suburbs and the bourgeoisie about the bohemian life of Greenwich Village and New York's chic East Side: of how writers, painters, their doxies and hangers-on disported themselves at the weekend in the Prohibition age. In this truly awful book (it was as if Robert W. Service was trying to describe the seventh circle of Hell) we were subjected to nothing but a welter of seductions, fights, music, booze, cocaine, among people periodically entwined irrespective of gender. It was thought at the time to be the most far-out poem about what was called Flaming Youth, and had better have been called sodden youth. I now appreciate that its author—whom I thought of when I met him as a grave, courteous man in late middle age—was then thirty-three.

Well, *The Wild Party* seems not decades but eons ago. Today, it would be taken for granted and illustrated in glossy porno magazines, and March would no doubt enjoy a national reputation as a champion of liberty and the First Amendment, and also of something you may have heard about called 'raised consciousness', in spite of the fact that all his characters were in a stupefied state of very low consciousness indeed. I don't think March had any trouble marketing his stuff. Somehow, he was artful enough in his language to convey an air of deploring the whole show, as Hearst newspaper editorials used to get very hot under the moral collar over some atrocity—a rape or a murder—which was plastered all over the front page.

In retrospect, though, I find it hard to believe that March should have been able to sell his work in the open market. Because there was a fierce and, as it turned out, historic case going on in the courts about a very much milder book that had been banned in the United States and could only be procured furtively in paperback in France and fetched into the United States between a shirt and a sweater in the incoming suitcase.

The book was James Joyce's *Ulysses*. It came up as a test case of obscenity. Until then, the American courts had closely followed the English law on obscenity, going back to a firm starting point in a British act of 1857, which authorised the seizure, on the premises or in the mails, of 'obscene matter, whether it be in writing or by pictures, effigy or otherwise'. Then, and more sharply later, the definition of obscenity was focused on the author's intention: 'the intention,' the law said, 'of corrupting morals'. Later still, both in Britain and the

United States, the courts refined the definition to mean 'anything tending to the corruption of minors'. And in time it came down to the definition which held before the *Ulysses* case, the criterion becoming 'anything that would offend or corrupt the average sensual man'. (Women, in the law, were, I imagine, not meant to be either sensual or corruptible.) The 'average sensual man' was the moral equivalent of 'the reasonable man' in the law of torts.

Then came the lightning flash of Joyce's *Ulysses*, which the most reverend critics said anyone would recognise as a masterpiece of literature, if you could get hold of it. Well, on the 6th of December, 1933, one Judge John M. Woolsey, in the famous Southern District Court of New York, delivered himself of a judgment lifting the ban on *Ulysses* and thereby opening up a new view of obscenity. The total effect of any work, he said, is what matters, and the total effect of *Ulysses* 'is somewhat emetic, nowhere does it tend to be aphrodisiac'. (In 1933, anything sexually stimulating—to men—would have been undoubtedly wicked, and therefore illegal.) Judge Woolsey added a waggish touch. 'Furthermore,' he said, 'it must always be remembered that Joyce's locale is Celtic and his season is spring.' Which does suggest that something written about a warm day in Dublin, even if it is meant to be emetic, might to some Irishmen be forgivably aphrodisiac.

So now, it was the literary quality of a work that was controlling. Judge Woolsey's ruling stood for a quarter of a century and permitted, on the same grounds, the publication— both in Britain and America—of D. H. Lawrence's *Lady Chatterley's Lover*. (I must digress for a moment to recall what to me was the finest moment in the controversy that swirled around Lawrence's book, about a gamekeeper and a lady, while the court case was being heard in London. There was a debate in the House of Lords, during which a Labour member grew indignant at the apparent off-handedness of an old Tory peer who had been baiting him. The Labour peer came in for the kill with the stinging remark: 'The noble lord may sound very casual about the effect on young people of this appalling book, but I'll wager that he wouldn't want it to fall into the hands of his daughter.' To which the unflappable landowner replied, 'My daughter, I am quite sure, would be unmoved by anything she'd find in this book, though I must say I should be disturbed if it fell into the hands of my gamekeeper.')

Well, once Lawrence—of all unlikely pornographers—had opened the floodgates, the flood came roaring through. Publishers grew bolder, both in print and in pictures. In the 1960s, the United States Supreme Court upheld the conviction of a man, not for printing an erotic magazine but for the 'prurient advertising' that promoted it.

We were descending into a twilight of reason and language. Once the Swedes erupted in a riot of frank photographic sex, and were emulated abroad, first timidly, then grossly, the definition of obscenity became so clouded, in the Western courts, that anything could gallivant freely under the cloud. Two years ago, the Supreme Court ruled that there was in effect no federal, no national, definition of obscenity. But under the First Amendment, the freedom of speech clause of the Constitution, the separate States could fairly ban what the community would consider obscene. And how do you find out what a whole community, or an overwhelming majority of it, will think obscene? By a Gallup poll? A referendum? It was to come down, inevitably, to what would be thought offensive by twelve good men and true. More commonly by nine good men and three good women.

That is where the law now stands. And a very rocky stance it is, and will remain so as long as the courts go on citing the First Amendment exclusively, and don't remind the jury that the First Amendment, like every other 'right' is not absolute; that it must, in fact, sometimes bow to the provisions of the never-mentioned Ninth Amendment, which says that 'the enumeration in the Constitution of certain rights shall not be construed to deny or disparage others retained by the people'. It would be a rousing thing, and it would clear the air of the moral fog that has settled on the courts, if the Supreme Court would one day attempt to reconcile the First and the Ninth Amendments.

In the meantime, a court in Cincinatti has banned a picture magazine, published both in Britain and the United States, that is frankly about as clinically sexual as you can get. Its publisher has been convicted, in this one city, and faces a stiff jail term.

Maybe after years of stumbling in the dark, through the writhing bodies and genitals of filmed and photographed orgies far wilder than any Joseph Moncure March ever conceived, we shall try again to make a fair and practical definition of freedom of speech that will manage to rid us of the clutter of filth that floats along with the First Amendment and is marketed for lucre in the name of liberty.

# The No-Food Plan
# for Longevity

## *20 May 1977*

I was watching the nightly television news and beginning to count up with a sagging feeling the foods that may be dangerous to eat, the medicines that may be dangerous to take, and now the materials it may be dangerous to wear. Mothers are now being warned off children's pyjamas that are treated for fire-proofing and may thereby—some people say—cause cancer of the kidney. In fact, in this case there's no need to put it gingerly ('some people say'). The United States Food and Drug Administration says the fire-proofing agent is called tris and has banned it outright.

This made me think of a long-forgotten friend, and made me think of him with a kind of wonder. Because he practically didn't eat. It wasn't a crusade on his part. Nor did he ever go about proclaiming the virtues of abstinence. He didn't eat by inclination. He simply wasn't interested.

He was at one time an important businessman. He went out every day to lunch, to give or to take. He had a calendar chockful of business meals. But whether at home or out on the town, he would say—whenever he was handed a menu—'Oh, anything, really, it doesn't matter much what.' For several years he had a girl who was comely and ripe, and her figure suggested that whatever else she was suffering from, malnutrition was not it. I think their strongest link, next strongest link at any rate, was that neither of them did anything but nibble. They didn't smoke either, not from virtue or self-restraint but from simple distaste. Same with drinking. They were always embarrassed when you said, 'What'll you have?'

You know the type: they want to be sociable, they've never really got used to the convention of having a drink in their hand. First they look embarrassed, then puzzled, then you suggest some ghastly aerated chemical confection called Scat or Fozz, and they leap on the suggestion with artificial enthusiasm. 'That would be just splendid,' they say, and sit there sipping the stuff like a patient sipping a carton of dye before submitting to a GI X-ray series.

This man is alive, and he is flourishing. I began to wish I were like him. By the way, he's also the type that says limply, 'I'm no good at pills.' So at a stroke he's freed from having to search through the pharmaceutical literature to find out what he ought not to take.

He makes me think that maybe we know very little about diet. And by 'we' I include the dieticians. I mentioned the other day to an otherwise mature and sensible woman that I was having trouble unscrewing the tops of fruit jars, jam jars and so on. She said it was arthritis. I said it was using too much right hand on my golf drives. My doctor agrees with her. Whatever it is, I'm prepared to put up with it for the time being. She said, with the passion of an evangelist, 'You must eat cherries.'

And then, there's the sugar–saccharine conflict. And— there is always with us the unsleeping fear of cholesterol. Nagging ladies of my acquaintance shudder at the sight of butter and milk and anything fried, and try to force soy sauce on us (I don't have to be forced, I like it) and go on about poly-unsaturated fats. Carbohydrates, we all know, are murder. So long ago as the mid-Thirties, the League of Nations put out a study that compared the diets of rich and poor in several nations. It came out that the more money you make in Italy, the more you tend to eat more fruits and vegetables. Whereas in Britain, the richer you get, the richer your diet gets in meat and cakes and cookies and candy, and from my observation, the orgy of carbohydrates goes on getting wilder and more intense as you go up the money scale. Yet, the latest figures of the United Nations don't suggest that the Italians, with their admirable eating habits, live any longer or suffer fewer of the usual afflictions (except decaying teeth) than Britons, with their love of meat and potatoes and bread and butter (and cakes) and cookies—and cakes.

My father, in old age, became an enthusiastic minor dietician. This was a way of making a religion of his dislikes, as a defensive move against my mother, a woman of iron character who in a quiet way had ruled the roost for ever, giving us what she thought we ought to have. I decided, looking back on it after both of them had gone, that my father—a sweet and exceedingly affable man, but not beyond a little private ingenuity to counter my mother's massive indifference to all dietary theories—was too timid to come right out and say he didn't like this or that and wouldn't eat it any more. He knew he was likely to get his block knocked off, in a manner of speaking. He would discover a new little book and come home full of scientific evidence to prove that rhubarb, or chocolate cake, or cheese, or cucumbers or whatever was the staff of life. He went about eating his latest favourites with gusto but also under the impression that he was doing it for his own good. My mother decided that in old age he was growing eccentric—his strategic deafness helped—and that he'd better be indulged before the end came.

As you know, I have spent a lifetime commuting between Britain and the United States, if not in the flesh, always and every day in the mind. Not the least of the pleasures of watching these two tribes practising their own habits and customs is to notice how horrified each of them is when contemplating the normal, bedrock diet of the other. Not diet in general but what every native of one country accepts as what you might call maintenance food: the stark simple national foods that are available when there is no choice. An Englishman attends his first baseball game and is appalled to see clerks, grocers, bankers, scholars, statesmen and truck-drivers all gobbling up hot dogs dripping with mustard or wolfing plastic hamburgers a quarter of an inch thick, on foam-rubber bread half an inch thick. An American attends an English golf tournament, or goes on a picnic, and is equally appalled at the notion that anyone can settle without nausea to such things as pork pies, sausage rolls, plum cake, chocolate 'biscuits', not to mention the wide but heavy range of suet puddings: what my wife offensively calls 'English glob'.

By the mid-1960s, we had all been so overwhelmed by medical sermons preaching the lethal qualities of fats that we were ready to cave in, and boil or poach everything, before adding soy sauce. But then, two eminent researchers—Yudkin and Roddy, if you're interested—came out with a paper that fell like a bomb on the medical profession. It bore the catchy title *Levels of Dietary Sucrose in Patients with Occlusive Arteriosclerotic Disease.* The paper said all the evidence showed that 'sugar rather than fat is responsible'. High sugar intake, in fact, was not only the prime villain in arterial and heart disease but it reflected pretty accurately the rise in cardio-vascular disease.

As I say, all this came to mind after a week of watching the telly during which I made a list of things not to eat, chemicals not to have about the house, drugs once thought to be a boon and a blessing that must now be put down the kitchen sink. And, watch out for the hair spray, the cockroach spray, the after-shave spray, the deodorant spray: aerosol is about to be banned completely from all sprays because of its effect, once it gets far enough up in the sky, of weakening our protection from the sun's rays.

By way of relief from the screaming meemies induced by this bout of muckraking on the part of the Food and Drug Administration—for which, I ought to say, I normally have a lively admiration—I went off to a movie. A desperate expedient in my case, because the only movies I see these days are these nights, on the late, late show. My daughter and I had no sooner settled in our seats than the hero—an Italian-American simpleton (I mean, a fine Italian-American but also a simpleton)—started what was evidently his daily routine in training for the heavyweight championship of the world. He staggered awake to his alarm clock, set for four a.m. He broke five eggs into a blender and swigged off the whole mess. My daughter—who is a one-woman Food and Drug Administration in herself—screamed aloud. 'My God,' she cried, 'that's worse than all the violence in all the movies.' (Like me, she speaks in nothing but precise scientific terms.) She reeled—sitting down—and gasped, 'All that raw egg white will kill him.' 'What's with egg whites?' I whispered. 'Well,' she hissed, 'raw white of egg combines avidin and biotin and prevents the biotin from reaching the blood.' 'Sounds serious,' I said, 'go on.' (Our hero was now jogging himself silly all over Philadelphia at dawn, apparently unaware that his biotin was not reaching his blood. He was panting like a bloodhound, a bloodless hound, I should say.) 'Well,' she went on, 'what it does is draw out all the vitamins from the body. White of egg also draws out impurities—it can be used on sores.'

We were shushed into silence by people carefree or callous enough to want to enjoy the movie. In a hoarser whisper, she asked, 'What's five times 260?' '1,300,' I said. 'My God,' she screamed again, '1,300 grams of cholesterol in one gulp!' 'If he'd added a tablespoon of sugar,' I said, 'he'd have dropped dead on the spot.' On the way out, she growled with some satisfaction. 'Anyway,' she said, 'he didn't win.' 'No wonder,' I said.

# The Money Game

'Half the world,' it says here, 'will have watched or listened to Wimbledon before the hundredth anniversary of tennis is over.' I fancy I hear the high protesting voice of Muhammad Ali crying: 'No way, brother. Not one tenth, not one thousandth, of the world is gonna watch that tennis, but the whole world watches me, because I am the best, the prettiest.'

Well, never mind the percentages. Let's hope that many more thousands saw Chris Evert correct the umpire's ruling in her favour than saw Connors snub the anniversary parade of champions and spend the time of the ceremony practising fifty yards away with his partner in boorishness, the inimitable if not unspeakable Nastase. Miss Evert reached to lob a return of Miss Wade's and was awarded the point. But she shook her head and pointed out that she had not reached the ball before its second bounce. It is a small thing and would have gone unremarked ten or twenty years ago. But today, in the money jungle of professional sports, it shone like a candle in a naughty world.

I remember the time when Bill Tilden, about fifty years ago, threw his racquet at Wimbledon. The game was stopped. He was warned at once that one more tantrum like that and he would be thrown out of the tournament. He didn't do it again. But no more than two years ago, I saw one of the most famous women tennis players reel with shock at a linesman's call. She was the one who stopped play. She walked over to her chair, gathered the five or six racquets that are now required to play one game of tennis, tucked them under her arm, and

234

as she walked off she poked her forefinger up at the umpire at what the spectators applauded as an obscene invitation. (If the Supreme Court came to divide on the question of its obscenity, it would only be because the dissenters had led a sheltered life.)

She hadn't quit. She was just biding her time, and temper, till the officials came running, or kneeling, begging her to return. Which, about three minutes later, she graciously consented to do, as thousands of spectators came to their feet to pay tribute to an act of bravery in giving the umpire his come-uppance. The umpire had not taken her out and paddy-whacked her. He didn't fume or shout. He blushed. He cowered. He knew he had behaved badly. He seemed truly sorry. And the crowd cheered their heroine again and forgave him. The terrifying touch here was not the sluttishness of the—er—lady but the attitude of the crowd.

I am told by Mr Herbert Warren Wind, one of the most distinguished of American sports writers, that a few years ago, when he was watching the Davis Cup matches being played in Romania, he got the ghoulish impression that this reversal of values—this upside-down courtesy which George Orwell might have anticipated—was not only common among tennis crowds in Romania but was organised by the state as a required exercise in patriotism. The crowd was expected to boo or hiss every point won by the Americans and to cheer every gesture—whether skilful or rude—of their idol Nastase. Mr Wind, who has been writing about tennis and golf for forty years or so, said the Romanian experience was the most frightening thing he had seen in his professional life. He came away with the uncomfortable feeling that he had been brainwashed, or morally washed, or whatever.

It is this sort of thing that led an American political columnist at the end of last year to offer some pointed advice to Mr Carter, who was then about to begin his term as President. The columnist laid down twenty numbered tips for the new President, most of them, of course, having to do with prudent political tactics. But the last three were about sports. Don't, he urged, use football lingo by way of encouraging your party. Don't talk about team play, or coming through in the last quarter, or giving it that old one, two. Don't invite athletes to the White House for dinner. Don't invite athletes ever. Have the courage to decide with Harry Truman that 'Sports is a lot of damn nonsense.'

This attack of bile, I don't doubt, must have been brought on by unpleasant memories of Mr Nixon's occupation of the White House, for nobody in American history, I dare say, has given the language of sport such a bad name by using it to recommend a strategy of deceit.

At the end of last year, too, Jim Murray, of the *Los Angeles Times*, the raciest, the most gifted of American sports writers, wrote a piece called, 'Whatever Happened to Frank Merriwell?' For the more tender members of the audience, may I say that a couple of generations ago Frank Merriwell was the fictional hero of all American small boys. Today, he would provoke salvoes of raucous laughter as a square and a sissy. Because—to use the quaint old phrases—he played fair, he gave his all and lost with a smile, he held to the naive delusion that sport is synonymous with what we used to call sportsmanship.

I was mentioning these odious comparisons to a sports official the other day. He was not greatly moved. He said, 'Well, sure. You're talking about the days before sports was a billion dollar industry. Today, we've got the Commies on our back. We teach the youngsters to develop competitive bite. We feed 'em money. The Russians draft 'em.' It is true. Most nations now train a picked quota of their young to devote their lives exclusively to excelling in some single sport. In the so-called Free World, we do this voluntarily or by the pressure of parents and the expectation of a million dollars. In the Communist world, they do it by compulsion, isolating promising babies, like so many blood strains, from their fellows. In all countries, the process intensifies, to the greater

236

glory of the Fatherland, and no doubt also to the development of a ragged nervous system and a blank ignorance of the variety and values of human society.

This is nothing new. It happened more than two thousand years ago. But it was not looked on, by the generations that came after, as the high point of their civilisation. The Greeks, when they developed competitive games, divided them into two categories. Neither offered money prizes. One, practised by inferior athletes, rewarded the winners with gifts of olive oil. Which would be, I imagine, the equivalent of presenting the local tennis champion with a gallon of one of those 'arthritic' rubs that don't cure anything but set up a secondary irritant to make you forget the first.

The great games, the spectator sports, were those competed for by the best, and to the victor went only a wreath. The Olympic Games, throughout their early history, were managed by officials whose title was a literal synonym for fairness. And the ground, the territory, on which the games were held was regarded as a holy place, so much so that it was held—even by the country's enemies—to be sacrosanct from invasion (Middle Eastern papers please copy). The great age of Greek sport was the fifth century BC. After that, the most learned of their historians says, all too cryptically: 'Later, athletics degenerated into professionalism, and experts in various sports spent their whole time going from one contest to another, sometimes winning at them all and styling themselves *periodonikai* or "leading money winners".'

In Rome, the decline from sport as an enjoyable end in itself to a spectacle designed to satisfy the blood lust of the spectators was very much more rapid. In the early days, Rome took over from her Etrurian invaders the practice of a gladiatorial combat as the last ceremony of a funeral. Pretty soon, they added contests with wild beasts, bred and fattened for the purpose. By the time of the emperors, the Romans were the supreme military power of the world, and though Augustus decided that enough foreign conquest was enough, the games were used as precautionary military exercises. To make the events at once more realistic and more satisfying to the mobs' love of cruelty, the losers now faced defeat in the form of death. In the beginning, even in contests to the death, the contestants were the sons of noble families. To lose a son in the games was as honourable as losing him on a foreign battlefield. But when you have a large army permanently on hand whose military and naval games are much like the real thing, there is bound to develop a corps of performers who are better than others. They too, ordinary legionnaires, prisoners of war, even slaves, became an elite corps of gladiators and were trained severely and lavishly paid.

There is a passage in Robert Graves's *I, Claudius* in which the gladiators are assembled in their underground locker room for a pep talk by Livia, the wife of Augustus and as wily an entrepreneur as the manager of any baseball club. She spent huge monies on the games, and at this point in the story she feels she is not getting her money's worth. At the end of her harangue, she says, 'These games are being degraded by more and more professional tricks to stay alive. I won't have it. So put on a good show, and there'll be plenty of money for the living, and a decent burial for the dead. If you let me down, I'll break this guild, and I'll send the lot of you to the mines in New Media. That's all I've got to say to you.'

Well, we've not quite come to that. But the true tone of sports in the 1970s is set by the elite corps, the best of the pros, that is to say by the richest gamesmen: the baseball, basketball, football and now tennis stars who have sweated their way up to prodigious salaries, are admiringly interviewed by cynical sycophants and receive the same adoring space as rock stars about their lavish pads, their king-size beds with sable quilts, their hand-made automobiles, their sleek girls in every port.

Money has got to be the reason, a primary reason anyway, why the insulted umpire sent his officials to beg the tennis star to return to the court and go on with the game. She earns a fortune. The fans pay to subsidise that fortune. The fans come not merely to see a game superlatively played. They have learned to expect high jinks and low jinks as part of the show. Any sports promoter will tell you that a sports crowd spurned is a dangerous social animal. In other words, the officials, who sometimes seem so cowed, must have in mind the maintenance of public order, which has come to have little to do with public courtesy. In America, we have much rough play, and some furious spectators, but—for no good reason I can see—we do not yet have basketball and baseball crowds tearing up the grounds or breaking up trains and ripping underground stations apart. I don't know why this hasn't happened—it no doubt will—since those of us brought up on the legend of British courtesy read with dismay of the hooliganism, bordering on criminal assault, of British football crowds, and of such desperate proposals to meet it as building ten-foot concrete walls around the inner ring of the stadiums and surrounding each playing field with a hundred cops.

I may have seemed to be reacting so far in the old man's standard fashion to the disappearance of amateurism in first-class sport. And, of course, it is true that—in tennis, particularly—much of the genteel air of the sport in the old days has been drowned out by the roar of the cash register. But I must say that genteelism, with its pleasant manners, was due to the comfortable fact that most players at Wimbledon and Forest Hills were upper-middle-class offspring who didn't have to work for a living. The same, at one time, was true of international golf. But plainly—it ought to be plain today—it is not only absurd, it is unjust, to expect people who earn a living at a game to have the same nonchalant code of behaviour as the loitering heirs of company directors who could afford to travel to France or Britain or America to play a game, while professionals (footballers as a gross example) were being paid at the going rate of plumbers' assistants. I applaud the fact that games can now be a career, and a profitable one, and that the expert should be considered like any other star entertainer and be paid accordingly.

But there has to come a point where the impulse to take up a game is very often the impulse to earn a million dollars and, so far, in the rush of a whole generation to make the million, there has not yet evolved a decent ethic that can discipline the game for the audience that has its mind more on the game than the million.

Six figures, I suggest, is some sort of turning point in the career, and too often the character, of the very young. A twenty-year-old who earns a hundred thousand dollars, or pounds—and nowadays it's more likely to be half a million—is encouraged by the media to see himself (herself) as a movie star entitled to adoration, the pamperings of luxury, and no questions asked about behaviour on or off the course, the rink, the court, the field. I suppose the television satellite has had a world to do with it. The best boxers know that—by virtue of world-wide exposure—the organisers will take in twenty millions or more, so the boxer doesn't pause for long before saying, 'Some of those millions should be mine.' And if the difference between winning forty thousand and twenty thousand turns on a linesman's call, it takes considerable character not to blow up. I heard a young fan say it would take a superman.

Well, it doesn't take a superman. It takes simply a type of human being who was taught when young the definition of a brat. I like to think that in one sport, at least, the type is still extant. Golf remains an oasis in a desert of gold and scruffy manners. Maybe it's because it doesn't allow for team play in-fighting. It's you and the ball and the course. And the rules. Even so, a man missing a three-foot putt today can lose in the instant twenty thousand dollars. He looks wretched or very forlorn. He does not batter the marshals with his putter or refuse to play next week. A few years ago, a single act of cheating—of slightly moving the ball into a better lie—caused a well-known pro to be suspended from the tour for good. Three years ago, Jack Nicklaus, the reigning star of the game, and—it seemed then—his heir apparent, Johnny Miller, were offered one million dollars to the winner of a head-to-head eighteen-hole game. One million dollars in one afternoon. They promptly turned it down as being, in Nicklaus's words, 'not in the best interests of the game'. May their tribe increase.

# Mr Olmsted's Park

*8 July 1977*

My workplace is a study that has the great luck to be perched on the fifteenth storey of an apartment house that looks out over the reservoir and the enclosing trees and meadows of Mr Frederick Law Olmsted's Central Park.

Olmsted was a remarkable Connecticut Yankee who wrote the classic, and still the fairest, account—on the verge of the Civil War—of life in the slave states of the South: *The Cotton Kingdom*. During the war, he ran the Union's sanitary commission. But before that, after a lively knockabout career, he had settled down as a landscape architect. When the city fathers of New York were thinking, in the 1850s, of having a city park, and when—naturally—the real estate men and the cement contractors and the politicians were trying to guess at the likely location and buy up every acre in sight, Olmsted's plan won out over the plans of thirty competitors. Maybe, I suspect, because Olmsted brought great relief to the realtors by placing his park on empty, bosky ground way out of town. In fact, Oliver Wendell Holmes, the father of the great Justice, wrote a satirical essay wondering why Olmsted should have christened the proposed park 'Central' Park, since it would be about two miles north of where everybody lived.

Olmsted had out-foxed them all. He privately, and correctly, figured that the next great lurch of residents would be north of the limit of populated Manhattan, which in the 1850s was the streets in the Forties. By the time the park commission had voted on the site and ordered the twenty-year job to begin, it was too late for the realtors to do more than buy up the surrounding fringes of what would become a precious breathing space in a jungle of cement and steel. Olmsted showed remarkable foresight in other ways. His original plan allowed for meadows and a lake for recreation, for a wriggle of footpaths, for carriage paths, and for so-called 'transverses' that would at three banked intervals allow the invisible passage of crosstown horse-buses. When the internal combustion engine arrived, nothing radical was required to adapt the original plan to the 1920s or the 1970s. The carriage paths and the transverses were paved over, and today the automobiles skim their winding way through the trees and meadows and the buses and trucks cut through and under the bridges without entering the park. Olmsted went on to lay out three more parks in New York, and the grounds around the Capitol in Washington, and those around Stanford University in California, and the now splendid lake front of Chicago. His masterpiece, to my mind, is the little-known but exquisite estate of trees, lakes, lawns, and rolling hills that now houses Emory University bang in the middle of Atlanta, Georgia.

Well, as I was saying, I have the luck to look out on Olmsted's first great work and, in moments of furious idleness, when I am trying to work up a little creative thought, I stare at the stark trees of the winter against the snowfields, or the heartening fuzz of the breaking spring, or the rioting forsythia and dogwood and cherry, and then the vast blobs of the summer's full foliage before the yellows and scarlets of the fall come on. I am just at the height of a plane coming in for a steady landing, but I am low enough to sit and envy the kids down there—in winter the little Brueghel dolls scudding downhill on their sledges, but now—in the steaming midsummer—tossing balls, lolling under trees with girls, gobbling ice-cream cones and, on the diamond off to the right, playing baseball.

Which gave me an idea. What has occurred to me, sitting here and weighing several leaden statements of the world's rulers—of Mr Brezhnev and Mr Carter and Mr Sadat—is that all the people I've ever known who are able to maintain an absorption with politics in the summertime don't play, or even watch, games. Of course, they can't stop governing through the summer—though in the blissful days before the United States became the Big Guy, the Congress of the United States managed it. But because great statesmen are almost wholly unfamiliar with games, they are unacquainted with such simple truths as that you win one, lose one, and begin again. This incapacity makes them fail to realise that politics—government, too—is a game.

I remember in the bitter Presidential campaign of 1932, in the pit of the Depression, when President Hoover was saying that prosperity was just around the corner, and Governor Roosevelt was saying that Hoover and his kidney had betrayed America, the rhetoric got so sharp and malicious that Will Rogers, the cowboy philosopher, wrote one of his three-sentence columns saying: 'Who do these fellas think they are, telling us who owns the Republic, and who is ruining the people? If we lost both of them, we'd get along. Why don't they shut their traps and go fishing?' Such was the popular prestige of Will Rogers that within days the news agencies received two photographs and printed them. One was of Roosevelt hauling a swordfish over the stern of a yacht. The other was of Hoover fly-fishing in a creek.

I hope it's not flippant to wish that Mr Sadat and General Dayan and Mr Carter could find some game they all played—cricket, say—and work up a healthy sweat and then sit down and talk about the future of the occupied territories, and the security of Israel, and the possibility of a Palestinian homeland. Instead of looking at the elements of the game, they all hammer away at a thesis. Which is to say, they are obsessed with their own ideologies. They are like a man who agrees to play a game but only on the understanding he shall win. Consequently, they have no disposition to begin by saying what and where are you prepared to lose? We've just had a particularly depressing example of what happens to idealists, ideologists, or—as we now say—ideologues when their ideology is reinforced by fear.

Let's admit that the problem of limiting the manufacture, and stock-piling, of nuclear arms is immense and maddeningly complex, and hard to simplify. You may remember that one powerful speech of Mr Carter—which had much to do with his election to the Presidency—insisted on beginning to limit nuclear arms and then working with the Russians to scrap them all. The Russians responded to this by saying that Mr Carter was saying just what they'd been saying all along. At the same time, to show the wickedness of Mr Carter's Republican opponents, who were always equated with 'the imperialist, war-mongering ruling classes', the Russians disclosed to their astonished people that thirty cents in every American tax dollar went for arms. What the Russians didn't tell their people was that: first, in Kennedy's day, it was closer to sixty cents in the dollar and, second, that they themselves accounted for rather more without any Russian being aware of it.

But the Americans, from the beginning of the SALT talks, have laboured under the hobbling difficulty of a democratic press, which lays out all the facts, supposed facts and rumours, and leaves them open to all sorts of benign and malign interpretations. During the Presidential campaign, the Democrats were quite willing to let the Russian characterisation of the Republicans stand. Then along comes Mr Carter, who—the Russians delightedly recalled—had promised during the campaign not to go ahead with the B-1 bomber, which is superior to anything the Russians have. However, a couple of weeks ago, the word got out that he would, after all, go ahead with the B-1. The Russians said they knew all the time it was a campaign promise. Then he *did* ban it. Now the Russians say this only shows how foxy he is, and probably he'll manufacture it in secret. But so he won't be thought to be a fall guy for Russian bullying, Mr Carter says that, by the way, he *is* going ahead with the air-launched cruise missile, which is years ahead of the Russian missile. This had been agreed upon, but now the Russians are howling that America has in the White House an even more warlike, imperialist leader than Nixon.

This is what in diplomacy is blandly called an impasse. Now the Administration announces that it has successfully tested a neutron bomb, and must therefore put up its umbrellas against a downpour of abuse not only from the Russians but from its liberal critics. Useless for Mr Carter to explain that the new bomb would greatly reduce the area of contamination in its job of killing off a military force inside a circumscribed place. What the Russians are going to say, and the liberals are saying already, is a phrase overwhelmingly attractive to ideologists, because it is so sharp and tangy. It is that at last we have a 'clean' bomb: one that protects the real estate but murders the inmates. As far as thought—and sarcasm—can reach, it's going to be a very tough ideological game to win.

In this 'impasse', I look out on Mr Olmsted's park again. And what do I see? Not people tossing balls, lolling under trees with girls, gobbling ice-cream cones, or playing baseball; all of which are honourable occupations. I see joggers. To be frank, I see them every morning, winter, summer, in sleet and Arctic cold, in the brisk fall and the furnace of the summer: these panting, slanting figures, in shorts and T-shirts, jogging, jogging, jogging around the long circumference of the reservoir. They are all very earnest, and so they are all ideologues. For earnestness is the only soil in which ideology can grow.

They used to make me feel guilty. But no more. Because I have to hand a copy, flown in here overnight, of the London *Times*. And in it is a short letter which, as far as I'm concerned, disposes once for all of the insanity of jogging. I don't know if there is a medical consensus about jogging, though in California—as you'd expect—there are psychiatrists, physiotherapists and other druids who, for a fat fee, promise to supervise your jogging by way of curing loneliness, depression, arteriosclerosis and hyper-tension, and restoring hair, fallen arches and failing marriages. I incline, myself, to the wisdom of three doctor friends of mine, one in San Francisco, one in Baltimore, the third in New York. The San Franciscan says that to jog over the age of fifty is madness, too much of a strain on the heart. The Baltimorean—who keeps his windows shut night and day, winter and summer—says more people have died of what they call 'fresh air' than any other noxious gas. The New Yorker, a man of great experience and some important original research, says that two martinis will cure anything.

Well, however that may be (and these are medical findings we should by no means dismiss without exhaustive testing), I can only say that the gentleman who wrote to *The Times* made a simple point worthy of Aristotle or Sir Isaac Newton: that is to say, he discovered an obvious thing which many people may have been dimly moving towards but which nobody ever said before. Let us not be coy about the identity of this great man. I have never heard of him, and it is possible that not many people have ever heard of him outside Blackheath— which is where he writes from. But I put his letter in a file of human wisdom that contains such gems as Aristotle's 'A play has a beginning, a middle and an end,' Dr Johnson's 'Much may be made of a Scotsman if he be caught young,' Mark Twain's 'The human being is the only animal that blushes, or needs to,' and H.L. Mencken's definition of self-respect: 'The secure feeling that no one, as yet, is suspicious.'

The great man's name is Mark Godding. And this is his admirable brief chronicle: 'Sir—Regarding the current enthusiasm for jogging to extend one's life, may I point out that if one jogged ten miles a day then, having lived to the ripe old age of eighty—one would have jogged for approximately nine years . . . Is it worth it?' Here in a nutshell is revealed the absurdity of seeking to prolong life by a process that shortens it, by nine years, during which you might better have been reading, playing games, flirting, shutting windows or drinking martinis.

A year or two ago, a doctor in California planned a book on How to Avoid a Heart Attack. Before he'd finished writing it, he had a heart attack. The main thesis of the book was that human beings fall into (yet another) two opposing types—A and B. A is highly strung and, therefore, subject to heart attacks. B is placid, less subject. Recently, this doc was approached about jogging. 'Well,' he said, 'I really hate to have a jogger for a patient. Because a jogger is, by definition, a type A.'

*P S About ten days after I broadcast this talk, I had a letter from London. It said: 'Dear Mr Cooke, I was very pleased that you mentioned me in your talk. Would you kindly send me your autograph? Sincerely, Mark Godding (aged 15).'*

# The Retiring Kind

### 9 September 1977

Americans, successful Americans most of all, are always talking about 'getting out of the rat race'. The rat race can mean any working routine that has started to bore you. I've heard this ambition voiced—bitterly, wearily, wistfully—by businessmen big and small, lawyers, big-time golfers, small-time grocers, university lecturers, burlesque strippers, journalists, ranchers, once, I remember, by a parson. He was a Southerner and he said, 'I've had ma fill of savin' souls, I'd just like to hole up in some dogpatch and nurse ma own.'

Englishmen, in my experience, go about it in a far less irascible way. They assume, or maybe they're taught from birth, that any job carries with it daily stretches of boredom. So they jog along for thirty, forty years and patter off sweetly or seedily into an inadequate pension, and then they are galvanised into doing what they've secretly wanted to do: to catch butterflies, collect stamps or book matches, read all of Trollope or grow turnips. An old lady wrote to me a year or so ago from Dorset, a lady plainly engrossed in her singular hobby. 'My retirement,' she wrote, 'which came in my sixty-fifth year, has made it possible for me to pursue my hobby: to catch *The Sound of Music* wherever it is being shown. Sometimes, I sit through all three performances. So far, I've seen it seventy-nine times, and I hope the end is not yet.'

The English live a life of boredom and then switch to mania. With Americans, it's the other way round. They are paranoid for years about the grind and horror of their jobs till they get to the pension, and then they mope and putter and mutter and confront their wives with a new ordeal—the daily nuisance of having to cook a lunch for a hanger-on.

These thoughts came to me when I recalled the pleasure this summer of visiting an old friend, an American news-paperman, who got out of the rat race with a bang one day, no notice given. He had never seemed to complain about the grind, even though he was the always-on-tap head of the Washington bureau of a distinguished Midwestern newspaper, even though he hated the fetid heat of Washington, which was odd in a boy born in the blistering heat of the prairie. It blisters in summer and petrifies in winter.

I imagine we all have a picture in our minds of how and where our friends will retire, the kind of set-up they've been used to and may now be expected to modify, or the kind of retreat they've always yearned for. If anybody had asked me, I could have improvised pretty quickly the ideal haven of my friend in retirement. I had known him best in the Kennedy days. It was a time when the White House press corps was more eager to be at the President's side than at any other time before or since. Not because Kennedy had loads of charm, which he had, but because he chose Palm Beach, Florida, as his winter White House. Let me explain.

Roosevelt's winter White House was the White House. His summer White House was the family home in Hyde Park, NY, up in the steaming Hudson Valley. After him, Truman slaved away in the White House winter and summer, but he did take quick winter safaris down in Key West, which is frowsier than the travel brochures indicate. Anyway, Truman lived with the Marines at their base, and the accommodation for the press was makeshift at best. Eisenhower simply didn't like the press around anywhere. But then came Kennedy. The moment it was known that he would be hopping off all the time to use his father's mansion in Palm Beach as the winter White House, the rush to become a White House correspond-ent was indecent. I myself remember writing a fast note to my editor, a cagey Scot with an unpleasant gift for distinguishing between a call to duty and a call to pleasure. I put it to him frankly: my conscience had been riven for some time. We never covered the President except when he was in Washington. Had not the time come for me to attach myself to the White House press corps, however much inconvenience it might entail? I would be the only foreign correspondent so accredited, and think of the opportunities for a scoop: ('President Kennedy today played sixteen holes of Seminole, the famous course named after the local Indian tribe which can be seen, on a clear day, watching things closely from its encampment—on stilts—in the swamp of the Everglades.') The time had come.

Kennedy, you remember, was elected on a promise to settle something called the New Frontier. Well, they had some pretty splendid shacks down there on the New Frontier, which, to all intents and purposes I've ever been able to figure, began and ended at Palm Beach. This was just one of the facts of life we had to face. For the news of the world outside we watched the Miami *Herald*. We were put up in a glittering, medium-size hotel overlooking a lagoon. The palm trees dozed in a blinding sun. The little boats skimmed along. There were some very lively fish, and there was the finest golf course in the South (Ben Hogan once said, 'Play Seminole and die'). The ambulating girls were tanned and nubile. There was nothing we wouldn't do to conquer the New Frontier.

Well, this is where I first met the man I've been talking about: later chief of the Washington bureau, then White House correspondent of the *Chicago Sun Times*. He was tall and languid-dapper, silver-haired, good looking in a wry way. If it hadn't been for his absolutely slack, unhurried manner (a deadline was a daily chore, like washing the dishes, never a seizure) you might have thought of him as a Navy man. I once noted his striking resemblance to a Riviera admiral in an old Jerome Kern musical.

If you'd asked me then what sort of place he'd retire to, I'd have said he'd get himself a very comfortable, split-level, ranch-style house overlooking a golf course, with easy access to a plush bar, and a snappy clothier's and a good book store down the road. One day, in about 1970, I think, years after the New Frontier had been abandoned, or absorbed, he went to his suburban home from his Washington office and announced to his wife that he was quitting. 'To where?' she asked. I see him now, slowly licking his thumb and turning at a turtle's pace the holiday ads in *The Saturday Review*. There was a tiny one, in two lines. It said baldly: 'Cottage for rent, three weeks, Glandore, Ireland.' That's it, he said. They thought they'd begin by using this unseen cottage as a tenting base for roving trips around Europe. They'd look around, in time they'd pick their Shangri-La and have their things shipped there. So they packed up everything—the furniture, clothes, books, records, kitchen ware, stereo deck, golf clubs, bird seed, the lot—and put them in a warehouse in Washington. They are still there.

They took the cottage for three weeks, and for the past seven years it has been their only home. It is what they'd call in Scotland a crofter's cottage: one door, one combination living-room, kitchen, dining-room, study, pantry, with three chairs, a bench, a stove, a lamp, a kettle, some pots and pans. Upstairs, two bedrooms, and a partitioned alleyway with a hole in the ceiling, through which drips a dribble of water known as a shower. From the downstairs room, they look out on a seven-foot high whitewashed wall. They sit and look at that, why I don't know, except it does shut out the thought that over the horizon is another assignment, another deadline. From their bedroom, they look out over dropping headlands and a bay and the sweeping Atlantic, which shores up again at the Antarctic.

At intervals, they read a paperback, bake the gritty, chewy Irish bread and take it—according to my Irish doctor's prescription—with refreshing swigs of the poteen. They breathe in and out. They have an old bone-shaker of an American car, not—so far as I could see—bearing Irish licence plates. If they occasionally infringe the law, like parking near a fire hydrant or picking up a pint ten minutes after closing, they are not apprehended. As my friend says, 'The great thing about this country is—there's always somebody who doesn't care.'

This should be an improving lesson to all of us who fret about retirement and the upkeep of the mortgage payment, and how to stretch the pound or dollar, how to maintain on half-pay our lifestyle, as we now preposterously call any way of life whether it has style or not. The moral is something an old schoolmaster told me. I thought it sententious at the time, as schoolboys think all general reflections on life are bound to be, since they seem meant to deny the particular schoolboy way of life. 'Never,' said this middle-aged Welshman, 'let your wants outstrip your needs.' This is no sort of advice to give to a sixteen-year-old, who's lusting after a new cricket bat, or the latest Venuti-Lang record, not to mention what's left over with which to finance the local bird at the cinema, the tea-dance or wherever.

But it's a good line to say to fretful oldsters on the verge of a pension. And I should have guessed that nobody was more in need of it than my dapper, high-living (on his paper) Jerome Kern admiral. So what happened? Well, with—I suspect—a firm push from his beguiling wife, he became one of the few people I ever knew who got out of the rat race and managed with obvious content to *reduce* his wants to his needs. It is all the more remarkable in that it happened to an American couple, for Americans, as all the world knows, are alternately harried and cushioned from the womb with every brand of material comfort. Not, I hasten to say, like the British who, as we all know, want only to sit by a broken teapot and meditate and grow a flower.

What was at the back of my mind when I began, what got me off on this high moral theme, was the fact that a couple of years after I first met the admiral, I was invited to dinner in Palm Beach by a new United States Senator who was down there to celebrate his victory at the polls with a holiday. He was an old friend of mine. He'd been Governor of his state twice. And because he'd jumped aboard the Kennedy bandwagon about four years before anybody else, he was rewarded by becoming the first man to be appointed to the Kennedy Cabinet.

This dinner was the first time I'd seen him since his translation from Cabinet officer into Senator. I asked him why he'd made the switch. Why quit the Kennedy Administration, in which he might have gone onwards and upwards (he'd actually had an offer of a seat on the Supreme Court)? He was very firm about it. 'You know why?' he said. 'You want to know why?' (He sounded for a moment like Jackie Gleason about to browbeat Alice.) 'Because now, goddamit, I'm my own man.' Go on, I said. 'Well,' he said, 'let me put it this way. When you get to be a Cabinet officer, you think you'll have the President's ear every day. I had great plans for a health and welfare bill, worked on it for months. I drafted it and sent it up to the President. I waited for the phone to ring. Hell, I didn't see him, except casually, in two months. Finally, I got a call from the *real* President of the United States.' Who dat? I drawled. With extraordinary venom for a normally benevolent man, he shouted, 'The Director of the Bureau of the Budget, that's who. He told me they'd looked over the bill. Fine, just fine. Great job. But they thought they'd have to whittle it down, the costs I mean, from—oh, I don't know— maybe twenty-five millions to two millions! End of bill. Never forget, my friend, the effective President of the United States, when you're in the Cabinet, is the Director of the Budget. What'll you drink?'

Well, it sometimes takes the wheel a long time to come full circle. In this case, fifteen years. The Director of the Budget has changed his title, but not his authority. He's now the Director of the Office of Management and Budget. But he's the same quietly dictatorial figure, unknown to the public, who decides what the President's budget is to be, how much will be spent on what. As I talk, the big man is one Bert Lance,

254

an old, dear friend of the President and, naturally, a Georgian. He is now accused, or suspected, of all sorts of shenanigans with his own bank, and with his securities and investments. Four government agencies and three Congressional committees are looking into these dark matters. The key committee—the one that can save him or break him—is the Senate's Governmental Affairs Committee. Its chairman thought he had enough evidence by mid-week to urge Mr Lance to resign. Either way, this chairman's judgment could be decisive. And his conduct of the Committee hearings was, for him, unusually severe. He is normally gentle, forbearing, wistfully inviting sinners to repentance. In these hearings, he was almost an inquisitor. Very odd. Perhaps it was due to an impulse to get in some final legislative licks before he retires, at the end of his present term.

So who *is* the chairman of that Senate Committee? He is that Senator who discovered to his chagrin, fifteen years ago, who was 'the real' President of the United States. He is the handsome, the able, senior Senator from Connecticut: Abraham Ribicoff.

# Two for the Road

*23 December 1977*

At the risk of seeming to take a short trot through a graveyard (something that only Dickens in one of his familiar morbid moods would do at Christmas time) I should like to say something about two tremendous figures who recently went off—along with Johnny Mercer—into immortality. Or upon what Mercer, the most poetic of jazz lyricists, called 'the long, long road'.

I hope there was no moaning at the bar over the death of Groucho Marx. He was very old, and for several years he had had only short lucid intervals in which he knew much about what was going on.

My first contact with him was about twenty-five years ago, when he wrote to me to say he would very much like to be on a television show that I was running. We were delighted to start negotiations, and at one point we thought everything was sewed up. Then, mysteriously, he backed out. In those days, television was done 'live' (no taping beforehand) and movie stars were petrified by it since they'd have to memorise a whole part instead of thirty-second bits. By the same token, stage actors were eager for exposure over a national network, and you could hire the best of them for a few hundred dollars. Groucho evidently didn't know this. And I soon heard from our business manager why Groucho wouldn't be with us: he had asked an enormous fee. We regretfully declined his services. There was an awkward interval of silence at both ends. Then he wrote to me: 'Like Sam Goldwyn, I believe in

256

art. But my agent, a coarse type, believes in money. And who am I to argue with such a baboon?'

Shortly after that, I was in Hollywood. He invited me to lunch, and ever afterwards, whenever my wife and I were out on the Coast, we saw him and enjoyed him as the slap-happy anarchist he was in life just as much as he was in the movies. The great pleasure in him came from his finicky, and funny, respect for the English language. That, at first hearing, may sound incomprehensible. But whatever his comic style was like when he started out in vaudeville, he had the luck in Hollywood to fall in with the supreme American humorist, S. J. Perelman, who wrote one or two of the early Marx Brothers movies. I dare say nobody alive has a quicker ear for the oddities and absurdities of the language that can spring from taking words—taking the tenses of English—literally. This gift passed over to Groucho and he made it his own. So much so that when I wrote a piece about Groucho's gift to the Library of Congress of his letters, I suggested in it that S. J. Perelman's scripts and letters should be sent along too. Groucho, whose laughable view of human pomp did not extend to his own vanity, kicked up a great fuss and swore our friendship was an unpleasantness from the past. A vow he forgot the next time he embraced me.

The most memorable example I can think of this language game happened when we were lunching with him at the most luxurious of Jewish country clubs in Los Angeles. When the menu was passed around, I raised an eyebrow at what even then were outrageous prices. 'Fear not, my friend,' said Groucho, 'it's only money. The initiation fee at this club is ten thousand dollars, and for that you don't even get a dill pickle.' When the main course was over and the waiter came to take the dessert order, he stumbled several times over who was having what. Finally, he said, 'Four éclairs and four—no, four éclairs and two coffees?' Groucho whipped in with, 'Four éclairs and two coffees ago, our forefathers brought forth on this continent a nation dedicated to the proposition—skip the dedication and bring the dessoit.'

On the way out, Groucho lined up to pay his bill behind a fat and fussy lady who was fiddling around in her bag for change. The young cashier gave a patient sigh, and Groucho—his cigar raking the air like an artillery barrage—said, 'Shoot her when you see the whites of her eyes!' The large lady turned around in a huff, which dissolved into a delighted goggle. 'Would you,' she gasped, 'be Groucho Marx?' In a flash, Groucho rasped out, 'Waddya mean, *would* I be Groucho Marx? I *am* Groucho Marx. Who would *you* be if you weren't yourself? Marilyn Monroe, no doubt. Well, pay your bill, lady, you'll never make it.'

The other great man was a world apart from Groucho—in geography, upbringing, temperament and talent. I'm talking about Harry Lillis Crosby who, for reasons as obscure and debatable as the origins of the word 'jazz', was known from boyhood on as Bing. Some years ago, a friend of mine, a publisher, thought of persuading Bing to sit down in several sessions with a tape recorder and put out a book of reminiscences. My friend was very steamed up about this project and came to me one day and said he'd got the main thing, he'd got the title. He narrowed his eyes and said very slowly, '*My Friends Call Me Bing*.' Four words too many, I said. And truly, I don't suppose there are more than half a dozen people in the world who would be instantly recognisable by a single word.

It's been just over fifty years since we were first exposed to the Rhythm Boys and their lead tenor, who provided the first happy breakaway from the ladylike sopranos and resonant baritones of the London and New York stages who were singing Youmans, Gershwin and Rodgers as if they were still commuting between Heidelberg and Ruritania. Then the Rhythm Boys' tenor, never identified on the record label, broke loose on his own, and the word ran through the English underground that a genuine jazz singer—and a white man!—

had appeared in the unlikeliest place: breezing along on the ocean of Paul Whiteman's lush 'symphonic' sound. For about six precious months, as I recall, from the fall of 1927 through the spring of 1928, Whiteman, of all people, permitted a small jazz group—Bix Beiderbecke, Frank Trumbauer, Eddie Lang and Crosby—to be given its head. And on the long spring nights, the punts drifting along the Cambridge Backs gave out the easy, vagabond phrases of Bing and the lovely codas of Bill Challis's orchestrations.

For several years after that, the underground went into mourning for the apostasy of Bing Crosby, who turned into a gargling crooner. We abandoned him as a traitor, until after the war years he relaxed again into the unbuttoned troubadour, the mellower jazz singer, known from El Paso to El Alamein as the Groaner, Der Bingle and always Bing. For thirty years or so, there appeared a parade of male singers, from Russ Columbo through Como and Sinatra and beyond, who could never have found their own style if Crosby had never existed.

By then, Bing had done everything he wanted to do in music and movies, and having wisely appreciated the approach of the gentleman with a scythe, he countered him by developing other talents and went off to fire 3-irons in Scotland and repeating rifles in Africa. Never a man to push himself, at twilight or any other time, he crooned only to himself. Then, fifty years after his first record, he cut a final album. Well into his seventies, he was the same Bing, because he had the great good sense to know the right keys, the navigable modulations, where to go and where not to go, unlike some other star-studded egos who like to fancy that the rules of mortality have been suspended for them alone.

I first ran into him on the set of one of the Hope-Crosby 'Road' movies, and I think I picked up a false impression of him right away. Because he was saucy, mischievous, almost gabby when he was working, especially with Hope. They ad-libbed so much and broke down in chuckles so often that at one point Bing turned to a writer who was sitting with the director and said, 'If you hear any of your own lines, shout Bingo!' Of course, Bing was witty, in a droll, tired way (nobody else would have described his face, with its flapping ears, as looking 'like a taxicab with both doors open'), but the movie image of Bing was a very high-pressure version of the man off the set. Once the lights dimmed and the director said, 'It's a take,' Bing visibly drooped into a character so shambling and low key that I got the impression he'd had a sleepless night and would soon be off for a nap. People used to ask me, 'What was Bing like playing golf, I'll bet he was uproarious, right?' In fact, he was relaxed to the point of boredom, good-natured boredom. It's true he always looked you in the eye, but he did it with the grey, tired eyes of a man who had seen everything—a lot of fun but also a lot of grief—and was never going to be surprised by anything said or done.

From his early success days with the Rhythm Boys and on into his movie career, there'd been all sorts of problems in and around his family: sickness, death, the bottle, truancy, spats and sulks with his sons. Until he came into port at last, after some stormy seas, with his second wife and his new family. It is possible that he talked about these things to very close friends, but even his butler couldn't recall any. To everyone, except some missing confidante, he put up the quiet defence of offhand, easy-going small talk.

I can't think of another man of anything like his fame who was so unrattled by it and so genuinely modest. The accursed foible of show business people is prima donnaism: the massive ego, the implication that the whole world is revolving around them and their new picture, their new plans—which they pretend to find delightful but embarrassing. Not Bing. He was in this more mature than any actor or actress, author or musician, statesman or politician I have known in coming to sensible terms with great fame. His mail must have been staggering, with its appeals for favours and money from every charity and every crackpot in the world. He never mentioned it. He was polite to every nice fan, and every child, and every moron who hailed him. All his later concerts, and pro-amateur golf tournaments, passed on the receipts to a raft of favourite charities.

When he died, there was a spate of film clips and replayed old interviews and the like. The most revealing of these was one done shortly before he died by the news interviewer, Barbara Walters, who does have a knack for asking the childlike questions we'd all like to ask but don't dare. She asked him to sum himself up, and he allowed that he had an easy temperament, a way with a song, a fair vocabulary, on the whole a contented life. And she said, 'Are you telling us that's all there is—a nice, agreeable shell of a man?' Bing appeared not to be floored. After the slightest pause for deep reflection, he said, 'Sure, that's about it. I have no deep thoughts, no profound philosophy. That's right. I guess that's what I am.'

It was so startling, so honest, and probably so true, that it explained why he'd been able, through hard times, to stay on an even keel. Perhaps he was one of those people who, though not at all selfish, are deeply self-centred: what they call 'a very private person'. Because he couldn't identify with other people's troubles, he was able to appear, and to be, everybody's easy-going buddy, and forget death and disaster in a recording date or a round of golf. He was the least exhibitionist celebrity I have ever known. And because death is so dramatic, so showy, some of us cannot believe he won't show up in the locker room tomorrow and say, 'Well, skipper, how's tricks?'

# A Picture on the Wall

*13 January 1978*

In a mad moment during the Presidential campaign of 1964, President Lyndon Johnson—his open car riding at the head of a long motorcade through some of the dingiest streets of Pittsburgh—stopped the car and, before the Secret Service men could grab him, bounded across the narrow street and into a grimy house and was up the stairs and suddenly his face was framed, like Mr Punch, in an upper window grinning alongside a half-dressed workman and his astonished wife.

We were in a Polish and Czech neighbourhood and it was one of those parcels of American slums of unpainted wooden houses slumping and crumbling into the sidewalk. Whereas English and Scottish slums, built for all time in brick and stone, look as if they'd be there long after the human race had been atomised, American slums look as if one high wind would dispose of them in a clatter of timber. As, indeed, happens—in the South mostly—to suburbs of quite pretentious houses once a tornado has whirled into town.

This scene in Pittsburgh, I ought to remind you, happened less than a year after the assassination of President Kennedy. And by then the Secret Service, while trying not to relax its anxious protection of the President in all public places, was in despair at the headlong gymnastics of Lyndon Johnson in crowds, in football stadiums, in streets and supermarkets, as he performed his favourite outdoor exercise of 'pressing the flesh'. This Pittsburgh incident had their hair on end. One minute, the President was standing high in his car. Then he caught a glimpse of the old couple in the upper window, and the next thing he was gone. What did he think he was doing?

He said later that when he spotted the couple peering out of their crummy bedroom, he thought of his own poor boyhood and his parents and he remembered—something. It was something none of us could have possibly guessed. He thought of a picture on the wall, the first picture his parents ever bought. Now, Lyndon Johnson was an expert at political second thoughts, and in any hot discussion he would separate the opponents and soothe them and massage them and take them off into another room—as he used to say—'to sit down and take counsel together' and come to some decent compromise. But when he saw poor people looking on from the outside, he never had a second thought. He plunged at them with some large, instinctive promise. He stayed long enough with the Pittsburgh couple to take a cup of coffee. When he came out, he said he'd told them, 'I want every family in America to have a carpet on the floor and a picture on the wall. After bread, you've got to have a picture on the wall.'

Some people will think this fatuous or sentimental or pathetic, but I'm pretty sure they will be people who have taken carpets and pictures for granted all their lives.

When we were riding along back to the airport for the next flight—off to South Carolina then on to Miami—I thought of my own boyhood and my father's obsession with one kind, or school, of painting. We certainly couldn't afford originals, though a Wesleyan parson friend who dabbled quite impressively in water-colours gave us, I recall, a small study of a cow contemplating the green but treeless landscape of the Fylde. Otherwise, we had prints, reproductions, everywhere. Of the Pre-Raphaelites, and of G. F. Watts in his Pre-Raphaelite mood. Under a mirror or over a sofa would hang these absurdly small reproductions of Millais and Holman Hunt and Burne-Jones. Mostly, it seemed to a boy approaching puberty, of languid ladies (with necks like giraffes) taking a bath. But even in a Methodist household, this was all right because they wore layers of enfolding draperies, and this was art, wasn't it? In the room where I did my homework, I must have looked up a thousand times from the algebra problem, or the Battle of Bannockburn, or the weird movement of the trade winds, and seen a melancholy lady, swathed in a blindfold at the top and towels down below, plucking at a lyre with only one string. She was slouching on a globe, a hopeless figure if ever I saw one. She was supposed to represent 'Hope'. There was also, facing me at every meal, the most Anglo-Saxon Jesus ever painted. He was carrying a lantern and knocking at the door of a cottage as run down as any in Pittsburgh. This was called 'The Light of the World', and my father pointed out the magical skill with which the lamplight traced the folds of his nightgown. (A critic of our own time said that Hunt's 'renderings of minutiae in "The Light of the World" are agonising'.)

Well, only a few years later—but seventy-odd years after this painting had been exhibited and marvelled at by huge crowds in America—I was at Cambridge, and there I learned to my shame that all these painters who my father thought were the high points of high art were, in fact, perfect examples of non-art. The Pre-Raphaelites went down and down on the auction blocks of the world. So that sometime in the 1930s, I think, you could have bought that long-necked lady on the globe for a few hundred pounds, if she'd been for sale. Thirty years later, she would have cost you—I believe a bid was made—something like £200,000. The Pre-Raphaelites came hurtling back into fashion. So much so that once, when I was visiting my old college, I found a pack of art lovers come up specially from London to gaze on a window in our chapel. And quite right, too. It was an incomparable medieval chapel, and one window fairly blazed, in the late afternoon light, with the scarlets and greens and bottomless blues done in dyes whose secret has been lost. However, that was not what this knowing art society had come to see. The college had had the misfortune to have Sir Edward Burne-Jones as an alumnus and he had offered to re-do one of the chapel windows. What's worse, he did it. What the young art critics were looking at, with their backs to the medieval window, was a droop of those lachrymose ladies peering out of the Gate of Heaven in colours as lifeless as their space-movie eyes. This window had been, in my time, an object of embarrassment to the college authorities, and if any painter or art critic looked at it he would stand and titter.

But one generation comes to titter, and the next to pray. We've just had an extraordinary example in New York of how the wheel of appreciation can come full circle from ribaldry to reverence. It was announced the other day that the Radio City Music Hall is going to close down right after Easter. It has been losing about three million dollars a year, and it has to go. After a stunned silence, the burghers of New York have risen and let out a howl of pain. It is as if St Paul's Cathedral were standing in the path of a projected motorway and would have to be pulled down. Somebody, in fact, has called Radio City Music Hall the 'secular cathedral' of New York City. More accurately, throughout the 1930s (it opened in 1933) and on into our time, it was called 'the nation's showplace'.

From the first, its size and grandeur caught the breath of the movie-goers, but also caught the scornful breath of most artists and architectural critics. One exhaustive guide to New York City put out in 1948 doesn't mention it. The government guide concedes that of all the super-theatres built around that time, Radio City Music Hall is 'recognisably modern (and) its aesthetic sins are easier to forgive than those of its predecessors'. Today it is an aesthetic wonder.

The educational fund that sponsored my first visit to America rightly ignored the aesthetes and took us to see it on our first evening, as you might take a first visitor to India to see the Taj Mahal. Six of us were piled off to see a new Harold Lloyd movie. But it wasn't the movie that mattered. The administrators of these fellowships were shrewd. They could certainly have afforded to put us in the best orchestra seats.

But they didn't. They booked us into the highest balcony, where we could peer into the enormous vault of the auditorium and look down on the other 6,175 people present. The movie screen looked like a postcard suspended in the nave of St Paul's.

During the interval, we were taken to wander into the immense grand foyer with its mammoth gold-backed mirrors and its twenty-nine-foot cylindrical chandeliers. A little later on, before we went out for supper, our hosts dropped a hint that we might like to spend a penny. A penny! A pound would not have been too much to see the towering ceiling, to stand at black-and-white marble stalls in a Roman urinal about ten times the Roman scale. As the man said, it made one's anatomy look awfully shabby.

Perhaps it was this grandeur—which in those days mocked the surrounding bleakness of the Depression—that made sensitive souls bemoan the very existence of this Babylonian extravaganza. But, as the Depression slackened off, and when prosperity was back again, even arty people began to look at it again and grant, first grudgingly and then openly, and today enthusiastically, that there is no more breathtaking example in the world of the style of decoration peculiar to the late 1920s and early 1930s. By now it has a name. It is a cult. It is called Art Deco. And a very heavy critic indeed has just joined his voice to all the civic-minded people who are begging the city, or the federal government, or somebody to arrest the wrecking ball and save it for the nation and posterity.

What is now admired as Art Deco was then scorned as vulgar and styleless extravagance. It has been the story of many styles. The most exquisite Colonial church in New England, in Litchfield, Connecticut—a white jewel of eighteenth-century grace in wood—was removed by the late Victorians as an eyesore. It was literally dug up and transported whole and re-planted out of town, dumped on the countryside. It became in turn a stable, a chapel, a movie theatre. Till along came my generation, or the one just before, abominating every product of the Victorians, and brought the church back again and planted it once more on the town green, where it glorifies the surrounding streets of other eighteenth-century gems. No doubt, twenty years from now they will tear it down.

But today, the art critics and the city fathers have spoken with one voice. Radio City Music Hall, they pronounce, is *the* masterpiece of Art Deco and, as one of them has just added, 'is along with the Chrysler Building, immortal'. Well, as I say, it isn't. Its mortality has a deadline. After the big Easter show, it will close its doors, unless all the missionaries for its salvation win the day. The Mayor is being urged to have the responsible commission declare it an historic landmark. This will probably happen. But after that, the question is what to do with it? The shell, with all its decorations, will be kept, they say. Then it might serve nicely as an exhibition hall, if the real estate giants don't win out, with their argument that, after all, it's forty-five years old, and progress would indicate that nothing could be finer than an eighty-storey hotel to clinch New York's claims to be *the* convention city. In the meantime, though, it is our picture on the wall, and most people want it to stay that way.

# The Spy that
# Came Down in the Cold

*10 February 1978*

We have just followed the first story of general interest to come out of the vast tundra of Canada's Northwest Territories since the Klondike gold rush.

It came at us first as a scare story, like something out of *Dr Strangelove* or *Star Wars*. Then it turned into a technological puzzle as remote from the interests, or competence, of ordinary people as the workings of a breeder reactor. So that, more or less out of boredom, we were ready to sink back into the soap opera or the insurance policy, when the *New York Times* published a long piece that suggested, for the first time in print, appalling possibilities for all of us. The White House promptly denied the gist of the story. And then the whole thing was surprisingly dropped.

What I'm talking about is the Soviet satellite that fell out of its orbit into the earth's atmosphere, burst into flames and disintegrated above North America. For a day or two, the main concern of Canadians and Americans was to know if the accident had happened over any well-populated part of this continent. But once it was run to ground in the empty pinelands surrounding Canada's Great Slave Lake, everybody breathed again, and we all chuckled and quoted the man who said, 'Chicken Little was right.'

Yet the Russian satellite was admittedly a spy, whose job was to orbit the earth 150 miles above it and keep track of the movements of all the ocean-going American warships—what we now call defence ships—including submarines deeply submerged. The satellite carried a load of radioactive materials, and that was what caused the fright. The debris from the disintegration rained across a 250-mile stretch. But once it was established that none of the sample fragments picked up was radioactive, the scare died down.

It shows how far we've come in eighteen years, how far in stoicism, or a sense of reality, maybe. In May 1960, when an American spy plane was shot down over the Soviet Union, President Eisenhower denied that American reconnaissance planes ever flew over Russia. Then he broke down and said, 'Well, you do it too.' This happened just when the Big Four leaders had assembled in Paris for a summit meeting. But in the uproar over the American U-2 plane, Mr Khrushchev, the Soviet Prime Minister, stomped off home. The other three looked foolish and packed their bags. And the summit never took place.

If we have acquired a new sense of reality, it is no less than a rather fearful admission that we are in a steady *warm* war with the Soviet Union—and at a time when we go on talking about the progress of détente. Whatever it is, it has nothing to do with a change of heart, or with policy, or, indeed, with Mr Carter or Mr Brezhnev. It is due to the inescapable fact that spy planes can now fly too high to be reached. The U-2 reconnaissance planes flew at 65,000 feet, which is roughly twelve and a half miles up. From that height the Americans at least had—so long ago as 1962—cameras that could define with astonishing accuracy objects as small as a woodshed. The Russians must not have known this. Because when they were shown, in the Security Council of the United Nations, the American reconnaissance blow-ups of the Russian missiles being installed in Cuba, they blustered and swore that the pictures were fakes. But the photographs plainly showed missiles mounted and unmounted, all the paraphernalia of bases and launch pads that could not possibly be mistaken for woodsheds. So it was not so much the initiative of President Kennedy that persuaded the Russians to abandon their bluff and dismantle their bases. It was the cameras of the U-2s with their nine- by eighteen-inch negatives and their incredible twenty-six-inch lenses.

Well, by now, photographs of landscape from 65,000 feet are so taken for granted that NASA, the National Aeronautics and Space Administration, puts out infra-red prints (you can buy them) of every section of the United States, in reaches of country thirty or forty miles across, on which you can see the sharp divisions of streets in cities of several million population. Obviously, these pictures would not be made public if they represented the known limit of the technical resources of reconnaissance, or spying. Clearly, since 1962, enormous advances have been made in the ways that one nation can scan the land and the industry and the defence establishment of another. We now spy, not from twelve miles up but from 150 miles up. Neither the Russians nor the Americans deny it. In fact, since this scanning through radar has passed over into space, we have a situation that could have been imagined a hundred years ago only by W. S. Gilbert and Jules Verne working in tandem. Through several accidents, the two superpowers have become so aware of the lethal consequences of mismanagement in space that they keep each other posted on the movement of their spy ships, the orbiting satellites that are monitoring each other's military movements.

The crash of the Soviet satellite, Cosmos 954, provided the ordinary citizen with, I believe, the first glimpse we've had into this involuntary partnership. I say involuntary, because whether or not the Pentagon or the Soviet Defence Department wants it, the possibilities of accidental devastation from satellites floating *untracked* through space are too awful to be ignored. So it's worth taking a look into how it works. And today it can be done quite openly and the findings published without so much as a squeak of protest from the North American Air Defence Command, whose headquarters are buried deep in the granite of the Colorado Rockies.

Six years ago, I was doing a television programme about the working of the Strategic Air Command's underground headquarters in Omaha, Nebraska. We were given extraordinary freedom to film the whole process that could lead to the President's final cue for a nuclear attack. But there *were* things that were off-limits. We were not allowed to guess at the number of missiles the Americans had at the ready.

The perils of free-floating satellites have changed all that. Today, we know—and the Soviets know—that there are 4,600 machines of various sorts in space and precisely 939 satellites. Perhaps, now, 938. Somewhere in the Urals or wherever, Soviet technicians are tracking them. And, in the bowels of the Rockies, American technicians are doing the same. They marked the launching of Cosmos 954 on the 17th of September last. They knew its job was to scan the oceans with its radar and tell Soviet ground stations what it saw by way of ships and submarines. The Americans knew that its penetrating radar equipment was powered by a nuclear reactor.

Three months after it was launched, in mid-December, Cosmos 954 began to sag out of its prescribed orbit. The Russians ordered it to break into three parts and dissipate. Evidently it didn't obey. It stayed intact, and every time it went round the earth, it swung a little nearer. In early January, the Americans figured it would fall into the earth's atmosphere over North America. The Soviet Ambassador was invited to a secret meeting in the White House, and the Russians were asked for all relevant information. The American anxiety was over the amount of uranium on board the satellite and its chances of disintegrating on or above the earth. Teams of observers and decontamination experts were flown out to likely points of impact. The afternoon before it crumbled, the men of the Air Defence Command watched it go across Australia and then the Pacific and then on into northern Canada. When a Canadian Mountie reported a meteorite, they knew it was all over. The fragments were tested, and it seemed certain that the satellite and its nuclear power cell had burned up completely on re-entering the earth's atmosphere.

271

The Air Defence Command relaxed. The newspapers cooled down. All was well.

Not quite. What came out a few days later was the admission from space scientists that the location of the crash was not contrived by human skill or the magic of computers. It was sheer luck. They calculated that if the satellite had managed to hobble once more around the earth, it would have come down somewhere close to New York City between eight and nine in the morning. This afterthought was not published. The official story was all over, except for a plea from President Carter for a law, an agreement at least, to ban from space any satellite that contains nuclear reactors. The Secretary of Energy said amen, but he couldn't quite see how it was to be done. Mr Brezhnev made the stunning comment, 'There must not be another war.' Ah, so. Apart from that, the Russians said nothing. However, the doubt remains whether any satellite, like Cosmos 954, would be able to spot the movement of submarines unless its radar was powered by a nuclear reactor. In other words, the evidence is undeniable that we are already embarked on the military uses of space. And just how far we've gone was chillingly exposed two days later by a front-page piece in the *New York Times*. It recalled that the United States had become the first nation to put a spy-satellite in orbit, in 1959. That, more recently, Mr Carter became the first President to admit that both countries are developing weapons meant to destroy each other's satellites. And that the Defence Department is well aware of Russian experiments in space with laser weapons.

Then the *Times* dropped its bombshell. It reported that the Russians have outstripped the Americans, probably by several years, in developing what are known as 'hunter-killer satellites', which 'could knock out the Pentagon's ability to communicate with, and give orders to, ships, planes, submarines, missile silos and ground forces around the world'. Now, this, of course, means that the United States could be paralysed from outer space and rendered impotent even to order an act of retaliation if she were attacked.

The subject was evidently too touchy for security experts in the White House and the Pentagon. They wouldn't talk about it. But the recently retired Chief of Air Force Intelligence would and did. He is General George Keegan. He said that eighteen years ago, a Russian spy working for the Allies in the Kremlin warned Washington that the Russians were about to invest on a grand scale in military space research. He says the man was ignored. But two years ago, American experts were startled when the Russians put into orbit a hunter-killer that could destroy a target on earth after making only one pass around it. General Keegan says the threat is 'grim'.

And what does President Carter say? He brushed the story off at a press conference. How could he have said anything of substance? To say, 'Yes, the Russians have them and we don't' would have dealt a crippling blow to the morale of the people.

What we have to face is that whether it's true or not, it is going to be. We are already far gone towards preparing for the kind of war that H. G. Wells conceived as scientific fiction half a century ago, and that Bertrand Russell, twenty-two years ago, foresaw as the almost certain consequence of American and Russian nuclear research. It surely should give an aching urgency to the coming talks on how to limit strategic arms. For, if the wind out of Canada has blown any good, it is the warning that satellites are already beyond absolute human control, that the technology of war is acquiring a momentum independent of national policy or the men who make it. Like that ghoulish computer in an old 1969 movie, the hunter-killer may come to have a mind of its own.

# A 'Proper' Wedding

*5 May 1978*

It was Shelley, I think, who called poets 'the unacknowledged legislators of the world'. This sounds so grand and final that I, for one, have never bothered to see what it means. But every time the seasons change it occurs to me that in one way, at least, the English poets—four or five centuries of them—have proved more powerful than the legislatures of the United States and, I shouldn't wonder, of Canada, Africa, India, Australasia, the Bahamas, and wherever the British have brewed tea and measured out a cricket pitch. All these far-flung soldiers, civil servants, parsons followed the English calendar and behaved as if they were living in Surrey or Cornwall. American children who have just come through the desert heat of March in Arizona, or are slogging through twenty feet of snow on the Kansas prairie, obediently pipe Chaucer's assurance that 'April with his showers sweet, the draught of March has piercéd to the root.' U Thant, browned by the midday heat of Burma, carried a raincoat when April came in. Not so long ago, American children in New England used to blink their way through the blinding light and the scarlet of their fall and enter a dark schoolroom to learn that autumn was a 'season of mists and mellow fruitfulness'.

Well, now, May has come in, and though my daughter in Vermont is squishing through the banks of melting snow, it is a time in and around New York when we can believe that winter has gone for ever. It is, as the English translators of the Bible quaintly put it, the time when 'The singing of birds is come, and the voice of the turtle is heard in our land.' I don't know what the youngsters of today, anywhere, would make of that sentence, Americans especially, since the teaching of the Bible in the schools clearly goes against the constitutional ban on establishing a state religion. And it's pretty safe, if sad, to say that the teaching of the Bible as literature is practically non-existent.

Indeed, except among Orthodox Jews, and Catholics, I find that in talking with young people it is better to skirt even the most homely biblical reference—the patience of Job, Samson in the temple—because they haven't the slightest idea what you're talking about. A local board of education gave a group of sixteen-year-olds such a test, with frightening results. Cain and Abel were identified as the senior partners of a law firm. 'Ruth amid the alien corn' was a complete puzzle: it was suggested that Ruth had left her native state of Iowa and was looking with contempt on the inferior strain of maize grown by some Eastern state. That's fair enough, it's even intelligent, if you remember that 'corn' in America is everywhere and always maize.

These biblical meditations came to me after attending a ceremony, last Saturday night, that was at once to me original and daring. We'd been invited to the wedding of a girl we'd known since she was a toddler. On the way there, I said to my wife, 'I wonder what the service will be like.' 'I think,' she said, 'they've written their own.' This was depressing news. The last roll-your-own service I attended was in the hills of New Hampshire, also the wedding of a youngish man whom we'd also known from birth. We were told to dress as we pleased and were asked to follow a certain footpath through some woods and appear on the crest of Old Baldy, or whatever it was called, at three in the afternoon.

The footpath was invisible, except to an Indian scout, and we clomped through broom and briar and scratched our way up to a clearing. This had to be it, because the scene bore all the marks of a country wedding. There was a youth with matted locks piping on a flute, and another, bare to the waistband of his jeans, twanging a guitar. Half a dozen young men and women—sex indistinguishable till you got up close—were hefting a case of beer and another case of Fright, Scram, Fickle or some such soft drink for the teetotallers. There was also a middle-aged couple in grotesque uniforms: he was wearing a business suit, a shirt and tie, and she was in a summer dress her mother might have worn in the 1940s. They looked as comfortable as an archbishop and his lady at a punk rock concert. They turned out to be the parents of the bride, a comely girl in some sort of Tibetan peasant's smock, with beads down to her ankles. Those were the days—not, alas, yet over—when girls wore their hair down to their knees by the bow and to their coccyx astern. And throughout the proceedings, which didn't so much get under way as just lurch into a service, the bride kept parting those tidal waves of hair with the palms of her hands in order to see what was going on, and also to respond without choking.

The—I was going to say clergyman, but of course he wasn't a clergyman. In my time, he would have been a particularly sincere type of amateur actor playing John the Baptist in the school play. He had bare feet, wore jeans, a sort of smock, which was possibly the vestment of his mysterious order. But he also had a book. It was a book of poems, by—of all true believers—Robert Lowell. This was encouraging. Perhaps they'd tried to write a service, and given up and fallen back on some fine bit of Lowell. But the book was simply a crutch to the non-parson's memory. He opened it, looked through his beer-bottle glasses at everybody—certainly he was as solemn as any ageing priest—and he said, 'Well, like, shall we get goin'?' He read about four lines of Lowell and that was it. Then he took out from under the folds of his garment a sheet of paper and read what had, indeed, been written by the equally, nay the grindingly, solemn couple. It did not repeat any of the well-worn—and in this setting, I gathered, highly suspect—phrases of the usual marriage service. It was an elephantine parody of them by somebody who seemed to have much the same idea as St Paul but was determined not to show it. The couple, we were told, was about to enter 'a meaningful relationship'. They were identified by their first names only. They would live in 'achieved integrity' (his prose, not mine). They promised nothing. There was no question of honour, love, obedience, or even of a contract. They had chosen, the man said, 'to finalise the concept of oneness'. In fact, they were getting married. He declared them to be not man and wife, a loathsome phrase, but 'two persons equal in marriage'.

That was it. The flute player piped away, and the brooding guitar player bent double over the strings and mumbled something about 'touching your hand'. The four or five adults present were visibly relieved. And we stood around making small talk to smocks and sandals, and waves of hair. Being buddies. Saying things like, 'You into sociology?' and 'Sure, sure.' Then we unzipped the beer cans, and somebody brought on an organic cake, and we nibbled and said 'Um-huh' and it was all over.

Well, that was the last time. You can imagine my feelings when I pulled up this time at an awning in the mid-Fifties in Manhattan, an awning that suggested what we used to call a 'respectable' apartment house (block of flats, if we must translate) but turned out to be a midtown club, mainly for tennis players. That was square enough, and maybe the service would be squarer still. We followed arrows pointing through subterranean passages and upstairs and down corridors till at last we came out on a penthouse apartment with trellis work, and chairs in rows facing a lectern, and out on the terrace leafy decorations and—ah, ha—a bar.

We were on time. I am not myself a particularly punctual person. But at airports and weddings, I'm the first man there. My wife believes you should pack your bags, sit down, take out a book and wait until the absolutely minimum time it would take to get to Kennedy, or wherever, at four a.m. on a Sunday. Then you whisk off in a cab, arrive, dash through the ticket counter and the body check, go aboard, they slam the doors and you're off. I keep saying but why not pack, get to the airport, *then* sit down and read a book? It does no good.

As for weddings, nothing to me is more uncomfortable than tiptoeing in and seeming to steal the limelight as the congregation swivels its collective head and hisses, just when the parson is already launched on 'Dearly Beloved' or 'Well, like, shall we get goin'?'

This time I won. The wedding was to be at 7.30 p.m. We arrived in the penthouse suite at 7.15. There were three other people there. One man, a splendid cynic we'd known for years, said, 'What are you doing here? Sit down and take a nap. Didn't you know this was a Jewish wedding?' The other two were a young man and an old man, the young man wearing a black yarmulka, and the old man—who plainly fancied himself as a swinging chic dresser of the type drawn by Charles Saxon—had on a high-bosomed, tight-waisted suit with lapels like shields, a flowered tie, and a powder-blue yarmulka. They looked at their watches and looked at *us* with mild scorn, as if we were at the wrong party. 'You see?' said my wife.

We sat down. And then I noticed that the lectern was draped in white silk bedsheets. I guessed that the marrying couple had not written their own service. Or if they had, they were anticipating the proceedings by several hours.

Soon a brass quartet started puffing at some charming Tudor music. Possibly by Henry VIII. Henry was an accomplished musician and, after all, he is to the heathen practically the patron saint of marriage.

Then two men and two women came in bearing standards in their hands. When they got to the lectern, they stood at the four corners, and a great flapping blanket of cloth was suddenly extended into a canopy. A young rabbi came in. Then the families. Then the bridegroom, about six feet four with a black yarmulka. And the tiny, and exquisite, bride.

I cannot pretend to call off the sequence of the ceremonies, and the faithful must excuse me if I don't know the proper names for the objects and the articles of the service. I could do it in accurate descriptive detail for another Gentile or *goy*. I will simply say that in its insistence on doing things according to 'the traditions and the wisdom of the Jewish people' it had great dignity. It was half in English and half in Hebrew. The shy couple repeated after the rabbi the traditional phrases.

Two things in this ritual fascinated me. One was the new—to me—and heartening stress on friendship as (the rabbi put it) the sheet anchor of marriage. It struck me as being light years of wisdom beyond St Paul. The other was a grim note, at least it was grim to me. And I hope I don't seem patronising in saying it. The rabbi made the slightest, glancing mention of the trials of the Jewish people, but also of the troubles that are bound to come into any life. And while the couple stood there—he looking like a giant trying not to hurt the pearl he was handling—I thought of a television programme that has just been shown around this country. It is called *Holocaust*. It is a long and ghastly reminder of the six million Jews sacrificed by Hitler like pigs on a spit. There has been a furious correspondence in the papers about how it is too strong, or too mild, or over-edited. And there have been bitter protests—rightly—about the brutal tastelessness of the intruding commercials. But I think it will have acquainted many millions who never knew it with one of the towering obscenities of our time. Maybe sometime we shall see a similar series about the larger liquidations of his own people by Stalin. And, if the present crush on China gets to be too silly, it might be wise to have a television series on the long period of systematic executions, performed on mainland China, that began with the Communist take-over in 1949 and went on and on with almost ritual monotony and the blessing of Chairman Mao. The best estimates vary between thirty and fifty millions.

As I sat there watching this grave and traditional ceremony, feeling uncomfortable at times—very much amid the alien corn—I was glad that the young rabbi had mentioned the troubles of life, and the trials of ancient peoples. I was happy that the young couple had not written their own service.

# Please Die Before Noon

*19 May 1978*

I hesitate, but not for long, to mention a knotty little professional problem that a good professional is not supposed to talk about. Any more than a printer has a right to beg forgiveness for a clutch of typographical errors because his mother has just died. It is this: I am having to tape this talk several days before the day it will be heard in Britain, and the later days when it will be heard in Barbados, in Australia, in Ethiopia and Uganda, who transmit these jewels on their own time during the following week.

I go into the tiresome logistics of broadcasting these days—the taping, the air-mailing of the tape, the passage through customs three thousand miles away, the first transmission, the subsequent transmission over the short wave to far-flung countries—so as to crave a little sympathy for the times when something cataclysmic has happened in the interval between the taping of a talk and the broadcasting of it. During the Watergate days and nights, cataclysms were routine. I remember having to re-do my talk several times so that some listeners around the globe wouldn't think I'd been asleep during the previous twenty-four hours. Even then, Mr Nixon's final decision to abdicate came about thirty-six hours after my deadline for recording the talk. As I sat before the microphone, people were either saying, 'He's bound to go' or 'Of course, he'll brazen it out.' I therefore had to contrive a final sentence which, if you will allow me, I now believe to have been the cagiest sentence I ever spoke into a microphone. Faced with the on again—off again desperation of the man in the White

House, all I could do was to report as dispassionately as possible the known events of the week up to the moment the mike was turned on. At the end of this recital, I said—with cryptic solemnity—'The rest you know.' By the time you heard it, in London or Melbourne, you did.* No critic, no listener, no official of the BBC, apparently paused to figure out the impossibility of my recording those words four full days before the roof fell in. The most sceptical, the most sophisticated, listener believes without a second thought that what is being said is being said at the moment he hears it.

In other words, in this game, a reputation for knowingness, for being on the ball, depends perilously on things not happening too soon. To a lesser extent, the newspaper reporter is a helpless victim of the same heartless technicality: the interval between the writing and the appearance in print. I well remember the first of November, 1950. I was sitting in the lounge of the National Press Club in Washington. I was a working newspaperman then, a journalist in the only literal sense of the term: one who writes every day, for immediate publication. It was about four o'clock in the afternoon. I had filed two stories for my paper, and that would be all for one day, because my deadline was 1.30 p.m. Rather early, you might think, for the American news that would be read over tomorrow morning's breakfast. Well, in those days my paper—which was merely the *Guardian* of Manchester, and not of the whole of the kingdom, of the world—was printed in Manchester. The London editions had to catch a train. So anything intended for tomorrow's London edition had to be filed in New York or Washington by 1.30 our time, at the latest 2.30: 7.30 p.m. British time.

Well, as I say, it was four o'clock. Suddenly, the lazy horsehair-stuffed calm of the press lounge was violated—like that tap dance Fred Astaire broke into in the reading room of a London club—by a man I know, a reporter from a Chicago

* See page 169.

paper. He positively clattered into the room, his eyes bulging and his breath coming in surges, like the sea on a beach. 'Harry Truman,' he bawled, 'has been shot!'

It was not—it turned out, after several plunges for the news ticker—it was not true. But it was true that two men, members of a Puerto Rican nationalist movement, had *tried* to shoot the President, when he appeared at the window of Blair House, where he was living at the time (because, you may remember, the roof of the White House was literally about to fall in). We didn't disentangle the plot from its fanciful additions until about four-thirty. By which time, I was back in the lounge with a friend recovering from the shock with a medicinal snort. While this recovery was proceeding, another man came darting in. He was the Washington chief of Reuter's—not an habitual darter, but very competent and always on the verge of the breaking news. He stopped in his tracks and glared at me. 'Haven't you heard?' he screamed. 'What are you doing here?' 'Too late,' I said. 'They should have done it a couple of hours ago.' It would never have made my paper.

I had learned this lesson long ago, most memorably on Monday, 8th December, 1941, the day after the Japanese attacked Pearl Harbor and brought the United States into the Second World War. The first mad hint of this preposterous— and, as it seemed at the time, impossible—event came while the New York Philharmonic was tuning up for its regular Sunday afternoon broadcast concert. When an announcer broke in to pant out, 'The Japanese have attacked Pearl Harbor.' Nobody will believe it now, but most of us—I'm certain—had to drag out an atlas to discover that Pearl Harbor was in Hawaii and was the main base of the American Pacific Fleet. It was now 2.30, and I dashed off to the White House and drifted impatiently with a tide of reporters waiting for the confirming word, which came at last from the President's press secretary. By the time I got to my office, which in those days was that of the London *Times*, it must have been five p.m. at the earliest. The place was dark and empty. My 'chief', the incomparable and in any crisis the imperturbable Sir Willmott Lewis, had gone off to Maryland for the weekend having filed his only story the day before. It was a thoughtful piece about President Roosevelt's meditations on a message he'd received from the Emperor of Japan. The Emperor was greatly concerned for peaceful relations with the United States. The President had issued a sympathetic reply, and that surely was news enough to see us through the weekend.

It was too late for me to do anything about the enormous bombardment that consigned the Emperor's message, and the President's reply, to the ancient history books. But next morning, sure enough—about twenty hours after Pearl Harbor—the first edition, anyway, of the London *Times* came out with a column dispatch from good old Lewis in Washington bearing the majestic headline: 'The President's Reply to the Emperor Hirohito.'

The most professional if gruesome, response I ever had—to the annoying habit of big-bugs of dying, or invading, too late—came from my *Guardian* editor, A. P. Wadsworth, a tiny Lancastrian with spiky hair, wily eyes and a refusal ever to be excited by any eager beaver, whether a messenger boy or a Prime Minister. One November night in 1948, my friend and guru, H. L. Mencken, was stricken with a massive stroke. The hospital in Baltimore told me it was doubtful that he would last through the night. (It was typical of his intimate, but bilious, view of the medicos that he lasted another seven years.) I sat down and wrote practically into the dawn: an obituary stretching to four thousand words. I cabled it without pausing to consider: first, that most Britons had never heard of Mencken and second, that British newspapers just then were the pinched victims of austerity. Our paper, for example, was allowed only *four* pages on Monday, Wednesday and Friday, and six pages on Tuesday, Thursday and Saturday. I got an acknowledging cable back from Wadsworth. It said, 'MANY THANKS MENCKEN STOP HOPE HE DIES MONDAY WEDNESDAY OR FRIDAY.'

I have been, on the whole, wonderfully lucky with the timing of these talks. But many innocent years ago, before the space age was ushered in, there was a weekend as slack as any I have known. I riffled through four or five newspapers trying to spot anything that might possibly excite the listener in Glasgow or Brighton, let alone in Ethiopia or Uganda. In the end, I sat down and thought up things near at home, tiny things that might still touch some relaxed human being, whereas a report on the latest farm subsidy or a row in the Senate would positively not. I recorded it according to custom. According to custom, it was flown off overnight and passed by the British customs as non-contraband material. It was played a couple of days later—in those days, first on Sunday evening, and again on Monday morning.

Sooner or later, it was bound to happen. And it happened that the radio critic of the *Listener*, the BBC's distinguished house organ, chose that weekend to review my talk. Alas! (A word I use only under the stress of great emotion.) By the time of my broadcast, I knew, and the critic knew—he would have had to be a sloth or a terminal case not to know—that the Russians had just rocketed Yuri Alekseyevich Gagarin round the earth: the first human to travel in space. Of course, I knew it as soon as the *Listener's* critic did. I'll bet I knew it sooner. But even veteran radio and television critics are as hypnotised by the medium as a five-year-old. What you hear is being spoken *now*. The man wrote: 'One thing you must say for Cooke. When the last, the final, bomb has dropped on us all, he'll be there in New York, still waffling away.'

Now you'll understand why I've been vamping till ready all this time. I have a hunch this weekend. I am not going to be caught out by a new war, or the death of a king. I shall know as soon as you do. I am sticking to what has happened, not to what might happen.

Very well, then. On the first Saturday in May, the Kentucky Derby was won by Affirmed. Up, as they say, was the wonder boy of American racing, the—just—eighteen-year-old Steve

Cauthen. By the time you hear this, he will probably have won ten more races, bringing his total in two years to four hundred and—careful!—some. As for American politics, and Mr Carter, and the Cold War—or what we now call détente—I can only say: The rest you know.

# The Hawk and the Gorilla

*2 June 1978*

I don't know who first said that travel broadens the mind, but he might have added the warning that the broader the mind, the thinner it gets. Certainly, some of the shallowest people in the world—types you used to avoid on ocean liners by remembering a pressing appointment with the ship's doctor, or a mislaid friend, or even a deck quoit—these are often people who have been everywhere on every continent and seen everything through the eyes of a travel folder. Another cliché, the converse of the first, but one less quoted since the arrival of Mr Laker and cheap flights for everybody, is that people who stay in one place all their lives are necessarily insular or bigoted. Was it Emmanuel Kant who never moved more than a few miles from his home but managed to move the minds of men and women across the globe and down the centuries? Thomas Hardy spent all but a few years in his native Dorset. But his mind, however narrow, went as deep as the Grand Canyon and discovered rockbed truths about men and women that apply equally to people in Istanbul or New Orleans today as they did to the early nineteenth-century inhabitants of Dorchester.

These homely thoughts came to me as I watched the cheerful tourists bustling out of the hotels on Nob Hill in San Francisco, which is second only to New York as *the* tourist city of the United States. In spite of its record reputation for alcoholism and random street crime. The tourists are off every morning—in coatless summer clothes, since nobody told them that Northern California is a whole climate away from

286

Southern California—off to see what the package tours tell them to see. Fisherman's Wharf is one mecca. Forty years ago, it was a colourful mess of boats and Italian-Americans mending their lines or tossing the huge California crabs onto scales. (California fish and seafood, like the roses and the strawberries, are bigger than anything we know in the East: the bigger they come, the less they taste or smell.) Today, Fisherman's Wharf looks as if it had been put together by a movie art director as San Francisco's 'tatty-picturesque location No. 1'.

Then there is Chinatown, which is as commercial as any Chinatown abroad is bound to be. And it had better be, since the Chinese population's livelihood depends—like that of the native populations of the Bahama and Caribbean islands—on truckling to a tourist view of them. I always find this embarrassing: watching the impassive natives having to put up with fussy or gaping tourists oohing and ahing over tawdry objects and staged ceremonies that the natives themselves may well despise. There's no way of knowing, they keep themselves to themselves, even amidst a pack of outlanders. So much so, incidentally, that when the big issue was integration—the forcible integration of the races in schools, in the first place—even San Franciscans were astonished when the firmest protest came not from the white parents but from the Chinese. They didn't want their children to become contaminated by our culture. I remember, then, visiting the Mayor of Chinatown. He didn't put it quite as grossly as that, but he did make it plain that the Chinese feared their children would lose their dignity in becoming half and half or, as he put it, 'nothing Chinese'.

However, some of the compulsory tourist attractions are indeed things that anyone ought to see. I recall that just after the war, the late Cyril Connolly, the English literary critic, came to New York for the first time and asked me what he ought to see. Of course, I knew he would, like a homing pigeon, make immediate contact with his own kind. He would stay in Greenwich Village and in a flash he would know his opposite numbers. So I apologised for suggesting that he must take a boat round Manhattan Island, and that he simply must go to the top of the Empire State Building at sunset—in the winter is best, when the office lights will be on as the sun goes down—and see the skyscrapers like a bird as succeeding curtains of jewels. 'It's a very touristy thing to do,' I said. I was greatly relieved when he replied, 'But I *am* a tourist.'

Well, whether you're in San Francisco for business or pleasure, it is a crime not to cross the Golden Gate bridge into Marin County and tumble down its hills, and sniff the great eucalyptus trees and spot the wine-red madrones and manzanitas in the forests and come to the valley floor and the nearest grove of redwood trees, called, after the great naturalist, Muir Woods. It is a dense forest, shaggy with delicate ferns and, above you, the vast towering trees eight feet wide and sky-high that were there at the time of Moses.

I was joined this time by an English friend who had never been West. He is at an age which, in Edwardian times, would have been thought of as the cusp of old age. Today, he is—being fifty—in early middle age. But even such a whipper-snapper begins to hear the ticking of the clock, though he wears a digital watch (to me one of the absurdities of the age) and he has to do mental arithmetic to figure out how long he has left to catch a train or make a date. In fact, it occurs to me that perhaps to a digital watch-wearer time is even more ominously fleeting, since the little figure is changing, visually, every second, the way a grandfather clock taps away as relentlessly as a woodpecker.

At any rate, when I suggested to him that we were only 600 miles away from one of the world's great spectacles, he said, 'Let's do it, I may never have the chance again.' This is rather like saying to a visitor to London, 'Since you're so close, you really ought to take a look at the canals of Venice.' But to an Englishman, the West is the West, a compact region all its own. And he, who has made such fun of Americans who go up to Oxford and take in the Cotswolds in a day, he thought nothing of a 1,200-mile trip that started at 8.20 in the morning from San Francisco airport and had us back there at seven in the evening, in time to dine at a splendid Hungarian restaurant.

The trip required two planes. We landed at ten o'clock at Las Vegas, and having an hour between planes we hopped a cab and drove along the main drag—the so-called Strip—and back again. By day, Las Vegas is the crummiest town on earth. By night, the vast electric signs, of the hotels, the motels, the night clubs, blaze away against the purple desert sky with enough candle power to maintain London for a month. It reminds me of what G. K. Chesterton said when he caught his first glimpse of Broadway at night: 'To a man who couldn't read, this would look like Heaven.'

We had no regrets at all as we trundled down the next runway and took off for our spectacle. An hour later, we landed at a small airport carved out of an endless pine forest on a plateau. There was nothing there but the surrounding high pines, a vault of bottomless sky and a clear, dry light that gave everybody twenty-twenty vision. There was also a bus standing there to meet the plane. In the bus sat a tall driver with a slightly gnarled, handsome face and a willingness to answer foolish questions in an amiable way, and to wait for Godot whenever Godot cared to appear. My friend was rattled with impatience. We were supposed to have about four hours at the spectacle, but the tolerance of our driver—'We'll be off to the races in just a few minutes, folks'—was reducing our stay alarmingly. I remarked, by way of a cultural note, that the driver was a typical easy-going, Charles Bickford sort of Westerner. My friend said, 'Isn't he, though? He's so patient, and so good-natured, and such a pain in the neck.'

We finally took off, and ten minutes later came to high groves of trees and rising ground going up to an old timbered lodge. Here, not a hundred yards from the miracle, were substantial grandmothers and bored small children watching bad television. We walked out onto a terrace, and there it was:

the biggest hole on earth, thirteen miles from rim to rim, two miles deep, down a hellish immensity to a trickling river. And a silence as absolute as death. The Grand Canyon of Arizona.

Travel writers usually announce that something is indescribable and then proceed to writhe through inadequate descriptions. I won't be caught in this trap. No matter how many home movies you've seen of it, or coloured centrefolds, the thing itself is beyond human experience. Eons and eons ago, it must have taken the Colorado River a century or so to carve a measurable canyon out of red clay soil. It took about another two million years to approach its present scale. And if we'd been there the morning Christ was born, it would have looked much the same. We mooched a mile or two along the rim and watched the sun go over, and the mile-long shadows shifting across layer after layer of red and purple and yellow mesas the size of cities. And we peered into the immensity and spotted a hawk gliding down there as tiny as a housefly. But no other movement.

In the end, it becomes unbearably beautiful, or preposterous, or unreal. And you have to turn away and seek the company of your own kind in an enclosed space—in the restaurant—because otherwise you'd doubt that human beings had yet been created. Maybe the Grand Canyon—along with the exquisite, incomparable Bryce Canyon—was God's main purpose, and once they were done, it was a piddling afterthought to make Adam and Eve and the billions of scattering ants we now call 'the human family'. Look at the Grand Canyon long enough and you are in danger, not so much of total misanthropy as of a fixed, stony indifference to our world and its inhabitants. It simply doesn't matter whether the Chinese or the Russians or the Arabs come out on top. When all the empires are dust, it will be there, with the little hawks and the big buzzards wheeling and gliding to the end of time.

Well, the afternoon wore on and we were eventually back with Charles Bickford, and then the airline stewardesses and their gleaming teeth ('Coffee? Coke? Tab?'), and the snowcapped Sierras, and the huge, fertile Central Valley, and the Coast Range, and driving towards the confetti-spattered hills: the myriads of wooden white houses of San Francisco.

A couple of days later, we were sitting on a little porch on the peninsula of Belvedere that overlooks San Francisco Bay and the rising city beyond. Another spectacle but a human one. A San Franciscan present said to the Englishman, 'Tell me, which of the things you've seen in America was the most impressive?' They were afraid he'd say the Grand Canyon but hoped he'd say San Francisco. (For there are no chauvinists like San Francisco chauvinists, especially the professional San Franciscans, who were born in Connecticut, Iowa or Indiana.) With great promptness, and an ill-concealed note of defiance, he said, 'Oh, no doubt about it—New York, the day I arrived.'

They were too mannerly to say, 'Oh, come on!' They smiled, in a sporting, hurt way and asked, 'Why?' 'We-e-ell,' he said, as if spelling out the obvious, 'because New York is full of the damndest eccentrics and wonderful oddities.' They looked baffled, and so did I. He had to go on and explain what he pretends is nothing but close observation, though in fact it is a theory he sprouted on his first visit. Now, to prove it, he roams the hot city for endless hours determined to track down examples. Rather like the London correspondents of the American television networks who, when they are asked to get the reaction of 'the City' to some financial turn in the weather, fight their way through millions of Londoners looking for a 'typical' one wearing a bowler hat and a rolled umbrella. Other, blander types of visitor to America may settle for saying that New York is huge, exhilarating, frightening. Not this man. He is a Dickens lover, so he ransacks the great haystack of New York for the needle of an eccentric.

'Such as what?' the now surly San Franciscans persisted.

'We-e-ell,' he said, 'when I first walked through Central Park, I thought it was just a park, interesting in a general way, because it's a big rock garden enclosed by skyscrapers. But then I came on a man playing a harp. It was a black harp—I'd never seen one before—a black harp, and the man was dressed as a gorilla!'

Looking the man—the Englishman—in the eye and guessing he doesn't have a fever or a brain tumour, you simply have to believe him. Then, he said, he'd seen and heard four youngsters on Fifth Avenue tootling away at a Mozart quartet. Plainly, a man given to visions. Since he is a musician, and no doubt knows every aria in *The Messiah*, tomorrow he will tell you he saw a man in a tattered tunic and a ragged beard bawling, 'Prepare Ye the Way of the Lord!'

Well, we came back to New York, and the first day he announced, with a slightly shifty look, that he was just going to 'amble around' the town. 'Off to spot an eccentric, eh?' He ignored this drollery. And he came back in the evening, and guess what? 'I saw the most amazing thing in Central Park.' *Do* go on, you press him. 'We-e-ell,' he says, 'there was a woman sitting on a bench, a middle-aged, well, sixtyish, glasses, quite nondescript. And she had on her lap a carry-all bag and was fumbling around in it and twisting it, as if something had spilled, and then she pulled out—what d'you think?—a snake, a great five-foot snake, and stretched it so people could take pictures of it. And then she bundled it back in her bag and went round collecting quarters from the bystanders. Can you believe it?' You've got to believe it, since in every other way this man is a practical and rational being.

Well, either my friend is a mental case or he's a compulsive spotter of oddities. For him, these strays represent the entire population of New York. It all reminds me of a boy from North Dakota, a Rhodes Scholar who went straight from the boat train to Paddington to catch the train to Oxford. His first day in England. As he leaned back in the unfamiliar carriage, he heard whistles blowing, saw cops running and a bullet shot through his carriage window and out the other side. 'So,' he said, 'and they talk about Chicago.'

Between the hawk in the Grand Canyon with its eye on the

end of time, and my friend with his eye out for gorillas playing black harps, it will be an effort to get back to such trivialities as the Israeli-Egyptian deadlock, the financial plight of New York, or President Carter's new tough line with the Russians. We can only try.

# A Letter
# from Long Island

*18 August 1978*

As you may have heard, all the New York City newspapers—
all three of them—are on strike. How, then, am I going to
acquaint you with what is being said, and thought, and
speculated about all the great issues of the day? I am not. It
may be cold-blooded to say so but this seems to me to offer a
golden opportunity to disclaim all responsibility for being
well-informed, or informed at all. I could spoil it for you—and
for me—by remarking that the television networks are
doubling and tripling their coverage from New York and of
the local controversies that spring from the strike. So it's
possible to sit down at six p.m. and emerge four hours later
choked and dizzy with facts and fancies.

In the middle of a sweaty August, it seems to me to be a
mistake not to make the most of the surcease from the *New
York Times*. Far better, I hope you'll agree, if I retreat to where
I belong and tell you something about life as it is lived at the
end of Long Island. I don't mean to give you the romantic
notion that the end of the Island—we are precisely one
hundred miles from door to door—is a romantic haven devoid
of all involvement with the modern world. On the contrary, it
would be possible for a nosey reporter to make it over into a
miniature of the nation's plight.

The county politicians voted not to raise the pay of our
local sheriffs, so for a day or two the prison guards called in to
say they were all feeling very poorly. Rural crime has increased
by three per cent in the past year—up in our village from ten
robberies to—presumably—ten and a third! There is a mild

hullabaloo about a proposal to build an atomic plant in the middle of our potato fields. The groundwater supply, our only source of water, is becoming polluted with nitrates from fertilizers used by farmers and golf clubs, and it's going to cost a quarter of a million dollars to keep the water safe for humans. And so on.

Enough. You must picture the island as a fish, a very long fish with its snout on the left and its tail on the right. Its mouth is hooked to Manhattan and its body reaches into the Atlantic in a direction more easterly than anything, for about 120 miles. Its tail is divided into two flukes, which enclose a bay about thirty miles long, five to six miles wide. This is called Peconic Bay (the Peconics were a tribe of Indians, fishermen, whom the refugees from Suffolk came on in the seventeenth century).

There are certain places of the earth I would rather be than anywhere else, at certain times of the year. In the fall, there is nowhere I would rather be than Vermont, for the beauty of its scarlet and gold landscape—except Long Island, for its shining days and its miraculous draught of fishes. In fact, there is nowhere I know—not the Mediterranean, or the Crimea, most certainly not California—where, between May and November, there is such a succulent haul of so many kinds of splendid eating fish. We are just at the point where the northern cold-water fish nibble at our shores and where the warm-water fish abound. First, for the gourmet, are the noble striped bass, and the bluefish. Then the swordfish, and the flounder, and the lemon sole. But there are also other very tasty species, which city people either don't know about or despise out of genteel ignorance. In the summer months, the fat flat porgy is always mooching along the bed of the bay. It is very easy to catch by bouncing a sinker on the bottom and stirring up enough sand and mud to blind it. It is a paranoid species that feels it's being chased by submarines and so comes to the surface along a zigzag course, as if in convoy during wartime. Baked porgy is delicious, and I simply have no idea why it never appears on restaurant menus.

Then there is the blowfish, known to the local tots as the swell-belly, for the exact reason that when it's grounded it blows itself up like a balloon in the hope of disposing of the hook. It is regarded by weekenders as a pest fish, but it has down its backbone a slim triangular fillet of firm flesh, the closest thing we have to the delicious rubbery texture—I'm afraid there is no other word—of a Dover sole. More remarkable still is the city's non-acceptance of the weakfish. I have caught it and savoured it for forty years. It is so-called because it has a weak, papery mouth, which it cheerfully—I presume—rips in order to dislodge the hook. It then swims off and grows its mouth together again. Maybe its name is the snag. Some years ago, droll Italians who owned fish markets on the South Shore took to laying out weakfish and marking them with a sign saying, 'Sea Trout'. They were out of stock within an hour of piling up the weaks.

The island, like all other bits of geography, has its own local lingo for its different districts that will not be found on maps or in atlases. Thus, the northern fluke—where I live—is known as the North Fork. But the southern fluke is known as the South *Shore* (never mind that some old families over there try to retain the South Fork). The natives of the North Fork say they are going 'South Side' whenever they are disposed to do so, which is not often, for reasons I hasten to explain.

The South Shore used to be the exclusive monopoly of early Dutch and English landowners. One of the latter, William Floyd, was a signer of the Declaration of Independence and achieved a very late badge of immortality by having a motorway named after him. The early settlers were a little miffed, at the end of the nineteenth century, when some of the Robber Barons and their heirs moved in. One of them, name of Vanderbilt, visited Scotland and saw the natives playing the peculiar game known locally as 'the gowf'. He accordingly imported some clubs, hired a landscape man, or golf architect, and commissioned him to lay out the first twelve-hole links course in the United States.

Until the Second World War, the fashionable resorts of the South Shore—Southampton, Bridgehampton, Easthampton—were pretty choosy places. But following the immemorial custom of all Western societies, the latest batch of the new rich moved as close to the old rich as possible in the hope of having some of their effortless poise brush off on them. In the past twenty or thirty years, these once fussy compounds have been invaded by brokers, interior decorators, bankers, chic painters, actors and actresses, television producers, and infested by ten-percenters of all kinds.

If you detect a note of inverted snobbery in this account, your instinct is correct. I have summered and autumned (fallen?) on the North Fork for forty-two years. We stand out on our hundred-foot high cliff or bluff and look across the five or six miles of the quarantine waters that separate us from the chic, the bad and the beautiful. The North Fork is not chic. It is not rich. I doubt there are more than half a dozen residents whose combined securities could match the portfolio of any one of several hundreds of the denizens of Easthampton and Southampton. The North Fork was for two and a half centuries the province of English settlers from Suffolk, and you can follow the family lines through platoons of tombstones, the victims of seventeenth-century epidemics, and all the wars since the Revolution, in the local graveyards or what—in my village—is known as 'the burying ground'. I know old people, and not so old, who only once in their lifetime have made the hundred-mile trip to New York. They didn't like what they saw, and went no more.

Shortly after the Robber Barons invaded the South Shore, the North Fork was invaded by immigrant Poles: Catholic farmers. Like all immigrants, they had a nostril tuned to the smell of their native soil. And the North Fork, planted as far as the eye can see with potatoes and cauliflower and corn, is interrupted only by a few old Colonial churches but more conspicuously by squat wooden churches with blunt spires. The Fork could be used today with great accuracy as the location for a film about central Poland.

The Poles were industrious and very thrifty and in no time took over the big duck farms, which had been run in a comfortable way by the Anglos. So now, our Fork is populated mostly by the descendants of the original English and by third-generation Poles. And in the manner of long-settled rural communities, the North Forkers tend to take a dim view of the South Shore. But then, the South Shore takes no view at all of the North Fork. In fact, friends of ours on the South Side have lived and died there without having the faintest idea where the North Fork was or how to find our point, though it's clearly visible from the Peconic shore of their side. I still have friends who ask us every summer, 'How are things at your place in Southampton?' Which is like asking a proud Lancastrian, 'How are things in Bradford and Leeds?'

Our point is called Nassau Point. After the English occupation it was rechristened Hog's Neck, but it reverted later on to Nassau since, under the Dutch, it had been designated as a sliver of crown property by King William (Prince, you'll recall, of Orange and Nassau). Since then the Point has managed to remain unmentioned in the history books or even in the newspapers. In fact, we are so obscure that when Nassau Point achieved the fame of a new comet, nobody noticed it. It needed no newspaper strike to leave us unhonoured and unsung. But that is another story. Another letter.

# *The* Letter
# from Long Island

## *4 August 1970*

We have just seen for the first time a film made in Japan exactly twenty-five years ago. It is about what happened on that fine, hot August day to the city of Hiroshima. It was shown here now, I suppose, as a bleak reminder, and a commemoration of the 120,000 dead or injured. Two things struck me all through the film. One was the remarkable bravery—or phlegm—of the cameramen. The other was the thought that this gross nightmare should have happened to a people who have always been noted for their delicate fine touch, whether in the growing of a tree or the making of an optical lens or, as here, following the tracery of a score of wounds on a single human being.

It was enough to lacerate us, and it started up again the controversy, which will never be settled, about President Truman's decision to drop the bomb in the first place. Without raising more dust over the bleached bones of Hiroshima, I should like to contribute a couple of reminders. The first is that the men who had to make the decision to pass on to the President—General George C. Marshall and the Secretary of War, Henry L. Stimson—were just as humane and tortured at the time as you and I were later. And secondly, that they had to make a choice of alternatives that I for one would not have wanted to have to make for all the offers of redemption from all the religions of the world.

What the President and his advisers did not know and what we rather confidently know now, is that by August 1945 the Japanese were at the end of their rope. The plans were going

299

forward for a step-by-step invasion of the Japanese home islands, where the Japanese had a million men under arms, apart from another three million if the worst happened in the rest of the Far East. The best estimates, put together by the staffs of Marshall and Stimson, were that an invasion would require five million American men, that it would probably not succeed until 1947, and that the casualties, of Americans, the fighting Japanese and Japanese civilians, would amount to something between one and a half and three millions. When the invasion was being planned, the bomb had not been tried. But once it went off in New Mexico, the question was whether the Japanese should be given an ultimatum and a warning 'technical' demonstration, on uninhabited land, of the bomb's power. The atomic scientists in New Mexico delivered their opinion: 'We can propose no technical demonstration likely to bring an end to the war; we see no acceptable alternative to direct military use.'

With that judgment in their hands, Marshall and Stimson and Co. looked over the proposed targets. They ruled out the old cultural capital of Kyoto and in the end decided on Hiroshima, as the headquarters and main arsenal of the Japanese army defending southern Japan; and Nagasaki, a seaport and a centre of the war industry.

I suppose we must all have wondered, in a distraught way at some time or other, how it all started. To be painstakingly historical about it you could, of course, take it back far beyond Einstein and Rutherford and the quantum theory. If you really got going, you could find yourself in the fifth century BC with Empedocles, who worked on the assumption that an atom is the smallest indivisible particle of matter. But let us leap, say, twenty-five centuries forward to the spring of 1939 and the slowly dawning idea, in the minds of a few physicists, that an atomic bomb might be made. It was left to a scattered band of Jewish refugees from Germany—some in Sweden, most in the United States—to realise that the bomb might get into the wrong hands, namely Hitler's. Three of these refugees, all

Hungarians, lived here in the obscurity that is the lot of scientists whose speciality is so exotic that neither the statesmen nor the public knows that it exists.

These three men were named Szilard, Wigner and Teller. They kept up with what was happening in their work abroad through letters from old friends, Jews mostly, who had been driven out of Germany into Belgium and Britain and Sweden. By the winter of 1938–9, the three began to hear that the Germans were working on something called 'the uranium problem'. In March, 1939, an Italian physicist, Enrico Fermi, had actually called on an American admiral in the Navy Department and had touched on the possibility of an atomic bomb. Evidently it was an interesting, wild passing thought, like the possibility at some remote time of a man landing on the moon. Neither the Navy nor any other branch of the government gave it another thought. Then the three heard that a meeting of physicists had been called in Berlin to discuss the possibility of using something called 'nuclear fission' to drive an automobile.

Maybe they were reassured about the German intentions. But not for long. The summer came on and they had a letter from a woman scientist in Sweden who told them something that, even if it had been circulated in the Foreign Offices of London and Paris, let alone the American State Department, would have meant nothing at all to anybody outside businessmen with an interest in metal stocks. Germany had suddenly banned all exports of uranium ore from Czechoslovakia, which it occupied. There was only one other European country that stocked uranium ore: Belgium, which got it from the Belgian Congo. Szilard, Wigner and Teller, it is safe to say, were the only trio of friends anywhere in the United States who were alarmed by the news. They felt they must get the warning word to somebody in American government. This was a problem. They were unknown refugees; only Wigner was an American citizen. They had cause to distrust the military mind, because of its ingrained habit of preparing to

301

fight the last war. They had no more standing with the White House or the State Department than any ordinary person who writes a crackpot letter to the President. (The Secret Service and the FBI between them screen several hundreds of such alarms every week.) They saw what was ahead. And suddenly they thought of 'the Old Man', who was world renowned and who—if he wrote to the Belgians—that was their first idea—might be able to get them to hold on to their stocks of uranium. They must get to the Old Man.

So it began, on a drenching hot midsummer day in July 1939. Two of the refugees, Szilard and Wigner, woke one morning and got out a map of Long Island. They knew that the Old Man had rented a cottage for the summer from one Dr Moore. That's all. They had been lately so out of touch with him both in their work and their social contacts that they didn't know where the cottage was. Long Island is a hundred and twenty miles long and choked with place names, English and Indian. But the Old Man had named it on the telephone. Wigner was his associate at Princeton. He looked over the map. It was something with a 'P'. Way down on the south shore of the island, he saw the name—Patchogue. That was it. So they drove off. They got out to Patchogue and asked in stores and gas stations for the whereabouts of Dr Moore's cottage. Nobody had ever heard of him. They got back into the car and sweated over the map. Could it be, said Szilard, looking up across the bay to the North Fork of the island, could it be Peconic? 'Peconic,' said Wigner, 'that's it, I remember.' So they drove north and east forty-some miles, along the North Fork, and came to the minute town of Peconic, which to this day consists of one small saloon and the clearing of what was then a crumbling wooden railway shelter. Dr Moore, please? Dr Moore was unheard of.

It was one of those hideous north-eastern midsummer days, of a grey leaden sky, and the wet heat up in the nineties, and the map was like a towel in their hands. They were irritable and pretty much in despair and they turned, to drive the hundred miles back to the city. Less than two miles from Peconic, on a two-lane road, you have to come back through a one-street town called Cutchogue. They stopped at Mr Kramer's drug store to get some trifle or other. They saw a boy, about seven years old, standing in a corner with a fishing rod in his hands. The Old Man was a great fisherman. 'Sure,' said the boy, 'he lives in Dr Moore's cottage.' He climbed in and he led them over a causeway and along a narrow peninsula called Nassau Point and they came to the cottage.

The Old Man came out in his slippers, and they told him their news. They had a hot hour explaining to him what it all meant, or could mean. Szilard, with whom I checked the facts of this trip years later, said he was surprised to realise that 'the possibility of a chain reaction had not occurred to the Old Man'. But they convinced him, and together they agreed that the best thing to do would be to write a letter to the Belgian government and send a copy of it to the United States State Department. Then Wigner and Szilard drove back to New York.

And there they began to have more misgivings. The Belgians might not respond. The copy might vanish in the yawning files of the State Department. They began to grow tense over the likelihood of a long delay. Maybe they should persuade the Old Man himself to write to the President of the United States, no less. They made discreet enquiries of other friends, other refugees, and came on a German economist who knew a banker who was a personal friend of President Roosevelt. Maybe the banker could be the courier. They sat down and drafted a much bolder and simpler letter.

And on the 2nd of August, they drove off again. 'They', this time, were not the same couple. Wigner had gone on his holiday in California. Szilard, a scientific brain beyond our comprehension, couldn't drive a car. So Szilard invited Teller to drive him down the island. With no fear, this time, of losing the way. Not Patchogue, with a 'P', not Peconic, but Cutchogue with an 'ogue'. An easy mistake. Our weekend guests make it all the time.

The Old Man was ready for them, and they went from the porch into his study and read him both a German draft and an English translation they had typed. At last the Old Man nodded, and put his pen to it. Next step, on to the middleman banker and the White House.

It read:

Nassau Point,
Peconic, Long Island.
August 2nd, 1939

F. D. Roosevelt,
President of the United States,
White House,
Washington, D. C.

Sir:

Some recent work of E. Fermi and L. Szilard, which has been communicated to me in manuscript, leads me to expect that the element uranium may be turned into a new and important source of energy in the immediate future. Certain aspects of the situation which has arisen seem to call for watchfulness and, if necessary, quick action on the part of the Administration. I believe therefore that it is my duty to bring to your attention the following facts and recommendations:

In the course of the last four months it has been made probable—through the work of Joliot in France as well as Fermi and Szilard in America—that it may become possible to set up a nuclear chain reaction in a large mass of uranium, by which vast amounts of power and large quantities of new radium-like elements would be generated ... by which, my dear Mr President, it might be possible to unleash an immense destructive force.'

The President got the letter from the banker, but not before the following October, and maybe he thought it interesting enough, though mysterious. Not until two years later, in the fall of 1941, did he appoint a committee—of the Vice President, and the Secretary of War, and General Marshall and two scientists—to look into it. He put aside some hundreds of dollars in executive funds for this study, which, later on, were increased to the tune of over two billion dollars.

The Old Man, who put his signature to the Nassau Point letter, was, of course, 'A. Einstein'.

# The Presidential Ear

*8 December 1978*

The newspapers and the TV commentators have just paid their annual respects—or regrets—to the Japanese attack on Pearl Harbor, on the 7th of December, 1941, a day, President Roosevelt said when he went before Congress, 'that will live in infamy'.

However, two days before that was December the 5th, 1978, a night which will surely live in American history. For there occurred an event that has never before taken place in the history of the Republic: an incumbent President of the United States took his seat at the opera. The doors of New York's Metropolitan Opera House—either the old or the new—have never been darkened, or lit up, by the presence of a President.

Nothing ought to be made of the fact that the opera was *Aida*, an opera on an Egyptian subject commissioned by Ismail Pasha and first performed in Cairo, though it's possible something may be made of it by ill-meaning journalists in and out of Israel. In which case, the President could make amends by commissioning a performance of Handel's *Israel in Egypt*.

The fact is that President Carter is something of a freak among the long line of American Presidents. He is a music lover. I don't mean that he has his favourite tunes, as haven't we all. President Eisenhower, I believe, let it be known that he had an album of favourites, which he liked to have piped in so that he could hum to them, as George V on a memorable occasion—his fifth visit to *his* favourite opera, *Rose Marie*—sat in the royal box and, having conquered his favourite song in

306

the whole of music, accompanied the chorus singing 'Totem tom tom, Totem tom tom.'

I mean that President Carter is the phenomenon of a very hard-working President who yet makes time every morning—every dawning, I ought to say—to listen to a half-hour or so of Mozart or Beethoven. It is hard to think of a better prescription for rinsing out the mind before the growing cacophonies of the day. It is fascinating, though perhaps not very instructive, to wonder why politicians, who regularly acquire some strange bedmates, should so rarely relax with the muse of music, with classical music, that is. Franklin Roosevelt and John F. Kennedy would have paid any price to avoid a symphony concert. Disciples of the late Harry Truman will be bound to protest that he actually played the piano, chopped his way through bits of Chopin, and at all times was ready to give a soulful performance of 'The Missouri Waltz'.

But having heard him and followed his tastes, I must say that his range was that of the excerpts we staggered through on the piano when I was a boy: a series of what was called 'The Three Star Folio', which incorporated the more swinging bits from the *Poet and Peasant* overture, 'Zampa', Handel's 'Largo' and the 'Four Indian Love Lyrics' of the immortal Amy Woodforde-Finden. They were conveniently known as middle-brow classics.

And I'm sure that out of Texas will storm the reminder that whenever at a barbecue or other local festival Lyndon Johnson heard 'The Eyes of Texas', the tears flowed down the clefts of his endless cheeks. President Nixon, too, was almost as eager to get to any piano in sight as was George Gershwin, about whom a close but clear-eyed friend said, 'No question about it, an evening with Gershwin is a Gershwin evening.' Nobody thumped away with more zest and pleasure than President Nixon, and I imagine he treasures as one of the precious mementoes of his Presidency the evening when, in full view of a delirious audience, Duke Ellington kissed him on both cheeks—the last time, I believe, Mr Nixon was ever kissed in public, except by next of kin.

In case any overseas listener is beginning to preen himself on the superior cultivation of his own politicians, as distinct from the rude American kind, I beg him or her to take thought. Name offhand, or even after much boning up, any politician of the first chop who is or was a known lover of classical music. Apart, that is, from the blinding exception of Mr Edward Heath. Mr Gladstone, my father told me, was properly reverent when called to Buckingham Palace to listen to performances of sacred music commissioned by Queen Victoria. He would have been a brave Prime Minister who dared to refuse *that* royal command to listen to any music, however sacred, however stupefyingly dull. But I don't remember from the memoirs that Balfour, Lloyd George, Asquith, Bonar Law or any of their generation had the slightest interest in music. In the many volumes of the works of Winston Churchill, I can't recall a reference to any of the top-flight or even third-flight composers, though Mr Churchill was also known to weep whenever the 'Battle Hymn of the Republic' was played. As for the succeeding generations of British politicians—and I hope I do them no insult—I cannot find either that Anthony Eden was an accomplished bassoonist or that Mr Callaghan devotes his spare hours to reading the scores of the Bach fugues. I do recall, and was actually present once when the astonishing thing happened: the first Lord Birkenhead was tone deaf and had to be nudged whenever the band went into the national anthem.

Going back for a minute or two to the startling event that provoked all this meditation, I must say it seems very unlikely that some President, at some time or other, did not find it expedient, let alone pleasurable, to attend the opera. A friend of mine, who knows not only all the obscure operas of the great composers but all the mediocre operas of the obscure composers, did a little digging and came up with the nugget that in 1918 President Wilson did appear at the Metropolitan

Opera House. But it turned out that he was there, as usual, not to listen but to perform. Not, so help us, to sing, but to make a speech before a rally called to stir up popular support for the League of Nations. There is also an unauthenticated rumour that at another time, President Wilson dropped a hint to the authorities that he might come up to New York to attend the opera, but when he discovered that it was to be performed on a Sunday, he was shocked into withdrawing his request.

Further painstaking research at last reveals that there is one other President who not only had the wild impulse to go to the Met but yielded to it. Not, however, in New York. The Metropolitan company was on tour in the winter of 1905–6, and when it appeared in Philadelphia President Theodore Roosevelt—in the full flush of what had been till then the biggest popular majority any President had ever had from the voters—took himself off to see and hear Enrico Caruso. Roosevelt must have slipped into the house—if a mountain can ever be said to have slipped in anywhere—or he had not tipped off the company. Because when the performance was over and he went backstage to greet the great man, the other great man, Caruso, we are told, believed for an awkward time that he was meeting an impostor. But when he realised that he was indeed being visited by the one and only T. R. or Teddy, he threw his arms around the President and—anticipating Duke Ellington—smacked a kiss on each cheek. There was a photographer present—a small fact I mention because the following April Caruso was performing in San Francisco, and early in the morning of the 18th he was asleep in his regal suite in the Palace Hotel. Just before dawn, the bed started to shake and the chandelier to swing and, in a word, the hell of the famous earthquake was let loose all around him. He dashed out, like all the other guests, in a nightgown into the courtyard of the hotel and begged for any form of transport that would take him to the ferry, which in turn would take him to the railroad and save him from disaster. In what must have been an agony of conflict, between egotism and self-preservation, he tried to think of some single possession he could not bear to lose. My opera historian records—and who is to question him?—that what Caruso rescued was the photograph of himself with Teddy Roosevelt.

I was pondering on this unexplained mystery—why politics apparently works through the nervous system to produce an allergy to first-rate music—when one of the television networks ended its nightly news roundup with a five-minute visual essay on two minority peoples, most of whom live outside China but some of whom spill over the northern and southern borders: namely, Mongols and Thais. This piece was put on, I imagine, partly to tell us more about our new Communist friend, and partly to offset the chill of the twenty-year treaty of friendship that the Soviet Union has just signed with Afghanistan.

These two ancient peoples are, of course, resident aliens, or what the Bible calls 'strangers within the gates'. They have their own strong cultures, and we were assured that the Chinese in no wise want to reform them. To keep them friendly, on both sides of the borders, we were told that the Chinese allow them to live—I quote—'independent lives according to their own customs, within the framework of Chinese Communism'. I must say this sounded to me like saying that the Jews were 'allowed to live independent lives, according to their own customs, within the framework of the Third Reich'. Anyway, what we saw mostly was young children dancing to charming music, and I was told later that this was not any Oriental equivalent of rock or pop but classical folk music. It was very pleasing. And because these were the only films we'd ever seen of these people, we got the impression that they did nothing else but dance to classical music. It was as if American propaganda films sent to China showed the American people as one mammoth Mormon choir singing the *St Matthew Passion*.

The shock was in what the delightful children were doing to the music. The Mongol tots danced with rifles, the Thais with rifles and fixed bayonets. Evidently, there are some nations whose rulers have learned how to soothe the savagery of their system by marrying music to politics. For export only.

# A Piece of Paper

*20 April 1979*

It must be a very long time since so many Americans, women especially, have awaited the outcome of a court case with such palpitation of the heart and purse as they have done in the case of Michelle Triola Marvin v. Lee Marvin.

So much gossip, so much wishful speculation, so many high hopes and low fears have been stirred by this case that I ought to explain as plainly as possible the argument, or rationale, on which Miss Marvin brought her suit. Right at the beginning we have a little trouble. 'Miss' Marvin suggests a legal relationship with Mr Marvin. I won't call her Ms. Marvin, because I object to the Ms. usage on the three grounds laid down by the excellent Florence King, the author of a small masterpiece called *He*, a devastating exposure both of the American male and of the females who labour to expose him. First, she says, Ms. sounds like the buzz of an insect. Secondly, it signifies, if anything at all, the abbreviation of 'manuscript'. And thirdly, if a woman—married or single—achieves any professional independence of her own, she has the right to the honourable title of Miss, which should not suggest marriage or the absence of it. I think I shall call Michelle Triola Marvin simply Michelle, as one of the two contending parties in the case. The other, of course, is no one but the actor Lee Marvin, known to us all before this case as a gritty upholder of the law, sometimes (in, for instance, *Bad Day at Black Rock*) as a very mean man biding his time, but never as an injured party.

Well, as Serjeant Buzfuz said, 'These are the facts and circumstances of the case—detailed by me.' Michelle Triola, who is now forty-five, was a youngster when she moved from Chicago shortly after the end of the Second World War. Once out of high school she started singing in night clubs in Reno and Las Vegas, had a brief marriage with an actor, went to Europe and sang in night clubs there, for pretty good fees, and came back to Hollywood in 1964. There and then she met Mr Marvin and they lived together from December of that year until June of 1970. Then he left her and married an old high school sweetheart.

For a little time after she took up with Mr Marvin she went on singing in public and cut a record, but she had no time to promote it because, she says, she had all but abandoned her career and given her life and time to Mr Marvin wherever he was making a picture, and wherever he wasn't. A few months before they parted, in the spring of 1970, she legally changed her name by adding Marvin to Michelle Triola. They were never married but she swore at the trial that at a very early stage of their living together he had said to her, 'What I have is yours and what you have is mine.'

I isolate that simple sentence from the huge transcript of an eleven-week trial because it reduces her case to its legal nub—in California more than anywhere. California is one of the South-Western states that inherited much of its law from the Spanish. And one element of Spanish law that is still extant and binding in California is what is known as the 'community property' law. It is not much known about abroad, but it is quickly and painfully learned by, say, English movie actors—by, indeed, any male, domestic or foreign—who marries in California or marries somewhere else and becomes a permanent resident of California. No bachelor who ever fantasises about conjugal happiness with some nubile Holly-wood actress should ever envy her husband. If they get a divorce, he delivers over to his wife exactly half of all his property—house, furnishings, income, savings—the lot. If he marries a new houri and divorces *her*, he then has to give her exactly half of what he has left. There are much-married

313

actors—generally thought of as carefree millionaires—who today are living on one-eighth or even one-sixteenth of what they owned and earned.

In other words, the California community property law is implicit in the marriage contract. When Mr Marvin said, if he did, 'What I have is yours and what you have is mine,' though it might sound very gallant and even poetic elsewhere—in California it was simply the repetition of a literal fact that applies to every married person. Half the man's property, in the moment of marriage, belongs to the wife. And half her property belongs to him.

But, you'll say, they were not married. That's right. But it was Michelle's contention that she had been for six years a wife in all but name. She hoped—her whole suit was a dogmatic declaration of her belief—that they had a contract equally as binding as a marriage contract. And since it happened in California she sued him for precisely one half of the 3.6 million dollars he earned while they were living together: for a property settlement comparable to that any California wife would get the moment her marriage was dissolved. That, said Michelle, is what she deserved.

The question before the judge was whether the *law* said she deserved it. She was, in principle, asserting a new view of contract, one that I don't imagine would have been tolerated ten or twenty years ago. But since living together outside wedlock has today shed the stigma it bore for centuries, there must be hundreds of thousands of American couples who followed the case with the concentration of ferrets, especially the disillusioned couples, the women panting in hope, the men in fear. There are, in fact, over a thousand similar suits pending in California alone.

Once the trial started, there was more debate about its possible outcome than about the rights and wrongs of the case. I'm thinking now of debates among lawyers, not among the rest of us who thought the suit either quixotic or vindictive or a brave blow for women's rights. Not to mention the millions of newspaper readers who merely lapped up the juices of their imaginations.

What many lawyers argued with the advocates of women's rights was this: should Michelle's contention about having been the party to a solemn contract stand up at a time when old laws about the marriage state are being challenged, and new laws are being proposed? All across the country, there are wives who contend that a housewife's work—which can run to ten or twelve hours a day if she has small children—ought to be legally recompensed at a going rate, of so much an hour, so much a week, so much a year. These contentions are before the courts. And they are being maintained by women who are not intimidated by the sanctity or stamina of ancient laws.

A lot of evangelists in the cause of equal rights for women find themselves stymied when they come to look at the California community property law. What could be more equal than a law which makes the marriage certificate itself say, 'What I have is yours and what you have is mine'? I'm sure that if Michelle had got what she wanted, there would have been a landslide move in other states to join the six or seven that have adopted the California law. But she lost. That is to say, she lost her main argument.

I hasten to report that she *says* she won. But then, Mr Marvin says *he* won. What did they win or lose? The judge stayed with the law of contract. 'To accede,' he said, 'to such a contention would mean that the court recognise each unmarried person living together to be automatically entitled ... to half the property bought with the earnings of the other non-marital partner.' It would be tantamount, he said, to recognising common law marriage, which the State of California abolished in 1895. As for Mr Marvin's heroic declaration—assuming he made it—that 'What I have is yours and what you have is mine,' the judge made the wry comment that under the circumstances (the circumstances of swearing fidelity to an alliance not bound by a contract) it could be put down to the sort of 'hyperbole' typical of people 'who live and work in the field of entertainment'.

So he threw out Michelle's suit for half of the 3.6 million dollars Mr Marvin had earned during the years of their unmarried bliss. But he threw her a bone, and it is one he chose to dignify by a legal doctrine that goes back, in English law, at least to the fifteenth century: the law of equity. He thought she ought to have some balm to ease the wound of Mr Marvin's desertion. And he awarded her $104,000 (which is $1,696,000 less than she asked), representing a thousand dollars a week for two years to help her 'retrain herself for a career'. So that, as he put it, 'She may return from her status of companion of a motion picture star to a separate calling—an independent but perhaps a more prosaic existence.'

The judge said the award was justified by the legal principle of what is known as 'equitable remedy'. I'd better say at once that while there will be rejoicing among many similar forsaken women, there have already been prompt and contemptuous protests from many lawyers who maintain that the law of equity has nothing to do with the case. One expert in family law says that the judge decided to forget about the law and say, 'Let's do what's fair.' Another said the judge might better have called his award 'severance pay' with little justification in the law. A third was alarmed at the precedent of naming a non-relative as the party responsible for seeing that Michelle did not become a public charge: '[The judge] seems to suggest,' sniffed this eminent law professor, 'that this is a substitute for welfare.' I hope there are also many honest lawyers who will cool their client's ardour for litigation by pointing out that if a judge does not specify a limit to the plaintiff's legal fees, they might be considerably more than any soothing balm he cares to apply, whether he calls it 're-training', 'welfare', 'severance pay' or 'equitable remedy'.

The law of equity is so ancient, so complicated, so barnacled with sore points that no layman should touch it. However, I will say gingerly that I am very much taken with two early definitions of it, which some other aggrieved concubines may care to ponder. In 1525, during the reign of Henry VIII, it was laid down that 'A man shall have remedy in Chancery for covenant made without specialty, if the party have sufficient witness to prove the covenants, and yet he is without remedy at the common law.' The plight of 'having no remedy at the common law' appears to be the healing essence of the law of equity.

Maybe Michelle, in the nine years of her cogitating, had dug deeper and gone back to the reign of Edward IV where— no later than 1480—there is a seeming defence of her contention. Five hundred years ago, Chancellor Stillington may have had Michelle in mind, for he said, 'He that is damaged by the non-performance of a promise shall have his remedy here.'

Well, the judge seemed to say, so she ought. But, while it was a promise all right, it was not a promise given on paper, in a marriage contract. The little bone he tossed her, even though he called it an 'equitable remedy', should give pause to the millions of the loose, liberated couples who swear love eternal, or love for a limited period, but who disdain anything so square, so bourgeois as 'a piece of paper'.

# In the Meantime

## 6 May 1979

Twenty odd years ago, my editor asked me to go over to
England to cover a British general election and make such
comparisons with an American Presidential campaign as
occurred to me. On the way in from London Airport, I scanned
the hoardings for election posters, for the billboards that would
show cosmetic blow-ups of the two opposing leaders over
some such slogan as: 'Labour is Your Neighbour' or 'Eden is
Leadin''. I saw none, no hint anywhere on the hustings that
there was to be, or had ever been, a general election. Come to
think of it, there was one, which puzzled me deeply. It said,
'Truman: Courage'. I asked a native in the airport bus what it
could possibly mean. He gave me a lack-lustre look of the sort
reserved for an American tourist who asks, 'What is the Cup
Final?' He said wearily, 'It's a beer advertisement.'

Next day, I took off for the country, and in all my travels—
from Reading to the West Country and up through the
Midlands and on to Scotland and back to the wind-up in
Manchester—I saw no buttons or bows, no surging mobs in
football stadiums, no aeroplanes sky-writing 'Madly for
Adlai'—or the British equivalent—at one thousand dollars an
hour. There were no motorcades—of six cars, three press
buses, eight police outriders—sirening into a city square, with
the candidate and his spread-eagled arms acknowledging the
roars of twenty thousand people—like Hitler entering Vienna.

Much more typical was a day spent with Mr Attlee and his
wife. They drove alone in a mini-car through the country
lanes and in and out of villages and dismal suburbs and came

to a schoolhouse or a market place. And he would stand up before a hundred, sometimes no more than a dozen, citizens and give a sort of scoutmaster's pep talk, and then drive off again to a rustle of handclaps. Certainly, there *were* rallies, so called, such as you might muster in the United States for a particularly heated parent–teachers' meeting. But they were held in halls not in Colosseums. There was no army of Youth for Eden wearing blue boaters, no flights of Attlee balloons, no flocks of waving banners to give the impression that you were present at an indoor Battle of Agincourt. There would be at most a couple of hundred people listening to what the man had to say. There would be the novelty—to an American—of people standing up in turn, like schoolboys, to ask the speaker to clarify this point or that. And another, startling, novelty: hecklers bawling out, 'Yaw, but 'ow about pensions, tell us that,' and 'Not bloody likely, mate.' These intruders, if they started to warm up to a harangue, were politely shushed. And the man said, 'Thank you, one and all.' And that was it.

In the United States, thirty thousand people pack into Madison Square Garden or some famous stadium in Boston or Pasadena. They are all of one party, one mind. These are rallies of the faithful, and any interloper who got up and heckled would be hustled out by a couple of alert cops. I came to the conclusion that a British election campaign compared with an American election campaign was as a prayer meeting to a Roman circus.

Well, from the extensive television clips we've seen of the recent British election campaign, I gather there've been some changes made. 'American style' was what the British commentators called them. I'm afraid they're right. Mrs Thatcher, in particular, appeared to have purloined several of the flossier American tricks, though her borrowings varied from early Coolidge to middle Nixon. Calvin Coolidge used to wear Indian headdresses and pat melancholy cows for the edification of three or four news agency photographers. Mrs Thatcher cuddled a calf for a swarm of television cameramen.

What bothered me most was what I've called the Nixon borrowings, because he most successfully adopted a public relations technique whereby his speeches were vetted for content and tone by the roving watchdogs of an advertising agency. Mr Nixon was, I believe, the first American to be convinced that Richard Nixon as God created him was not quite right for exposure to the multitude. No later than his run for the Senate, nearly thirty years ago, he delivered himself, as promising raw material, to a couple of advertising geniuses, and they moulded and barbered him into the 'image' of a man whom their private surveys told them would be most appealing to most voters. It turned out to be a Faustian bargain, for in the end he came to prefer what was cagey to what was true.

Plainly, the new British campaign techniques have a long way to go towards that torturous end. Nowhere, did it seem to me, were Mrs Thatcher and Mr Callaghan mouthing made-up opinions or saying anything they didn't positively believe, although neither of them was above registering spontaneous shock at charges and counter-charges that had become parrot cries during the campaign. The role of the advertising men appeared to have been restricted to what, figuratively speaking, you might call that of a movie director. A little more working man's downrightness here, a little more county-type patriotism there. Occasionally, you could almost hear the hired television therapists hissing, 'Just a touch slower, more relaxed,' and 'A chuckle there, perhaps.' Still, I'd like to have heard anyone suggesting to Churchill which convictions he ought to hold, or telling Ernest Bevin when to breathe or what to think. The British adoption of advertising wizards as political advisers would do well, I humbly suggest, to stop where it started.

Americans who don't like to see Britain going American in anything—if only because of the uncanny British gift for picking up the worst of America instead of the best—were greatly relieved to hear that nobody has yet thought of introducing the voting machine: the system whereby a million voters walk in turn into a curtained cubicle, tap little levers of their choice, then pull a big lever which locks their preferences and rattles up the cumulative vote, so that a couple of hours later the city count is in, and the Irish Democrats on Third Avenue are already steeped in sorrow or reeling in ecstasy. It was good to hear, and was in keeping with the American fondness for Old England, that men and women of matchless honesty, dexterity and patience would, on the contrary, be separating out bits of paper, some white, some off-white, and making two piles of votes, one for local councillors and one for Members of Parliament, and then dividing these piles into other piles till their lips grew tired in the dawn.

But, happily for all of us, not least for the sanity of the British nation, one thing in a British general election has not changed. The campaign lasts three, four weeks at most. It is a painful reminder that an American Presidential campaign lasts for eighteen months beginning no later than the first month or two of any President's third year. He imagines he was elected for four years, but once past the half-way mark he sees the Presidential hopefuls of the opposing party (and frequently one or two of his own) trotting into the paddock. Mr Carter already faces at least four Republicans who are officially entered for the race. From his own stable, Mr Carter sees a young pretender in Governor Brown of California, and half his party has its stopwatch out on Senator Edward Kennedy.

The President is not alone. Senators and Congressmen up for re-election, in November 1980, are already re-acquainting themselves with the geography and folkways of their beloved native States, and making up to fat cats for the wherewithal to finance all those stadium rallies and television commercials, and banners and posters and buttons and bows. Elections are now big business and also, since television, prime-time entertainment, and the media and the advertising agencies can't wait for the suspense of the thing itself: they draft it and plot it with all the cunning bestowed on a promising new crime series. They manufacture the suspense and stretch it throughout the better part of two years.

But however soon or late the grisly process starts, the effect on the politicians—whether in America or Britain—is much the same. In the United States, where—once the two Presidential nominees are chosen—the actual campaign runs for four or five months, or in Britain, where this time it ran for four weeks, the debate starts with an elaborate, even reasonable, parade of the issues. Soon the polls show the contenders to be running too close for the comfort of either side. The PR men now step in and report that one issue is boring the people while another is inflaming them. So the runners concentrate on the combustible material. They fuel it with an indignation that is less and less truly felt. The recipes for Utopia become more slapdash. And, whether in the last month of an American campaign or the last week of a British campaign, the debate deteriorates into fairly shameless evangelism. Each side is holier than thou. Self-righteousness, the cardinal sin, takes over. Nothing in American public life is more obnoxious than the swollen veins and the hurt tremolo of a Presidential candidate in his last speech on election eve, as he works up a paroxysm of outrage over the shamelessness of the opposition and the frightful prospect it offers of a ruined Republic.

And in the end, it seemed to me, the British campaign resolved itself into a hoarse exchange between two Billy Grahams. In the final days, the Labourites were warning us of a coming orgy of capitalist greed and 'a free for all', and the Conservatives were frightening us with the nightmare of a slave state hell-bent for Moscow.

But then, at last, there is a winner. And the new President or Prime Minister who through the fever of the campaign had declared the great aim to be nothing less than to usher in the Great Society or the New Britain must get down to the business of government: which is to decide whether or not to give truck-drivers a four-day week, to put a national sales tax on bran flakes, to call out the troops in a garbage strike, to recognise the latest African dictator, to subsidise the shoe industry bankrupted by Italian imports, to make social security cover middle-aged immigrants.

The glitter of the election fades, and it is then seen to be only a brilliant interruption in the process of government. Like a christening, a wedding, a graduation ceremony, a holy war, a revolution even: it is a firework display, a gaudy promise of what life ought to be, not life itself. And since in all the Western democracies the popular vote is about evenly divided, since there is—thank God—no thumping majority for a single ideology, the incoming government liquidates its rhetoric and the outgoing government promises a livelier firework show next time. In the meantime, everybody enters what a modern poet calls those 'spaces between stars' which say what 'common-sense has seen'. We settle down to the long grey pull of mending-and-making-do, the day-to-day duties and favours and shenanigans and small kindnesses, and the grumbles and chores of life. In a democracy, anyway, most government—and most of life, I shouldn't wonder—is conducted In The Meantime.